John R. Finger

Cherokee

AMERICANS

The Eastern Band of
Cherokees in the
Twentieth Century

University of Nebraska Press

Lincoln & London

18.95

Copyright © 1991 by the University of Nebraska Press

All rights reserved

Manufactured in the United States of America

First Bison Book printing: 1992

Library of Congress Cataloging in Publication Data

Finger, John R., 1939–

Cherokee Americans: the eastern band of
Cherokees in the twentieth century / John R. Finger.

p.   cm. –(Indians of the Southeast)

Includes bibliographical references and index.

ISBN 0-8032-1985-7 (alk. paper)

ISBN 0-8032-6879-3 (pbk.)

1. Cherokee Indians—History—20th century.

2. Cherokee Indians—Social conditions.

I. Title.   II. Series.

E99.C5F55   1991   973'.04975–dc20

90-43227   CIP

∞

For my Cherokee friends

Contents

ILLUSTRATIONS

Series Editors' Foreword

CHEROKEE HISTORY did not end with the "Trail of Tears." As John R. Finger demonstrated in his earlier work, *The Eastern Band of Cherokees, 1819–1900* (Knoxville: University of Tennessee Press, 1984), those Cherokees who remained in the East used their geographic isolation and economic marginality to maintain political and cultural integrity. In the twentieth century, however, the Eastern Band became increasingly drawn into a market economy, and some Cherokees began to advocate individualism, assimilation, and detribalization. Conflicts over ideology, life-style, and even worldview gave rise to a tribal debate that provides a window on Cherokee social and political dynamics. These conflicts are the focus of *Cherokee Americans: The Eastern Band of Cherokees in the Twentieth Century*. Yet the issues raised by this debate are not exclusively Cherokee. Finger's meticulous research and thoughtful analysis provide a model that may prove applicable to the study of other native peoples.

THEDA PERDUE   MICHAEL D. GREEN

Preface

COMPLETING this book in 1989 is appropriate because it coincides with the 150th anniversary of the Cherokee Nation's arrival in present-day Oklahoma after a long and deadly trek over the Trail of Tears. It also marks the 100th anniversary of the legal incorporation of a smaller Cherokee group in North Carolina. From 1889 to the present, the Eastern Band of Cherokee Indians has operated under a North Carolina charter while simultaneously enjoying federal recognition as a tribe. Comprising nearly 10,000 members claiming descent from a small remnant who avoided removal during the 1830s, the Eastern Band today occupies a reservation of more than 56,000 acres in the mountains of western North Carolina. Although they share a common cultural heritage with the Oklahoma Cherokees, its members have a separate legal and tribal identity. Historians and popular writers alike have written much about removal and the Cherokee Nation but have largely ignored the Band. I therefore view this book as a corrective. It is an attempt to weave the disparate threads of Eastern Cherokee experience into a comprehensive tribal history from 1900 to the present and stands as a sequel to my 1984 work, *The Eastern Band of Cherokees, 1819–1900*. I hope it will be useful to scholars, interested laypersons, and especially members of the Band who wish to learn more about their own past.

That Cherokees—or any Indians—remain in the Southeast is something of a surprise to those people whose conception of Indians is limited to well-known western tribes like the Sioux, Apaches, or Navajos. Yet thousands of Native Americans live in the eastern United States, from Maine to Florida and westward to Wisconsin and Louisiana. In 1980 North Carolina had the largest Indian population of any eastern state, a total of 64,635 Lumbees, Cherokees, and representatives of several smaller tribes. Eastern Indians reside on federal and state reservations, in cities and towns of all sizes, and on individual plots of land in rural areas. Some are highly acculturated to white ways, others are not. Some are recognized as tribes by the federal government, some are not. But almost all seek either to gain or to retain such recognition. Indeed, winning this status and receiving a variety of services from the Bureau of Indian Affairs and other agencies is one of the "strategies of survival" for such groups. The Lumbee Indians, numbering 40,000 or more, are conspicuous in this regard, whereas the Eastern Band already enjoys such recognition but opposes extending it to others, the Lumbees included.[1]

Any scholar working on the Eastern Band of Cherokees inevitably follows in the footsteps of James Mooney, the redoubtable ethnologist who began his fieldwork in the 1880s and published what is still an essential sourcebook of information and insights concerning these people.[2] Even today anthropologists remain among the most active scholars dealing with the Eastern Cherokees and other "remnant" Indians in the East. Mostly their focus is on the "ethnographic present"—how the Indians live at a given point in time.

Except for Mooney himself, anthropologists have done little original research on the history of the Eastern Cherokees. Trained historians are relative latecomers to the subject and are still finding new documentary evidence to supplement the wealth of anthropological data. Despite some excellent articles and theses on specific aspects of modern Cherokee history, this book is the first overview of the Eastern Band's twentieth-century experiences. What I have found is that the ethnographic present of nineteenth- and twentieth-century anthropologists has become part of the historians' documentary record. Obviously there is a large debt owed here, and I hope to give anthropologists due recognition without misrepresenting their findings. I have sometimes taken mild exception to their conclusions and, where appropriate, have noted where they disagree among themselves.

Other twentieth-century southeastern tribes have also become the subjects of recent studies by historians, anthropologists, sociologists, and other scholars. Readers will find especially significant the works of Helen C. Rountree on Virginia's Indians; Harry A. Kersey, Jr., on Florida's Seminoles; W. McKee Evans, Adolph Dial, David K. Eliades, and Karen I. Blu on North Carolina's Lumbees; Ronald N. Satz, Kendall Blanchard, and

John H. Peterson, Jr., on Mississippi's Choctaws; J. Anthony Paredes on Alabama's Creeks; Ernest C. Downs, Max E. Stanton, Fred B. Kniffen, Hiram F. Gregory, and George A. Stokes on Louisiana's several tribes; and Charles M. Hudson on South Carolina's Catawbas (Hudson has also written the standard textbook on southeastern tribes during the prehistoric and historic periods). Walter L. Williams has edited a convenient collection of essays dealing with all these groups.[3] In addition, scholarly journals routinely publish articles on specific aspects of contemporary southeastern Indian history and culture.

My approach in this book is both chronological and thematic and emphasizes political, legal, and economic developments as well as major social and cultural changes. To provide a more meaningful context and allow comparisons with other tribes, I shall attempt to weave these many strands of Cherokee history into the larger tapestry of changing federal Indian policy.

Perhaps the most significant theme in these pages is one applicable to almost all tribal groups today, the ongoing attempt to retain an Indian identity—indeed, to define that identity—while living successfully in a white-dominated America. For the Eastern Cherokees this attempt has taken a course similar to that of other tribes in some respects and yet quite different in others. A second theme is the complicated and anomalous legal status of the Eastern Cherokees, a status shaped by unique historical experiences and local circumstances. Readers familiar with my earlier book may recall that this first became a problem when the Eastern Cherokees separated from the Cherokee Nation after the treaties of 1817 and 1819. Certainly no casual acquaintance with the fundamentals of federal Indian law will explain the mixed or concurrent jurisdiction over the Eastern Band exercised by state and federal governments. Only in recent years has a legal consensus emerged. The federal relationship with the Band is preeminent, although the state of North Carolina exercises authority similar to that of other states with federally recognized tribes. Within that web of federal and state jurisdiction the Cherokees enjoy a large measure of home rule through their own tribal government, and within this tripartite structure of authority they are becoming more self-confident and self-sufficient.

Yet another theme dating to the nineteenth century is a sometimes virulent Cherokee factionalism. Tribal politics can be nasty, brutish, and frequently entertaining. Local issues take center stage, and tribal leaders, like white politicians, are not always consistent in their stands. One important aspect of this factionalism is a division between so-called white Indians who have minimal Cherokee ancestry and those who have more. This division also roughly corresponds with cultural and socioeconomic disparities among the Cherokees, between the haves and have-nots and those who are more and less acculturated. It is perhaps the most fundamental fact of life for today's Eastern Cherokees and raises the perplexing question of who is a "real" Cherokee.

Factionalism and defining a Cherokee identity have both taken peculiar shape because of the tribe's dependency on a tourist industry that has blossomed with the creation of the nearby Great Smoky Mountains National Park. Every year millions of visitors, almost all in private automobiles, pass through the reservation. The unusual pattern of tribal landholding has permitted a relatively few individuals to gain possession of the choicest tourist sites along federal highways. Other Cherokees have sometimes resented this relative affluence. There is also a certain paradox in tourism: Cherokees must prove to white visitors that they are "real" Indians by dressing in the stereotypical fashion of the more famous Plains tribes. Warbonnets, tepees, and souvenir tomahawks are affirmations of a generic Indianness if not of a specific Cherokee identity. Tourism, then, has heightened Cherokee self-awareness but has also necessitated a public display of "Indianness" far removed from historical or contemporary Cherokee culture. It also complicates the issue of what a real Cherokee is. In general, tribal members have handled this paradox well.

When discussing cultural differences, I necessarily employ terminology that lacks precision and might even seem objectionable to some readers. In discussing varying degrees of Cherokee ancestry, for example, I frequently refer to mixed-bloods, white Indians, and full-bloods. Readers are forewarned that I use these as the Cherokees themselves do, without scientific definition. A "mixed-blood" might have any degree of Indian-white (or Indian-black) ancestry, but in this book the term almost always refers to individuals who are not predominantly of Cherokee lineage. Contrary to its literal meaning, a "full-blood" is almost never entirely Cherokee and might more accurately be called a "fuller-blood," defined by one scholar as a person with at least three-fourths Cherokee ancestry. I use these terms interchangeably in the text. One should remember, however, that full-bloods, by Cherokee definition, might include individuals with considerably less Cherokee blood, depending on their behavior. Obviously there is a cultural as well as a genetic component involved in describing people in these terms. Similarly, "white Indian" is a term that is partly culturally defined, and it is possible (though unlikely) that a full-blood might be called a white Indian if highly acculturated.

Other terms that might be offensive to some readers because of possible racist overtones are "blood quantum" and "degree" of Cherokee blood. My justification is that these have great meaning among the Cherokees themselves and are part of the lingua franca on the reservation. Tribal membership, after all, is determined by degree of Cherokee ancestry. Virtually all Cherokees know what their "degree" is—as well as that of their neighbors. Whenever these terms appear in this book it is as a descriptive necessity and without any pejorative connotation.

Likewise the term "conservative" is potentially misleading because of its cultural imprecision. In this context it simply refers to those Indians of whatever blood quantum who seem to retain significant "traditional" Cherokee values and behavior patterns. One of the most important symbols of such a cultural orientation is the ability and willingness to speak Cherokee. Yet there are many nonspeakers of Cherokee who are recognized as conservatives, just as there are many Cherokee speakers who are highly acculturated. Another conservative "marker" is a retiring, even passive demeanor in the presence of whites. Such behavior is perhaps a carryover from what anthropologists call the harmony ethic—a striving to reach consensus, a noncompetitiveness, and an avoidance of giving offense. Conservatism also has a rough correlation with degree of Cherokee blood, but caution is again required. Some phenotypically white individuals are culturally conservative and not usually categorized as white Indians. Similarly, certain prominent full-bloods or fuller-bloods are thoroughly acculturated and just as competitive as their white neighbors.

For the sake of consistency, I have adopted a uniform way of referring to and spelling Cherokee communities that otherwise can vary widely. Wolf Town, for example, often appears in other sources as Wolfetown and is frequently called Soco. Cherokee is also known as Yellow Hill. Snowbird, in Graham County, is sometimes called Cheoah (and for part of the nineteenth century was Buffalo Town). In this book reservation communities appear as Paint Town, Wolf Town, Cherokee, Bird Town, Big Cove, and Snowbird. Except in a very few cases I do not refer to smaller divisions of these communities like the Big Y part of Wolf Town. Likewise, Cherokee surnames can vary even among family members, and I have opted for what seems to be the most common spelling. On those occasions when I discuss the Cherokee Nation or other Cherokee groups in Oklahoma, I shall refer to them by their appropriate names. Readers should also remember that whenever I refer to the Eastern Cherokees, the Eastern Band, the Cherokees, or the Band, I mean the Eastern Band of Cherokee Indians in North Carolina.

More specifically, I am dealing with tribal members who live on or in the immediate environs of the reservation and not those individuals residing elsewhere. Their stories are certainly significant, but they lack the common threads of the reservation experience.

Researching this book entailed using a greater variety of sources than for my earlier volume on the Eastern Band. Anyone working on a twentieth-century topic involving the United States government quickly becomes aware of the mass of official documentation. A small portion of this is available on microfilm, while the rest is mostly at the National Archives in Washington or the Federal Records Centers at East Point, Georgia, and Suitland, Maryland. As one might expect, newspaper coverage and manuscript collections dealing with the Eastern Band are also more complete for this century, though there is no single collection to match the rich documentation of the William Holland Thomas Papers for the nineteenth century.

Most important of all, in terms of my personal interest and gaining otherwise unavailable perspective, were my interviews and casual conversations with dozens of Cherokees. Some agreed to go on the record, whereas others did not want to be quoted or even listed by name. A few others refused even to talk with me. I understand and respect such wishes. Fortunately, during the past generation or so many scholars and reporters have published their own interviews with tribal members. Foremost among these is John Parris, longtime reporter for the *Asheville Citizen*. I am grateful to him, all other interviewers, and all our Indian subjects. I believe this book has benefited immeasurably from these Cherokee voices. In citing my own informants I have tried to use good judgment, be discreet, and protect them from unnecessary embarrassment. Sometimes I have chosen not to cite them at all. The Cherokee reservation is a small community where most people know one another and memories are long.

At the risk of overlooking some of the many people who generously assisted in preparing this book, I would like to thank the following: First, those members of the Eastern Band who have taken extra time to answer my incessant questions or have otherwise shown extraordinary kindness. These include former principal chief Robert S. Youngdeer and current chief Jonathan L. Taylor. Maxine Hill, formerly with the Museum of the Cherokee Indian, offered valuable commentary on reservation life. Kenneth Blankenship, current director of the museum, has also been helpful. Goingback and Mary Ulmer Chiltoskey provided gracious hospitality, important information, and infectious good humor. Lois Calonehuskie patiently answered questions about Snowbird and gave me a personal tour of that community. Wilbur Sequoyah, Lois Farthing, James Cooper, and Richard Welch all took considerable time to describe past events on the reservation and assess current and future prospects, while Pat Saunooke lent me photographs of her father, the late principal chief Osley Bird Saunooke. Though not a Cherokee, Tom Underwood has had a long and enduring relationship with the Eastern Band and willingly shared his recollections of events and personalities. My original manuscript also benefited greatly from the careful reading and useful suggestions of Ben Bridgers, the tribal attorney.

Bureau of Indian Affairs personnel at the Cherokee agency have been very helpful ever since the mid-1970s, when Robert Evans, the former economic programs officer, took time to address my university classes on our annual field trips. Jeff Muskrat, an Oklahoma Cherokee and former superintendent of the agency, offered genial assistance and encouragement in the early stages of research. His successor, Wilbur Paul, has been equally cooperative and continues to show me every courtesy. While I was working with the BIA papers in Washington, D.C., Sarah Hawkins was invaluable, cheerfully providing box after box of musty documents and overseeing the copying of important materials. Likewise, Gayle Peters made me feel at home at the Federal Records Center in East Point, Georgia, and patiently explained the intricacies of the federal filing systems.

Special thanks go to a cadre of loyal supporters and friends at Western Carolina University. James Lloyd and Diana Carlson, both formerly in the Manuscripts Division of the library there, frequently assisted me, as did George Frizzell, himself a Cherokee scholar and currently on the library staff. William Anderson, of Western Carolina's history department, is another friend and Cherokee specialist who has kindly included me in a number of symposia and conferences at his institution. Joan Orr, a former graduate student at Western now employed at the Museum of the Cherokee Indian, on several occasions answered my calls for assistance.

Any historian of Indian affairs owes a debt to his colleagues in anthropology. Robert K. Thomas generously provided me with copies of his papers written in the 1950s when he was working with the Cross-Cultural Laboratory of the Institute for Research in Social Sciences at the University of North Carolina, Chapel Hill. Likewise, Duane H. King and Larry R. Stucki have both been very helpful. Special gratitude goes to John Witthoft for his perceptive commentary on this manuscript; his own scholarship on the Cherokees remains a standard to which others aspire. Closer to home, two doctoral candidates in anthropology at the University of Tennessee have shared their ongoing research: Patricia Quiggins on her analysis of the

Baker Roll, and Betty Duggan on the Cherokee community at Turtletown in southeastern Tennessee. Betty also took time from her job in Nashville to critique most of this book while it was still in manuscript.

Turning to historians, I wish to thank Theda Perdue, a good friend who also happens to be coeditor of the University of Nebraska Press series to which this book is the newest addition. In her usual diplomatic way, she has nudged me toward completing the manuscript while offering welcome advice on several drafts. Catherine L. Albanese, of the University of California, Santa Barbara, and Ronald D. Eller, of the University of Kentucky, both generously assisted me. I also thank my colleagues in the history department at the University of Tennessee, Knoxville, for their friendship and supportiveness. Their enthusiasm for the profession and geniality sustain my own dedication to finding a happy blend of teaching and research.

As expected in all such expressions of gratitude, I accept total responsibility for any errors of fact and interpretation. Finally, on a more personal level, I wish to thank Judi Gaston and my parents, William Donovan and Annada Finger, for their unflagging encouragement. My children—Brian, Susan, and Mike—have sometimes wondered about their dad's fixation on Cherokees but have endured it all with bemused good humor.

1

The Eastern Band
in 1900

DESPITE a flurry of railroad construction during the preceding decade, western North Carolina was only gradually emerging from its geographic isolation in 1900. A beautiful region of lush valleys and coves, gentle hills, and precipitous mountains reaching to more than 6,600 feet, it had long been an eddy in American expansion. The only noteworthy exception was Asheville, the state's third largest city, with a population of 14,694.[1] West of Asheville was an overwhelmingly rural area dotted with small farms and villages, its quiet barely challenged by the railroad's arrival.

There was promise of change, however. Fifty miles or more west of Asheville, amid the forested Great Smoky Mountains and other ranges, the pace of life was already quickening as railroads helped create a lumber industry that would dominate the local economy for a full generation. Included in this newfound empire of timber were the homelands of nearly 1,400 members of the Eastern Band of Cherokees. Here their ancestors had sought peace and security after withdrawing from the Cherokee Nation in 1819 and claiming North Carolina citizenship. In 1838, when the Nation had been forced westward over the Trail of Tears, the Eastern Band and other tribal isolates had remained behind.[2]

The major portion of the Eastern Band's reservation was Qualla Boundary, a tract of about 78,000 acres in Swain and Jackson counties including portions of the present-day Great Smoky Mountains National Park. The Band also held more than fifty other widely separated tracts totaling some 18,000 acres in Swain, Jackson, Graham, and Cherokee counties. Even with the recent growth of the lumber industry, Cherokee lands were not readily accessible to outsiders, and the Indians remained quietly isolated from the larger events of American life. Those seeking to know these people were required to sacrifice comfort and take a long, conscious step backward in time and circumstance.

The would-be visitor would probably embark on the Southern Railroad in Asheville and head westward, arriving in about an hour at Waynesville, population 1,307, the seat of Haywood County. The town was scenically nestled beneath the Balsam Mountains and about ten air miles across that range from Soco Gap, the easternmost part of Qualla Boundary. Rather than challenge such rugged country, the hypothetical traveler would likely continue by train to Sylva, a new railroad town of 281 people in Jackson County, and then on to the whistlestop of Whittier.[3] This was the closest point to Qualla Boundary, which straddled the Jackson and Swain county line and was home to most Eastern Cherokees. Here the visitor would attempt to hire a wagon or buggy for the five-and-a-half mile trip over a rough and treacherous road to the Indian community of Yellow Hill, usually referred to as Cherokee.[4] This tiny cluster of buildings was the capital of the reservation and site of the federal agency operated by the Bureau of Indian Affairs. The residents occupied a level stretch along the Oconaluftee River, a fast-flowing stream originating almost at the crest of the Great Smoky Mountains and joining the Tuckasegee River a short distance below the settlement.

From Cherokee rough and sometimes impassable roads led to four other Qualla Boundary communities. Two—Bird Town and Big Cove—were, like Cherokee, in Swain County. Situated along the Oconaluftee two and a half miles below Cherokee, Bird Town was home to a mixed group of traditionalist and relatively acculturated Indians. Big Cove, the most remote and traditional of Qualla Boundary communities, was about twelve miles to the northeast of Cherokee. It was a scattering of cabins near Ravens Fork, a beautiful stream tumbling out of the mountains and emptying into the Oconaluftee above Cherokee. At an elevation of 2,500 feet, Big Cove was a secluded little pocket surrounded by forests and irregular ridges stretching to the crests of the Great Smoky and Balsam mountains. Even today, it is here that one most feels the immediacy of the mountains and appreciates their shaping of tribal life. In 1900 a visit to Big Cove was a retreat to a quieter, more idyllic America.

To the east of Cherokee and south of Big Cove were the Jackson County settlements of Paint Town and Wolf Town (sometimes called Soco). These were separated from the Swain County communities by a ridge that is both the county line and the watershed between the Oconaluftee and Soco Creek. Wolf Town and Paint Town are at the upper and lower ends of the creek, which originates below Soco Gap, flows westward, and then winds around the southern tip of the ridge to join the Oconaluftee below Cherokee.

To see reservation properties in Graham and Cherokee counties, more than sixty miles from Qualla Boundary, the intrepid traveler would return to Whittier and continue southwestward on the railroad. Paralleling the Tuckasegee, the train would almost immediately pass Qualla Boundary on the right and the 3,200 Acre Tract (or Thomas Tract) on the left. The latter was a rugged, heavily forested part of the reservation inhabited by only a few Indians. Then, very quickly, the train would arrive at Bryson City, population 417. This was the Swain County seat and an important marketing center for the Eastern Band. From here an unimproved road followed the Tuckasegee and Oconaluftee upstream to Bird Town and Cherokee.

Continuing aboard the train, the traveler would disembark at Topton, the nearest point on the line to Cherokee lands in Graham County. But visiting those remote spots meant a bruising ride of thirteen miles over another of those infamous mountain roads to the county seat of Robbinsville, too small even to be listed as a distinct community. The Cherokee tracts were mainly within a few miles of here, more remote from twentieth-century America than even the Qualla Boundary settlements. Most Indians lived in the Cheoah Community, often called Snowbird, which rivaled Big Cove as a center of Cherokee traditionalism. Its residents, like the Cherokee Nation in Oklahoma, spoke the "Western" dialect of Cherokee, while their Qualla Boundary brethren spoke the "Central" dialect.[5]

A more attractive option than such a rigorous side trip was to continue by train southwestward from Topton to Murphy, a town of 604 people that was the Cherokee County seat. Situated at the junction of the Valley and Hiwassee rivers, it was at the heart of what before removal were the Valley Town Cherokee settlements. In its environs were some tribal lands and a number of mixed-bloods who were phenotypically more white than Indian.[6] Separated by mountains from both Qualla Boundary and Snowbird, these people had only a tenuous connection with the tribe—so much so that some of the more traditional or politically ambitious moved to Qualla Boundary. Very little here would strike the dead-tired traveler as being representative of Cherokee life and culture. By now the visitor was seventy miles or more from the town of Cherokee and probably planning to continue by rail to the more civilized amenities of Chattanooga.

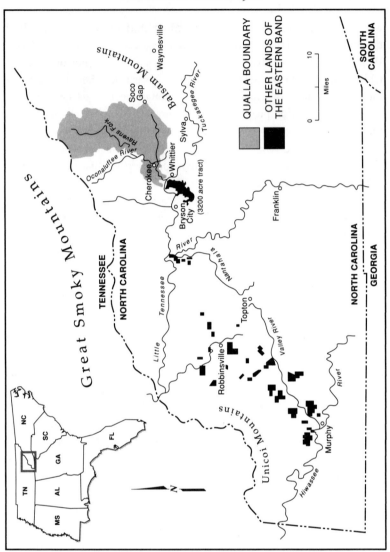

Approximate land holdings of the Eastern Band, 1900. Adapted by permission of the University of Tennessee Press from John R. Finger, *The Eastern Band of Cherokees, 1819–1900*. Copyright © 1984 by the University of Tennessee Press.

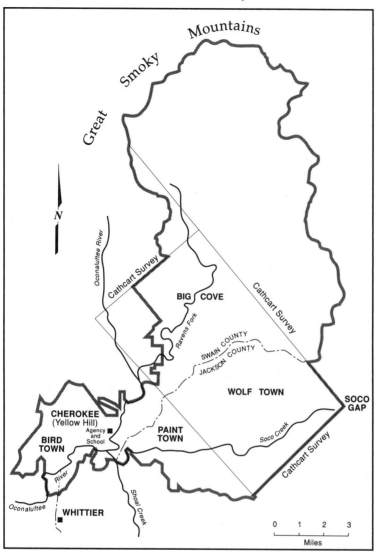

Qualla Boundary, 1900. Adapted by permission of the University of Tennessee Press from John R. Finger, *The Eastern Band of Cherokees, 1819–1900.* Copyright © 1984 by the University of Tennessee Press.

The Cherokee "towns" or settlements consisted of individual cabins and small homesteads scattered along the forested fringes of river and creek valleys. Like most mountain whites, the Cherokees lived in nuclear households and owned their cabins free of any mortgage. What they had they had built themselves, with the help of family and friends. In any given community, two or three of the seven Cherokee clans claimed a disproportionate share of the residents, who were frequently members of extended families occupying nearby homesites. They had a common sense of community with other residents and had developed institutions of mutual assistance.[7]

Cherokee town life in 1900 represented a profound concession to the unrelenting demands of an alien white culture. When Cherokee power had been at its zenith in the seventeenth and eighteenth centuries, the Indians lived in concentrated, palisaded communities featuring extended family groups in winter and summer dwellings clustered around a ceremonial town house. Situated in larger valleys on either side of the mountains, these towns had a complex institutional and ceremonial life, and they cultivated extensive outlying fields of corn, beans, squash, and other vegetables. It was a matrilocal and matrilineal society, the mother owning the home and the children inheriting her clan affiliation. She also did most of the work in the fields. Then the whites came with their different customs and lust for land. Gradually they reshaped Cherokee life to suit their own predilections. The new tribal society featured individual farms, nuclear families, and patrilineal descent; men eschewed warfare to become farmers, women learned the domestic arts. In the meantime, the United States forced the Cherokees to cede their domain piece by piece, until this small tribal remnant had been shunted onto poor mountain lands and assumed a life-style that, outwardly at least, resembled that of their white neighbors. By 1900 even this last sanctuary was under assault as entrepreneurs negotiated for the right to cut Cherokee forests.[8]

To Cherokees the Smokies had always been home, part of the collective tribal identity. Warriors had crisscrossed them while traveling between the Lower and Overhill towns, had fished their sparkling streams, hunted deer and bear in their countless clearings and secluded coves. The peaks and low-hanging clouds that gave the mountains their name nourished a body of myths, legends, and tales defining tribal origins and folkways. Ancient Kituwha, on the mountain flanks near present-day Bryson City, was supposed to be the mother town of all Cherokees.[9] It was almost as if white aggression of the previous two centuries had finally thrust the remaining Indians back to the mountain core that had always distinguished them from other peoples. The Eastern Band, like a retreating glacier on an isolated slope, was the sole remnant of an ancient people occupying its original domain. At that very moment, far to the west in present-day Oklahoma, the transplanted Cherokee Nation was about to lose its reservation to allotment, and traditionalists in North Carolina were determined that it would not happen in the tribal birthplace as well.

Like other parts of the southern Appalachians, the four counties that included the Cherokee reservation had a remarkably homogeneous population, with 87 percent of the people claiming nativity in North Carolina and only 37 individuals born outside the United States. In 1900 the population of the four counties totaled only 36,457 out of more than 1.3 million in the state and included 33,855 whites, 1,223 Negroes, and 1,379 members of the Eastern Band. Of the latter, 875 resided in Swain, 340 in Jackson, 128 in Graham, and 37 in Cherokee counties.[10] But there were others in the region with Cherokee blood who did not belong to the Band and were apparently reluctant to identify themselves as Indians. A few years later, when it had become potentially profitable to be a Cherokee, federal investigators listed some 2,000 individuals in the surrounding area with varying degrees of Indian blood who were not enrolled tribal members. Many had less than the one-sixteenth Cherokee blood quantum required for membership in the Eastern Band. Some of the nonenrolled people had always lived in the region, while others had recently moved into North Carolina from Tennessee and Georgia.[11]

Suitable agricultural land was at a premium for the Eastern Band, with most farming along creek bottoms, on the lower slopes of valleys, and where possible, on the mountainsides. The heavy clay soil common to the reservation does not wash away easily and sometimes allowed cultivation on slopes of thirty-five to forty degrees, but elsewhere such plowing invited serious erosion. Estimates of the amount of available agricultural land range from about 10 to 14 percent of the reservation, and in 1900 a significant portion of this was mountain pasturage. Other economic opportunities were already affecting Cherokee agriculture. An increasing reliance on wage labor, for example, was partly responsible for the reservation's cultivated acreage dropping by 25 percent in 1900–1901, from 3,953 acres to about 3,000. Thus the 290 families that farmed (almost the entire population) averaged little more than 10 acres each, virtually the same as for North Carolina Cherokees in 1835.[12]

Cherokee agriculture was largely for subsistence. Production in 1901 amounted to 23,000 bushels of corn, 5,000 bushels of vegetables, 1,800 bushels of wheat, 1,000 bushels of oats, barley, and rye, a quantity of fodder, and 2,800 pounds of butter. Most of the corn was apparently the "Indian" variety rather than newer strains. Farming methods were much like those of a generation before, and the typical Cherokee used an ox and bull-tongue plow to prepare the fields (oxen were superior to horses and mules on the steep slopes). Livestock included thousands of domestic fowl as well as hundreds of pigs and cattle, which roamed tribal forests and meadows. Less numerous were sheep, horses, mules, and burros. Because there was little interest in selective breeding or other aspects of modern husbandry, Cherokee animals were generally of inferior quality.[13]

Tribal diets primarily featured a multitude of corn dishes, but chestnuts were also important, in their natural state and especially for bread. Other foods included a variety of berries, homegrown apples and peaches, bacon, and coffee. Some of the more well-to-do or acculturated Indians also used honey, molasses, and flour bread. Pork was the preferred meat. Although figures are lacking, the Cherokees no doubt took thousands of fish from the many nearby streams. Game animals, it appears, had dwindled to the point where they were not a significant part of daily diets.[14]

* * *

For an administrative center, Cherokee village was remarkably isolated. Its closest link to the outside world was the railway and telegraph station at Whittier, and until a telephone line was installed between the two places in the summer of 1900, communications arriving after noon at Whittier would not be delivered in Cherokee until 5:00 P.M. the next day. Cherokee itself was little more than a few dwellings on either side of the Oconaluftee and a number of frame buildings occupying the benchland on the west side that housed the tribal agency and the boarding—or training—school. There was also a small farm used for vocational instruction and as a source of food for the school. The federal agent's official title of superintendent of education and disbursing officer accurately reflected his duties. His primary responsibility was Cherokee education, especially supervision of the 157 boys and girls enrolled at the boarding school. The buildings, illuminated by kerosene lamps and heated by stoves, were all badly in need of repair. The school's staff included the superintendent, five teachers, three matrons, three seamstresses, three cooks, and a laundress, gardener, cobbler, clerk, and physician. Only the clerk, an assistant matron, and a seamstress were Cherokees.[15]

Since the federal government had taken over Cherokee education from the Quakers in 1892, the resident agent had directed his attention to the school and attended to other tribal matters only as he had time. Very seldom was he able to visit the outlying portions of the reservation in Graham and Cherokee counties. He also handled the periodic payments of money that were due the Indians based on earlier treaties and, more recently, sales of tribal timber. The agent in 1900 was Henry W. Spray, age forty-nine, who had headed the Quaker boarding school until 1892. A strong-willed individual, he had become involved in an ugly controversy concerning his high-handed ways and alleged attempts to win Cherokee support for Republican political candidates. After giving up control over the school following threats of legal action, he had retained a powerful influence among many Cherokees and in 1898 was appointed resident agent by the McKinley administration. In this new position he would continue to be an object of dispute.[16]

Cherokee was also where the tribal government convened each October to conduct business. Under the Eastern Band's corporate charter, the principal chief and vice chief were to serve four-year terms, while fifteen council members—eight from Swain, five from Jackson, and two from Graham counties—each served two years. (The Cherokee County members of the Band did not have direct representation at the time.) Council proceedings were in both English and Cherokee and depended on an able tribal interpreter. So contentious were some of the rivalries for chieftainship that by 1900 no one individual exercised the same degree of authority that Principal Chief Nimrod J. Smith had during the 1880s and early 1890s.[17] Personal jealousies were simply too strong to allow such leadership.

The relationship between the tribal government and the resident federal agent was an uncertain one, largely shaped by circumstances and personalities. Part of this was due to the confused legal status of the Band. Since 1868 the federal government had claimed guardianship over the tribe, but it was unclear what that meant. Did it suggest, for example, that the Eastern Cherokees were not citizens? After the Civil War the state of North Carolina usually treated them as citizens, allowed them to vote, and tried them in state courts according to state law. The 1889 incorporation of the tribe under a state charter also seemed to validate North Carolina's authority. But in the 1897 case of *U.S. v. D. L. Boyd* the United States Circuit Court decided the Eastern Cherokees were not citizens but a tribe under the direct jurisdiction of the federal government. This decision had a dual effect. On the one hand, state authorities continued to insist on their authority in many areas, and the mixed system of jurisdiction continued without federal opposition. On the other hand, local registrars used the decision as justification for claiming the Cherokees were noncitizen wards of the federal government and therefore ineligible to vote in the 1900 elections. For many years afterward few Indians were able to register, let alone cast a ballot.[18]

The truth is nobody seemed certain what the Cherokees' status was or attempted to resolve the matter definitively. This is why Henry Spray and subsequent federal agents allowed the tribal council considerable authority in its deliberations. Tribal lands, moreover, were owned by the Eastern Band as a state corporation, complicating the question of federal authority to interfere in property matters. The sensible approach was to allow the council to make most decisions relating to Indian lands as long as they did not appear threatening to the tribe's interests. The Indian bureau always insisted, however, that it exercised ultimate authority and could veto such transactions. And sometimes it wielded that power.[19]

Although all land on the reservation belonged to the tribal corporation and was held for the Eastern Cherokees in common, individuals could acquire inheritable possessory tracts or homesteads. They were basically free to develop their land as they wished, but they actually owned only their improvements. These were passed on to their heirs or sold or traded to another enrolled member of the Band, often without any written record. No one outside the tribe was allowed to buy possessory rights, though some Indians worked out informal leaseholds with non-Cherokees.[20] With this kind of landholding arrangement, the Cherokees had, in effect, a modified form of allotment or private ownership. Since passage of the Dawes General Allotment Act in 1887, the federal government had encouraged allotment—or severalty—for certain tribes. Breaking up tribal or communal landholding patterns in favor of private ownership, it was thought, would help bring about the Indians' "Americanization." The Eastern Cherokees were bitterly divided over whether to give up their system of possessory holdings in favor of fee-simple allotments. Some opponents noted that the limited arable land base would yield individual allotments of far less than the 160 acres stipulated under the Dawes Act. Predictably, those who were more acculturated were most likely to favor allotment.[21]

By 1900 the Cherokees were becoming increasingly involved in the growing lumber industry. White entrepreneurs, especially from the North, were buying up huge tracts of forests in the southern Appalachians and systematically logging and milling them to supply a seemingly insatiable American market. The tribal stands of timber were the chief Cherokee assets and consisted of deciduous species like chestnut, tulip poplar, oak, basswood, and ash, as well as conifers like spruce and hemlock. More valuable species like black walnut had been legally and illegally cut since at least the 1850s. Indeed, timber trespass was the most prevalent crime on the reservation.[22]

Amid widespread controversy and opposition, full-scale commercial exploitation of Cherokee forests began in the 1890s, when the tribal council sold timber rights to the enormous Cathcart Tract on Qualla Boundary. Because the true value of these rights greatly exceeded the sale price, questions arose concerning the council's honesty and competence.[23] Such was the Cherokee introduction to an industry that would provide most of the tribal income during the early twentieth century.

The lumber business also produced palpable tensions and changes within the Eastern Band. Members could cut timber on their own possessory tracts for fuel and building materials if they obtained tribal permits, but they could not cut commercially because the trees belonged to the tribal corporation. Some ignored or evaded such restrictions or forthrightly demanded control over the timber on their claims. A few cut and sold their own trees or peeled tanbark in open defiance of the tribal government. Resident federal agents consistently supported the council's position, but at considerable cost to their personal relationships with certain Cherokees.[24]

* * *

The degree of acculturation varied considerably on the reservation, ranging from those in Cherokee County who could pass for white in both appearance and actions to the full-bloods at Snowbird and Big Cove who still stubbornly resisted the encroachments of white civilization. During the preceding twenty years or so some whites had moved onto the reservation and intermarried with Indians; perhaps surprisingly, their offspring were sometimes more Cherokee in behavior than their neighbors who were phenotypically and historically Indian. There were also individuals who had a significant degree of Cherokee blood but were highly acculturated. Others lived off the reservation in scattered enclaves in both North Carolina and southeastern Tennessee and intermingled peaceably with neighboring whites. These Indians might or might not be on the tribal roll, but they would often travel to visit friends and relatives on the reservation. Indeed, it was not uncommon for Cherokees to walk from the mountains of east Tennessee to Robbinsville or Cherokee and back, a custom that continued well into the automobile age.[25]

The 1900 federal census lists Indians separately and provides considerable information on the Eastern Cherokees. Among the least acculturated were the 128 in Graham County who occupied a number of scattered, small tracts interspersed with white-owned properties. In general the two races coexisted amicably, though the Indians were fiercely protective of Cherokee culture. One hundred and sixteen of the Indians lived in the Snowbird community and occupied twenty-six domiciles as nuclear families. Twenty of these homes were owned outright, and six were rented. All adult males were either farmers or farm laborers. Only three of the Indians listed in the census and seven of their parents had been born outside North Carolina (either in Georgia or in Tennessee). Obviously the Snowbird Indians were a stable, long-entrenched group little affected by the wanderings of other Cherokees through the southern Appalachians. All but nine were full-bloods, the others mostly having one-fourth white blood. Only nine claimed to have attended school at all, and this for periods of just one to three months. The other twelve Graham County Cherokees belonged to two families of full-bloods in nearby Stecoah Township, but the census taker could obtain little information about them because "they are superstitious and don't like to talk much to white people."[26]

For Cherokee County, census takers listed only thirty-seven Indians, though many more had varying degrees of Cherokee blood even if they were not members of the Eastern Band. Seven of those listed resided in Valley Town Township, while most of the rest lived near Murphy. About one-third claimed a small degree—one-eighth or one-fourth—of white blood. The males were either farmers, farm laborers, or day laborers.[27] Living in several small, discrete groups in a county overwhelmingly white, these Cherokees must have found it difficult indeed to maintain a traditional life-style.

The Qualla Boundary Cherokees residing in Jackson County totaled 340, comprising ninety-six families occupying ninety-five houses. They ranged in age from infants to John Axe, who was ninety-four. All but a few had been born in North Carolina, as was true for their parents. All those listing occupations were farmers or farm laborers, except for one "capitalist" and one "beggar." There were proportionately fewer full-bloods than in Graham County, 201, though it appears that no more than half a dozen families had a white husband or wife. One black couple renting their own house was also enumerated with the Indians. Despite the boarding school's proximity, only about seven children claimed to have had any formal education, suggesting that most acculturation resulted from the home environment or day-to-day contact with whites. Two of the most prominent of the Jackson County residents were current principal chief Jesse Reed and James Blythe, thirty-eight, a former superintendent of the Cherokee agency who was then serving as clerk of the boarding school. Part white, Blythe had been a consistent advocate of orderly acculturation and would continue to serve the Eastern Band in a variety of capacities for two decades. Living with him were his son, Jarrett, and an adopted son, Fred Blythe Bauer. Both would later become central figures in some of the bitterest political disputes in the tribe's history.[28]

The 875 Cherokees in Swain County ranged all the way from highly acculturated individuals to some of the staunchest conservatives on the reservation. Sixteen resided in the environs of Bryson City, while another sixty-four lived on small tracts near the Nantahala River. Forty-four of this latter group were full-bloods, with the rest having a small quantum of white blood. Only three said they had attended school.[29]

Almost all the other 795 Cherokees listed for Swain County resided on Qualla Boundary. Census takers enumerated them together as "Oconalufty Township," but it is still possible to arrive at a rough community breakdown. One hundred and fifty-seven of those listed were pupils at the boarding school in Cherokee who ranged in age from five to eighteen. Some of these students, of course, came from families in other counties. Of the remaining 638 Indians listed for Oconalufty Township, 491—or 77 percent—were full-bloods. Yet the distribution of full-bloods varied widely on Qualla Boundary. In Big Cove, for example, virtually all were full-bloods except for several white adults and their children by Cherokee spouses. Most prominent in this category were Wallace Bradley and John Swayney, whose families made up a sizable percentage of those in the cove who were conversant with English. (Whites sometimes referred to Big Cove as "Swayney.") Hardly anyone there even attended school—partly out of preference and partly because it was difficult to get to Cherokee. In contrast, many mixed-bloods lived along the lower Oconaluftee, especially around Bird Town. They were more likely to speak English, and their children were much more likely to attend the nearby school.[30]

The 1900 census indicates that more than 460 Eastern Cherokees could speak English, with a smaller number able to read or write it. As Henry Spray noted, however, this figure was inflated by the inclusion of individuals who knew at most a few words or phrases. His estimate was that only about 350—or one-fourth of the tribe—could use English in ordinary conversation, and even this is probably too high. All but three or four of the 157 boarding-school students, for example, are credited with being able to read, write, and speak English—despite testimony to the contrary about Cherokee pupils for at least another generation.[31] Though figures are lacking, a significant number of Indians could read and write the Cherokee syllabary.

If one assumes the pattern of error among census takers was more or less consistent throughout the reservation, it is possible to obtain a very rough idea of the distribution of English speakers. Not surprisingly, mixed-bloods and Cherokees living near towns like Bryson City were most likely to be fluent in it. In Swain County the greatest number of English speakers were in Bird Town and Cherokee, while Big Cove had the least. In fact, most families in the Cove did not have even one member conversant with the language. The Snowbird community in Graham County likewise had a very low percentage of English speakers, while the Jackson County Indians apparently ranked a bit below Bird Town and Cherokee in that category. The relatively few Cherokee County members of the Band were only slightly more familiar with English than those at Snowbird, but there were many other unenrolled individuals in that county with varying degrees of Indian blood who were almost completely assimilated into local white society.[32]

Competency in English would remain low, of course, as long as only a minority of school-age children attended classes. There were no reservation schools in 1900 besides the one at Cherokee, and many Indian children were too far away to take advantage of it even if their parents consented to their attending. That was no small problem, for Cherokee parents valued close-knit families and were suspicious of attempts to separate them from their children. It was sometimes even more difficult to convince parents that a good student should attend boarding schools at Hampton, Virginia, or Carlisle, Pennsylvania. Many students who did attend those institutions came back to the mountains at first opportunity, where they faced idleness and temptations like alcohol.[33]

Other facets of life, some so commonplace they were perhaps overlooked, reflected the uncertain extent of acculturation. Members of the school band wore uniforms and played John Philip Sousa marches on modern instruments. Children were learning to play white sports. And Cherokees who were once indifferent to white time constraints now found that, like it or not, their reservation operated according to eastern standard time. Some Cherokee crafts had declined until they were in danger of disappearing altogether. With the advent of wage labor, for example, came a decline in spinning and weaving as more Indians bought ready-to-wear clothing. There were only a few potters and basket makers, and Henry Spray apparently welcomed the day when there would be none. At the same time, however, clan identification continued in many households, and some Cherokees still participated in traditional rituals like the green corn ceremony and associated dances, though in modified form and with less frequency. Along with whites, they also flocked to see the hotly contested, lacrosse-like ballplay, which agents discouraged because of gambling, drinking, and occasional violence among participants and spectators. Swimmer, the noted shaman and conjurer, had died the previous year, but there were others who still invoked the ancient rituals. And practitioners of traditional Cherokee medicine successfully vied with the school doctor for influence over the ailing.[34]

Although an ever-growing majority of the Eastern Band attended Christian churches, sermons were in Cherokee, and there were strong elements of traditional Indian cosmology in religious practices. Quite likely the growing dominance of the Baptist denomination was partly due to its emphasis on baptism by immersion, which was similar to the traditional purification ritual of "going to the water." Likewise, all-night vigils at the homes of those who had just died, similar to the vigils of mountain whites, probably reflected a traditional Cherokee desire to protect bodies from witches. In these and other ways Christianity coalesced with Cherokee beliefs. As Catherine L. Albanese notes,

> In the first place, if the Cherokee accepted Christianity, they also accepted it in their own way. . . . [They] engrafted the new meanings and practices onto the old culture in an accommodation which gave expression to their distinctive character. In the second, even as Christianity attained near-total public acceptance as religion, the old religion—weakened but not extinct—continued under the guise of social-recreational and medical practices as well as various customs and behavioral norms.[35]

What had emerged by 1900, then, was a syncretic, highly individualized form of Christianity reflecting the tribal heritage.

Until recently the Cherokees' immediate white neighbors were the forgotten people, except for popular writers of the day who treated them as oddities, historical throwbacks, and semibarbarians.[36] The sad truth is that in 1900 there is even less documentary evidence for most of these mountaineers than for the Cherokees. The latter, at least, were subject to countless inspections, censuses, and "expert" testimony simply by virtue of their Indianness and connections with Washington's bureaucracy. Agents often commented that the Eastern Cherokees had access to better education and other opportunities than mountain whites and were at least as "civilized."[37] Otherwise the two groups had much in common. Although a few prominent Indians lived in frame dwellings, most occupied log cabins indistinguishable from those of nearby whites. Their diets were much the same, and both groups followed the rhythms of a rural life dependent on the forces of nature. Yet the Cherokees were still different from Appalachian whites. Their lands and their precise status were tied up in a unique welter of legal complexity. They could not attend public schools with whites or blacks or be admitted to certain other public institutions. More important, they retained significant attributes of cultural nationalism: their own language, a body of myths and legends defining their history, a legally recognized body of land, and in varying degrees, certain shared assumptions and traits. Most important of all, they perceived themselves as Cherokees.[38]

Already anthropologists had "discovered" these people and begun dissecting their beliefs and life-styles. By far the most illustrious was the Smithsonian Institution's James Mooney, a soon-to-be eminent ethnologist who conducted fieldwork on the reservation in the 1880s and 1890s (and later) and whose classic *Myths of the Cherokee* was published in 1900 by the Bureau of American Ethnology. He had relied extensively on Swimmer for much of his information but also profited from the assistance of others like James Blythe and Will West Long. *Myths of the Cherokee* was a prelude to the even more extensive fieldwork to be conducted among the Eastern Cherokees after 1900 and remains to this day an indispensable sourcebook.[39]

A continuing focus in all this anthropological research was the matter of cultural persistence and change among the Band. Mooney believed the Cherokees were rapidly accommodating themselves to the modern world and losing their unique identity. He saw the death of Swimmer in 1899 as symbolizing the passage of cultural traditionalism and the advent of modernity. "Peace to his ashes and sorrow for his going," he wrote, "for with him perished half the tradition of a people."[40] But though Mooney no doubt had witnessed many changes in the preceding fifteen years, his vision of a rapidly acculturating people was a bit premature. The Eastern Cherokees would cope with the twentieth century in their own way, at their own pace, and would undergo a process of adaptation and cultural selectivity that even the perceptive Mooney could not foresee. And as Fredrik Barth has contended, it is not enough simply to measure culture and ethnicity by inventories of traits; more important, perhaps, is how certain groups continue to define themselves as unique even amid a growing interrelationship and interdependence with other cultural groups.[41] The Cherokees were engaged in a creative process of adaptation that established ethnic and cultural "boundaries" that preserved an Indian identity in a white-dominated world.

2

Progressivism and the Cherokees

DURING the first two decades of the twentieth century progressive reformers attempted to cope with the manifold consequences of American industrialization, immigration, and urbanization. The economic changes precipitating this new reformism were apparent not only in burgeoning eastern industrial cities but in the southern Appalachians as well. After 1880, and especially after 1900, these once remote mountains and valleys increasingly attracted capitalists who exploited the virgin forests and varied mineral resources. Once a backwater, the region was undergoing a transformation promoted by "New South" advocates who envisioned the South being integrated into a national industrial economy.[1]

Industrial capitalism both complemented and violated the federal government's objectives for the Eastern Cherokees and, indeed, all Native Americans. It contradicted long-cherished agrarian ideals, yet it would ultimately assist the cause of assimilation by giving Indians firsthand contact with the larger world beyond the reservation. The ironies and paradoxes of industrial America were thus reflected in the Eastern Band of Cherokees. There was no way the Indians could avoid these changes, and some in fact welcomed them, bringing yet another dimension to tribal factionalism. Traditionalism now confronted as never before the pressures of modernity—pressures more sweeping than those of the early nineteenth century, when the first tentative steps toward Cherokee "civilization" were taken.

Nothing reflected these economic changes better than the lumber industry. By 1904 four white-owned sawmills on the reservation provided Cherokees with much-needed employment.[2] Eager to continue such development, the tribal council, amid mounting skepticism about its competence, spent considerable time negotiating sales of timber reserves.[3] As early as 1900 it encountered opposition to selling the 33,000-acre Love Tract along the upper Oconaluftee River. J. S. Holmes, a forestry expert and member of the North Carolina Geological Survey, protested the pending transaction because the $30,000 price was too low and the resulting despoliation would reduce chances of creating an Appalachian forest preserve. Besides, he argued, the Indians did not need the money and were incapable of handling it wisely.[4] The secretary of the interior agreed at least in part, noting that the Love Tract contained more than 400 million board feet of lumber worth about $1.2 million. Stumpage alone should pay anywhere from $100,000 to $400,000, and he therefore refused to approve the contract.[5] Nevertheless, the council continued its efforts and finally, in 1906, sold the tract for $245,000 to two West Virginians. Not wishing to sell to mere speculators, councilmen stipulated that the purchasers build a railroad to their otherwise inaccessible property.[6]

For all its attractions, the lumber industry had some troubling consequences. A largely unspoiled environment quickly gave way to an environmental degradation unimaginable in the nineteenth century; wage labor undermined the Cherokees' subsistence economy and traditional values; tensions mounted amid arguments over who could rightfully claim to be a Cherokee and share in the proceeds of timber sales. It also brought a modernity that could be strangely counterproductive: the Indian Office stressed education for Cherokee youth, yet teenagers were leaving school to work. And finally, there was an ambivalence on the part of officials who appreciated industrial opportunities for their Cherokee wards but still believed that agriculture was their only viable long-term occupation.

Henry Spray and later agents served on the tribal business committee and made every effort to protect Cherokee timber resources. For example, they often chided the Mason and Dixon Company for cutting undersized trees, taking tanbark, and other violations of its contract with the tribe. Even after the contract expired in 1908, the company provoked controversy by removing timber cut before that date.[7] Agents also tried to cope with frequent timber trespass by Indians and whites alike. The outlying tracts in Graham and Cherokee counties were especially vulnerable to spoilsmen seeking anything "from a walking stick to a sawlog."[8] Such depredations led to frequent pleas by both the council and agents to sell the isolated, largely unoccupied units and to concentrate on developing Qualla Boundary.[9]

Meanwhile, Henry Spray found himself increasingly under siege. A strong-willed, sometimes difficult individual, he faced opposition to both his policies and his methods. Accused of meddling in local politics, he was finally replaced as agent in January 1904 by Willard S. Campbell, who gave way to DeWitt Harris the following September.[10] Both men blamed many of the Band's problems on their predecessor. Spray's alleged "coddling" had supposedly limited Indian initiative, encouraged idleness, and denied tribal councillors a chance to develop sufficient skills to run the Band's business. Not only did members of the council quarrel incessantly, Harris said, but their honesty was suspect: "I have heard it openly stated more than once that two hundred dollars will get [them] to pass any measure desired."[11]

But Campbell and Harris agreed with Spray on the necessity of a more efficient and diversified Cherokee agriculture. By 1901 the number of acres under cultivation on the reservation had actually diminished because the Cherokees were resting some of their land and had found alternative opportunities in logging and milling.[12] Recognizing the limited quantity of arable land, agents vainly advocated importing blooded cattle and exploiting the reservation's pastoral opportunities. In 1904 the Eastern Band had more than 1,600 swine, 817 cattle, 335 sheep, and 109 horses, mules, and burros. All the stock was of inferior quality. Pigs fended for themselves, roaming the forests and fattening on an abundance of nuts. Cherokee cattle, including those of the training school, grazed on unoccupied tribal lands and were only occasionally tended by a herder. Whites also grazed stock on the largely unfenced reservation, sometimes under leases and sometimes illegally. The number of sheep had recently declined because a "superabundance of worthless curs" preyed on them and because fewer Indians were making their own clothing.[13]

Most Cherokee households had a few apple and peach trees, and federal agents consistently advocated developing orchards. Henry Spray believed the mountains of western North Carolina could grow apples as good as any in the eastern United States, a view shared by inspector O. H. Lipps, who in 1915 emphasized the advantages of Cherokee fruit and vegetable growing. Although a recent blight had killed the region's apple crop, the tribe had 4,000 apple seedlings in its nursery at the boarding school. Lipps suggested a multifaceted enterprise that included hiring a competent horticulturist, planting the hillsides in orchards, establishing a cannery and cold storage plant, manufacturing shipping crates, and using Cherokee women and children as fruit and berry pickers. But those dreams never materialized, perhaps because the average Cherokee, like the typical white mountaineer described by Horace Kephart, was "no horticulturist. He lets his fruit trees take care of themselves," resulting in unpruned trees "often bearing wizened fruit."[14]

During the first decade of the new century, the village of Cherokee underwent a modest transformation. By 1904 the tribal boarding school had become a sprawling complex of frame buildings connected by a network of boardwalks to keep students from tracking mud into their classrooms and living quarters. Kerosene lamps had already given way to electric lights powered by a small generator connected to a dam on the Oconaluftee. Steam heating plants provided warmth for several of the buildings. A new girls' dormitory eased the crowded living conditions by replacing the old one that had burned late in 1901. Around the school were cleared fields maintained by students learning modern farming techniques, while a new 50,000-gallon reservoir occupied a nearby plateau and furnished a convenient source of water for firefighting. There were also a number of Indian residences and a general store owned by D. K. Collins, a Bryson City businessman who held one of the few white inholdings on Qualla Boundary.[15]

The tribal capital could never advance beyond this modest cluster of buildings, however, without more direct access to the outside world. The road to Whittier, like all others on the reservation, was unpaved, frequently in bad repair, and unsuited for significant commerce. Arsene Thompson, a prominent Cherokee, recalled many years later that when the agency superintendent had an important message to transmit he would dispatch an Indian on horseback to Whittier. Communications improved somewhat late in 1900 with completion of a telephone line linking the training school with the railroad and telegraph at Whittier, but it was nearly a decade more before there was serious possibility of a railroad into Cherokee itself.[16] Such a spur connecting with the mainline of the Southern Railroad would provide employment, open the town for development, and eventually link up with a logging railroad into the untapped forests of the reservation.

By early 1909 construction had begun on the Appalachian Railroad, a seven-mile line linking Cherokee with the Southern tracks at Ela. Members of the Band also benefited by working on the road for $1.25 a day, good wages for that time and place. Completed in April, the railroad was soon running three round-trips every day except Sunday. At Ela it connected with four daily trains on the mainline and brought the tribe into contact with the outside world as nothing had before. Soon agent Frank Kyselka was considering requests to establish businesses near the depot and school. One of the first to see commercial possibilities was Whittier businessman R. J.

Roane, who wanted a five-year lease to set up a store on an Indian possessory claim. Kyselka, in asking permission from the Indian Office, voiced his approval because the proposed store would compete with that of Collins. The Indian Office authorized three-year leases of tribal land, subject to its approval, and this had immediate effects. In December 1910 Kyselka noted that "Cherokee is now a fairly good market place, as it has three stores, two of them superior to the average country store. Competition causes prices to be quite reasonable."[17]

By early 1917 there were three merchants in Cherokee besides Collins. His chief rival was the firm of Jenkins and Tahquette, across from the railroad station. Jenkins was a white man and John A. Tahquette, who owned the building, was a half-blood who later became principal chief. Their store had stock worth about $6,000 and also served as the town's post office, an important magnet for attracting people. Adjoining Tahquette's property was a small grocery belonging to Georgia Burgess, a Cherokee. The other business in town was a small wagon and harness firm owned by W. H. Duncan, a white man married to a tribal member. Four miles away on Soco Creek was a store owned by David Blythe, the current principal chief and partner of a white man named Quiet. At Bird Town was the store of W. H. Cooper, a white man occupying a building owned by a Cherokee. Neither the Indian Office nor the tribal government attempted to regulate these businesses in any way. Agent James Henderson believed their prices were slightly higher than those in nearby towns but unlikely to become exorbitant because there were six sizable stores within a mile or two of the reservation's edge.[18]

Railroad construction did not cease with completion of the line to Cherokee. By 1920 there was a track extending northward from town along the Oconaluftee to Ravensford and then a few more miles to Smokemont, part of today's Great Smoky Mountains National Park. Another spur reached from Ravensford along Ravens Fork back into Big Cove, the most remote part of Qualla Boundary.[19] Along these lines and elsewhere near the reservation were logging camps that offered jobs for Cherokees as well as a taste of different life-styles. Visitors commented on the excesses of that largely masculine environment, with its hard, dangerous work and occasional violence, but sometimes there were a few touches of civilization. Lois Farthing, a prominent businesswoman in Cherokee, fondly remembers growing up at Smokemont, where her father worked for Champion Fibre Company.[20]

* * *

The 1906 sale of the Love Tract for $245,000 exacerbated an ongoing controversy over the proceeds of such transactions. Since the late 1890s, revenues from timber sales had been deposited in an Asheville bank and later distributed in periodic payments to each enrolled member. The first allocation of money from the Love sale took place shortly after a federal court awarded a large sum (eventually amounting to about $5 million) to the Band and other, nonenrolled, "Eastern Cherokees." The award confirmed Indian claims to money based on treaties in 1835 and 1846, plus interest at 5 percent. Guion Miller, a lawyer and agent of the Indian Office, prepared a list of eligible Cherokees overlapping with but separate from the tribal roll.[21]

Not surprisingly, many individuals of dubious Indian ancestry clamored for a share of these "per capita" payments. The result was that by 1910 the government recognized 3,436 Cherokees living east of the Mississippi (and about 27,000 more residing west of the river) as eligible to share in the court's award, amounting eventually to $133.18 per person. The Eastern Band could do nothing to limit the number of awardees but was determined at least to keep its own tribal roll protected from such pretenders. Yet pressures to revise and increase that roll continued to mount. When the council accepted a tribal roll in 1907 showing 1,479 members, agent DeWitt Harris forwarded it with the comment that a number of individuals had been left off who deserved inclusion. To correct the roll himself would mean neglecting other duties and perhaps arouse antagonism, so he asked the Indian Office to assign the task to someone else. The office quickly sent Frank C. Churchill, who began work in November.[22]

When Churchill finished early in 1908, a special tribal committee complimented him for his diligence but claimed his roll of nearly 1,900 names was inflated. The committee wanted to eliminate those who resided in Georgia or had less than one-sixteenth Cherokee blood, the latter being denigrated as "White Indians." This continuing controversy led the Indian Office to review and amend the tribal roll, creating even more paperwork, bickering, and charges that non-Indians—including Negroes—were being added to a roll that totaled 2,115 when approved by the office in April 1913. The council challenged some 400 of these, prompting a series of hearings. No agreement could be reached, and nothing further was done pending eventual passage of an allotment bill that would include "a final determination of this long-standing enrollment controversy."[23]

The various per capita payments together represented more money than many Indians had ever known, and they were not always careful in spending it. Agents differed in their assessments of these cash distributions. As early as 1902 Henry Spray stated that, with certain notable exceptions, the payments were actually "pauperizing" the Band. But in 1910 an inspector pointed to a number of new homes and other improvements as evidence that most Indians used the payments wisely. A bit later Frank Kyselka emphasized the negative aspects of distribution and suggested the money was responsible for increased drunkenness and crime on the reservation.[24]

Even more complex than enrollment and per capita payments was the uncertain legal status of the Eastern Cherokees, a concern that had haunted them since the early nineteenth century. The Boyd decision of 1897 firmly upheld their lack of citizenship and their status as federal wards, but the old system of mixed state and federal jurisdiction continued without definitive resolution. Federal agents often disagreed as to the status and potential of the Eastern Cherokees. Willard Campbell believed this confusion impeded tribal progress and that, whatever their status, the Indians were better qualified for citizenship than southern white mountaineers. Frank Kyselka said the Cherokees were both wards and citizens. James Henderson was not even sure they were wards. But regardless of such confusion, all agents well understood that the legal uncertainty placed limits on federal authority. The secretary of the interior, for example, could disallow certain kinds of land transactions but could not order allotment of the reservation as long as it was owned by the Eastern Band as a state-chartered corporation.[25]

Some Indians and whites protested any outside control of Cherokee affairs. Particularly insistent on this point was George Smathers, longtime lawyer for the tribe, who in 1908 used two recent decisions in state courts to argue that the Indians were citizens and could therefore do anything they wanted with their property. Aware of Smathers's prominent role in recurring attempts to sell Cherokee lands to outside interests, DeWitt Harris warned that "it will be a sorry day for these Indians" when the government removed its protection over tribal property.[26]

Whatever their true status, the Cherokees were consistently denied the right to vote after 1900 as local white politicians, especially Democrats, used the Boyd decision to disfranchise the Indians because of their alleged lack of citizenship. In truth, it was mostly because the Democrats realized the Cherokees were overwhelmingly Republican in sentiment. Despite these restrictions, federal agents blithely claimed that qualified Indians could vote. The ostensible reason many did not do so was their inability to meet the required literacy standards, which also prevented blacks from exercising the franchise. Yet Sibbald Smith, the literate and highly articulate son of former principal chief Nimrod J. Smith, claimed that registrars prevented his voting in 1900 solely because of the Cherokees' supposed lack of citizenship. On the other hand, he noted, that very year a state court had tried, convicted, and sentenced several Indian suspects in a murder case. What was he, Smith asked, a citizen or a ward of the United States? His question remained unanswered. For many years afterward the overwhelming majority of Cherokees encountered similar difficulties if they had the temerity to attempt to register. Eventually most did not even try.[27]

Instead of participating in the white political arena, Cherokees had to content themselves with the shadowy and rough-and-tumble game of tribal politics. Since the Civil War, factionalism had become a fact of life for the Eastern Band, reflected in frequent charges, countercharges, and defamation of character. In 1899 the council declared Jesse Reed the victor over Sampson Owl in a disputed election for principal chief. A special agent investigating the results found certain irregularities but concluded that most in the Band supported the outcome. Besides, he said, Reed was of the "better class of these Indians." Nonetheless, Owl challenged the outcome in a state court, which dismissed the case because of uncertainty over the extent of state jurisdiction.[28]

Most important decisions were made by the fifteen-member council, which naturally became a target of more acculturated Cherokees, who charged councillors with incompetence, lax business procedures, and worse. DeWitt Harris was even more negative, viewing the council as an obstacle to Cherokee progress and a tool of designing whites like Henry Spray and George Smathers. Such subservience ultimately threatened the Band's landholdings. That was another reason he advocated allotting Cherokee lands and letting individuals assume responsibility for their own property.[29]

Harris's view highlighted the one consistent theme affecting the Eastern Cherokees during the Progressive Era: the continuing pressure for assimilation. It extended back more than one hundred years and by the early twentieth century had been heightened by the ongoing dissolution of other reservations after passage of the Dawes General Allotment Act in 1887. Allotment of reservations among individual Indians (severalty) was viewed as a vital means of incorporating Native Americans into the white cultural mainstream. In line with this, Harris favored sale of all surplus timber, a division of common property, individual deeds for allotments, and dissolution of the tribal government (which he thought worthless anyway). Then, in his words, "let them shift for themselves."[30] He well understood, of course, that the complicated legal status of the Band raised questions about the government's power to undertake such a program. Yet when he submitted his resignation in August 1908, he reiterated that severalty was desirable and that he believed most Cherokees were committed to it. "I have done the fighting, and won," he said. Though some still opposed allotment, his successor, "by tact," could continue to make progress toward it.[31] The new agent, Frank Kyselka, drew up a preliminary plan for allotment in 1910, but nothing came of it because of legal complexities, opposition within the tribe, and the difficulty of compiling an accurate tribal roll.[32]

Whatever agents might say to superiors, most Indians were probably frightened by the prospect of allotment. Conservative Cherokees were less likely to say or write anything than acculturated Indians, but Will West Long, a leading member of the traditionalist Big Cove community, asked the secretary of the interior to delay severalty because his people were not ready. His community was willing to send its children to school and make whatever progress the Indian Office wished, but for the present "it will become a bad condition if we are to support ourselves." They needed more time to adjust, to learn to maintain their lands and run their own affairs. To go ahead with allotment now, he pleaded, would be like the biblical story of Joseph being cast into a pit by his brothers. The secretary should continue to protect them from this abyss.[33] But the Indian Office was unmoved. In 1910, when a prominent member of the Bird Town community protested allotment, an official responded that it was desirable for the Band because "it has been shown from past experience that making allotments . . . has resulted in great good to the Indians . . . by permitting them to take a more direct, personal interest in the improvements and cultivation of their lands and also the building of comfortable homes thereupon."[34]

Another facet of assimilation—education—had more immediate and apparent impact than the allotment issue. The pride of the tribe was the boarding school at Cherokee, an institution that reflected the government's commitment to Indian progress. It had operated almost continuously since its founding in 1884 and provided a rudimentary education for both boys and girls. Half the day was for instruction in English, arithmetic, geography, and other academic subjects, and the other half emphasized domestic skills for girls and a variety of industrial arts and farming for boys. Students ranged in age from five to eighteen, with a few older pupils gaining admission by special permission.[35]

School routine was semimilitary, with strict discipline and scheduling. Instruction was in English, and teachers frowned on the use of Cherokee. Goingback Chiltoskey, a prominent artist who began attending the training school at the age of ten in 1917, said teachers or the matron would even wash out a student's mouth with soap for such an offense. For a child like himself, who did not speak a word of English when he arrived, it must have been an intimidating environment. But Chiltoskey adjusted quickly, probably because he returned to his parents only infrequently during the academic year. Despite the difficulties of learning what was for him a foreign language, he recently recalled, "They taught us to speak English. I guess they were right; I couldn't get along without it." [36]

Even with this emphasis on education, many Cherokee children did not attend school at all, either through personal disinclination or because their parents wanted them at home. Others stayed away if there was farm work to do or because of other pressing demands.[37] By 1905, according to DeWitt Harris, only about one-third of all school-age Cherokees attended classes even part time. Some parents would send their children to school only near the end of the term because it was customary to give each pupil two changes of clothing and one set of underwear before they returned home. This was not the way to foster education, Harris said, and he argued strenuously in favor of a proposed state law making school attendance compulsory for Indian children. (Because of the Band's anomalous status, the federal government was unable to enforce school attendance on the reservation as it could among western tribes.)[38]

Strongly supportive of a compulsory attendance law were state senator William W. Stringfield, a former Civil War officer who had served with the Cherokees, and Adolphus Patterson, state representative from Swain County. Early in 1905 they helped the assembly pass "An Act to Compel Attendance of Indians at School," which made Qualla Boundary a special school district and required, with certain exceptions, that all children from ages seven through seventeen attend classes for at least nine months of each calendar year. This was contingent upon the United States government's assuming all financial obligations for such education. Any parent or guardian withholding a child from class was subject to a fine or imprisonment. The racist basis of this legislation was evident from a provision exempting anyone with less than one-eighth Indian blood.[39]

The compulsory school law was promptly challenged by the continuing nonattendance of certain Indians. Finally, at the urging of Harris, state officials haled into court Jacob Wolf, the father of one truant. The resulting case made its way to the state supreme court, which declared in 1907 that the Cherokees were citizens and therefore subject to the attendance law. Though this decision implicitly challenged federal control of the Band, Harris applauded its supposed salutary effect in promoting education. Going even further, he lobbied for increasing the upper age limit for required attendance, and in 1909 an amendment to the act raised it to nineteen years. Unfortunately, school attendance on the reservation remained disappointing and was a continuing source of concern to agents. They often filed warrants against uncooperative parents or sent police to capture truants. And in 1913 Agent P. R. Wadsworth asked a nearby lumber company to fire two Cherokee boys who had run away from school to work.[40]

The increasing emphasis on Cherokee education was a factor in considering the reestablishment of day schools on the reservation. Agent William C. McCarthy had started these in the mid-1870s, and they had operated sporadically until closing in the late 1890s. By 1908, however, the compulsory attendance law and a renewed federal interest in such schools meant that DeWitt Harris could safely advocate reopening them. His successor, Frank Kyselka, also supported this and worked out a temporary arrangement whereby the counties provided several public day schools on the reservation. He pointed out to his superiors that Cherokees could not attend classes in nearby communities because state law prohibited Indians, blacks, and whites from attending the same public schools. The result was that even in small districts "the County has to provide three schools—one for whites, one for Indians (where any are provided) and one for negroes." Unfortunately, no county in western North Carolina had the money to support even one good educational system, let alone three.[41]

The solution, Kyselka believed, was for the federal government to take over operation of the day schools—using, if possible, some county revenues. Eventually the counties agreed to refund that portion of tribal taxes that would normally go for public education, and the Band used this to support its own federally supervised school system. By 1912 there were four day schools: in Big Cove and Bird Town on Qualla Boundary and at Snowbird Gap and Little Snowbird, near Robbinsville in Graham County. In contrast, most recently enrolled tribal members in Cherokee County had only a small quantum of Cherokee blood and could readily "pass" for white; they were thus able to attend public schools and experienced little discrimination.[42]

Day schools were less well equipped than the training school and were staffed by whites whose own educational attainments were sometimes suspect. John A. Hyde, the teacher at Snowbird Gap, complained that his school had only benches without backs, "which you know is death on the child." Pupils had to balance books and writing materials on their laps, and the ancient stove was hardly adequate for winter. There was not even an outhouse to provide a minimum of sanitation.[43]

For the more promising students, the boarding school in Cherokee provided a pipeline to further education at out-of-state institutions like Hampton, Carlisle, Haskell (Kansas), and Chilocco (Oklahoma). The first primarily served blacks, while the others were for Indians. The curriculum was a mixture of academic subjects and vocational instruction designed to prepare pupils for possible employment off the reservation. To accomplish this, white educators believed it was necessary to keep students away from the tribal milieu and encourage them to adopt the individualistic ethos of white America. Paradoxically, this often occurred within the context of a regimentation that discouraged deviation from accepted norms. During the summer Eastern Cherokee students usually participated in the "outing system," living and working among whites in order to earn a little money and to prevent possible backsliding by returning to the reservation.[44]

The schools received mixed marks from Cherokee students. David Owl, for example, found both Hampton and Carlisle worthwhile experiences. He and his younger brother George, who attended Hampton, received a good basic education, starred in athletics, and became sophisticated advocates of tribal progress. Other Cherokees also did well at those schools, although it appears that students attending Carlisle were less satisfied than those at Hampton—perhaps because it was farther from home or because of the discipline and near fanaticism of some of the Carlisle staff.[45]

On the other hand, some Cherokees languished in the strange environment of academe and yearned for home. Occasionally there were disciplinary problems or, more frequently, students complained of unfamiliar surroundings, strange food, and sickness. One girl at Carlisle pleaded with her mother for money to return home, claiming she had lost more than twenty pounds in only three months. Then, in an appeal any mother would find difficult to resist, she said, "If you want to see me well and strong again you will have to help me get away from here, because if I stay here another month I'll be nothing but skin and bones." If matters continued the same way, she believed she would be dead in three months. "I'm so lonesome and disappointed that I have had to cry nearly every day since I received your letter . . . for pittys sake help me away from here." She was soon back on Qualla Boundary.[46] Other students simply disappeared from school, usually to reappear quietly on the reservation. Getting back from Haskell and Chilocco took some effort, but there were students willing to take their chances.

One Eastern Cherokee left Haskell, somehow made his way to Knoxville, and then walked more than sixty-five miles across the Smoky Mountains to his home.[47]

The mere experience of going away to school, pleasant or not, at least made students more aware of the outside world. About 132 Cherokees attended Carlisle between its founding in 1879 and 1914. By the latter date 57 had apparently returned to North Carolina, 47 had no known address, and 28 others were scattered across fourteen other states.[48] Assuming that at least half of those with unknown addresses were living out of state, about 40 percent of the Carlisle students had a chance to leave North Carolina permanently, even if merely for employment on another reservation. By mid-1916 about 190 Eastern Cherokees had attended Carlisle, 54 Hampton, 23 or 24 Haskell, and 17 Chilocco. After the closing of Carlisle in 1918, more and more Cherokees attended the last two schools.[49]

Students returning from these schools to reservations found opportunities lacking, and agents encouraged them to seek employment elsewhere. An Indian Office report in 1917 concluded that "a large proportion of 'returned students' not only fail to show any progress but, in many instances, actually go backward." James Henderson reminded one Eastern Cherokee at Carlisle that he enjoyed a unique privilege: "Do you realize that you have a better opportunity to make something of yourself than any poor white boy on or near the Cherokee Reservation?" He asked the student if he was willing to work as a mere common laborer, warning, "Should you return to Cherokee the only opening for you would be shovelling dirt and hammering stone with the negroes on our public road."[50]

* * *

The many health-related problems on Indian reservations were no less pressing than those confronting progressive reformers in burgeoning industrial cities. At the Cherokee boarding school untreated waste went by terra-cotta pipes into small creeks running directly into the Oconaluftee River, a system no doubt more sanitary than arrangements at individual Indian homes, where even outhouses were almost unknown.[51] The ethnologist James Mooney had earlier cited the Cherokees' poor sanitation as a factor in their recurring diseases. And in 1914 a visiting government physician concluded that although the Cherokees "have reached a plane of education much in advance of that of most other tribes local conditions have been and are such that their knowledge of the simplest details of hygiene is scarcely in advance of that of the lowliest of the Western tribes."[52]

The Eastern Cherokees did not readily accept outside advice concerning health matters, for many continued to rely on conjurers or traditional medicine men. The physician who visited in 1914 said they "cling almost, if not quite as tenaciously to a belief in the medicine man as does the average Navajo or Pueblo." Even attempts at preventive medicine were likely to meet with suspicion. In 1901, for example, the Indian commissioner ordered all Cherokees to be vaccinated against smallpox. Most resolutely refused to submit, and Henry Spray could only remind the commissioner of the government's uncertain authority over the Band. Besides, he pointed out that the reservation's isolation had prevented any outbreak of smallpox since a major epidemic during the 1860s. His only hope was to use "moral suasion" to promote inoculation.[53]

Cherokee students living in crowded dormitories faced a variety of health threats. Foremost among the diseases were tuberculosis and trachoma, both common on other reservations. Others included typhoid and scarlet fever, measles, influenza, whooping cough, and pneumonia. These diseases, and such things as the unexplained deaths of thirteen students between the summers of 1899 and 1900, call into question the normally optimistic health reports sent by agents to the Indian Office.[54]

Most of the time there was a doctor at the training school, and in his absence a physician was available at Whittier. After installation of the telephone line to that town, it was a simple matter to call the doctor in an emergency. At other times the tribe used a physician based in Bryson City. But effective health care was still impossible as long as the Band lacked a hospital or even an infirmary. Special agents and inspectors visiting the reservation focused on this shortcoming so persistently that the government finally authorized construction of a small modern hospital. Within a year of its completion in 1916, James Henderson was complaining that it was too small and lacked tuberculosis and maternity wards.[55]

A common threat to health on Indian reservations everywhere was alcohol. Since the Civil War, various agents had often complained about drunkenness among the Cherokees and its attendant violence. The killing of a young Indian by another at Bird Town in 1908 apparently happened because both men were drinking. (Another factor, according to Frank Kyselka, was that both had stopped attending school and were therefore subject to little restraint.) If Kyselka is to be believed, the periodic per capita payments also contributed to more drinking and violence. Between the springs of 1910 and 1911 liquor was blamed for seven violent deaths on Qualla Boundary. Preventing alcohol from reaching the reservation was almost impossible because the federal government lacked clear authority over the Eastern Band. Though North Carolina had already enacted Prohibition, moonshining flourished in the mountains, and Indian and white bootleggers imported whiskey by railroad from Chattanooga and then distributed it among the Band. With Kyselka's encouragement, the legislature passed a law in 1909 making public drunkenness a crime in Swain County, but it did little good, for inebriated Indians—and whites—often disrupted tribal ballplays, fairs, and even religious meetings. Agents sometimes requested Swain and Jackson county law enforcement officers to be present at larger gatherings to prevent trouble.[56]

As befitted a time when there was growing national sentiment for a Prohibition amendment, officials launched a determined campaign to wean the Cherokees from alcohol. Classes at the boarding school emphasized the dangers of liquor, and authorities ferreted out and destroyed several moonshine distilleries that catered to Indians. One indignant Cherokee warned a Big Cove moonshiner that he would report the offender to the agent, whereupon the distiller offered the other man all the whiskey "he could tank himself up on"—an offer that was promptly accepted. Efforts were also made to prevent importation of spirits into Swain County by rail. The Indian Office meanwhile circulated forms encouraging Indians to sign an abstinence pledge. By mid-1915 more than 130 Cherokees had obliged, including, apparently, some children. Unfortunately, taking the pledge did little to ease the problem on the reservation.[57]

The Progressive Era witnessed both losses and gains in Cherokee crafts. With the advent of a money economy, tribal expertise in spinning and weaving all but disappeared as Indians chose to spend a portion of their wages on ready-made clothing. Prospects for other crafts, however, began to brighten. In 1902 Estelle Reel, superintendent of education within the Indian Office, inquired about the extent of crafts like basketry and suggested they might well provide additional income for Indians. Henry Spray replied with only slightly disguised disdain that a few Cherokee "vagabonds" traveled about selling baskets that were only slightly superior to those made by neighboring whites.[58] One who in some ways fit this description was Aggie Ross Lossiah, who lived in southeastern Tennessee as a child and sometimes walked all the way to Maryville to sell a few baskets for enough money to buy a cotton dress. Spray's successors were a bit more open-minded about Cherokee crafts, one noting in 1907 that tourists had already bought all of the native-made blowguns.[59]

By 1911, according to an agency report, forty Eastern Cherokees had part-time employment making baskets and two more were producing pottery, yet the total value of all baskets that year was only $600. Within another two years, however, the Indians could sell all the baskets they made to the Grove Park Inn, a newly opened and popular tourist resort in Asheville. Before long at least one store in Cherokee was also buying native baskets and pottery, and Indian craftsmen were finding other potential markets by exhibiting at regional fairs.[60]

Organizing their own fair was one way the Cherokees could showcase their crafts, attract whites to the reservation, and in general bring their people into closer contact with the outside world. A 1912 circular from the Indian Office suggested such a fair, but both Frank Kyselka and his successor, James Henderson, expressed doubts, the former saying that a fair would require a tribal subsidy and pose problems in controlling liquor consumption. Nevertheless, by September 1914 Henderson was busily planning to stage a fair the following month. Shrewdly sensing an opportunity to promote it, he tried to induce United States congressman James M. Gudger to speak by pointing out that there would be a large number of white voters present. This first fair was highly successful and exceeded Henderson's expectations, but some traditionalists were outraged over the tribal council's appropriation of $200 to finance it. As Henderson reported, "there was such a howl" raised by the "non-progressive element" that it was decided not to use the money.[61]

After this initial triumph, the Cherokee fair became an annual October event and drew increasingly large crowds. Maintaining order was always a major concern, and as early as 1915 Henderson requested money from the Indian Office to hire a white deputy sheriff for the upcoming fair. When the office responded that the tribe had its own two-man police force, Henderson replied, "A drunken mountaineer would care no more for a timid Indian police[man] than he would for the average boy."[62]

By 1916 one white observer claimed the Cherokee event was "far better" than some of the county fairs. Because the exposition had outgrown its modest facilities, the tribal council, now willing to override possible opposition, appropriated $500 to build an exhibit hall.[63] Until creation of the Great Smoky Mountains National Park in the 1930s, the fair provided the main contact between the Band and whites, many of whom came from Asheville and beyond. Clearly the fair had mixed results, encouraging Cherokee interaction with the outside world and also reinforcing cultural continuity by emphasizing native crafts and activities.

Thus, as progressivism on the domestic front was about to become a larger crusade to make the world safe for democracy, the Eastern Cherokees were slowly adjusting to the new industrial age. The changes of the early twentieth century had brought them into contact with the outside world, introduced them to wage labor and the profit incentive, and raised anew the troubling question of whether it was possible—or desirable—to remain an Indian. The coming of a world war and renewed efforts to allot their reservation would test both their resolve and their ability to be part of the modern world while retaining a Cherokee identity.

3

The Citizenship and Allotment Disputes

IN APRIL 1917, when President Woodrow Wilson asked Congress to declare war against Germany "to make the world safe for democracy," he likely had given little thought to those at home who had no quarrel with Germany and every reason to suspect Wilsonian claims of "democracy." Such individuals included more than 300,000 Indians living on reservations and private allotments throughout the United States. Many still lacked citizenship, and almost all were impoverished. Among them were the Eastern Band of Cherokees, who, despite decades of mystifying legal dispute, were generally regarded as noncitizen wards of the United States.[1]

Officials within the Office of Indian Affairs viewed the war as a means of promoting the assimilation of Native Americans into the white-dominated cultural mainstream. Supporting the war effort—on battlefield and reservation alike—would hasten the Indians' "Americanization." Not coincidentally, it would also redound to the glory of the Indian Office as a responsible and patriotic part of the Wilson administration.[2]

About the only members of the Eastern Band expressing any interest in the war were a few individuals attending boarding schools or otherwise living outside North Carolina. As early as August 1915 Jack Jackson, an Eastern Cherokee living in Oklahoma, jokingly alluded to the conflict that had already been raging for a year in Europe: "It is rumored that they are having 'war' across the waters. Is that so? I can't quite understand what they are fighting over. Has that been the talk in North Carolina and Cherokee, ha, 'ha.' But let them fight, as long as they stay away from the United States of North Carolina & Oklahoma. Ha. Ha."[3]

Most of the Band manifested even less interest in the war. The closest many had come to the outside world was the annual tribal fair, when whites from the surrounding area flocked to the reservation. Certainly the stench of death on Europe's western front had little bearing on daily Cherokee life. Besides, as apparent noncitizens, why should they care about Wilson's crusade against Germany? Yet they did become involved, raising anew the perplexing questions about their status and exposing them to the violent realities of the twentieth century.

The war's most immediate impact on the Indians, as for many white Americans, came through selective service registration. Despite the president's early belief that conscription would be unnecessary, it soon became apparent that only a draft could raise the required manpower. After acrimonious debate, Congress finally passed a selective service act on May 18, 1917.[4] The only previous American draft, during the Civil War, had resulted in riots and other forms of opposition to a measure that seemed to contradict traditional ideals of voluntarism and independence. There was also considerable opposition in 1917, though any critic of selective service was likely to be considered unpatriotic or, worse, a "socialist." To further inhibit such foot-dragging, Congress quickly passed legislation outlawing public actions construed as hindering conscription. Wilsonian democracy might espouse "freedom," but it was a freedom that was carefully circumscribed.[5]

Indians were to register like any other Americans, but all noncitizens among them were legally exempt from compulsory military service. Despite the obvious importance of determining the Cherokees' status in regard to citizenship, agency superintendent James Henderson ignored the matter and hoped his charges would question neither registration nor conscription. He posted notices around the reservation informing all males of appropriate age of their obligation to register and requested various whites, including county sheriffs, to assist in processing them. He also asked officials at out-of-state boarding schools to register students from his reservation.[6] David Owl, who was then at Carlisle, dutifully registered and forwarded his card to Henderson along with comments on the situation at his school: "Owing to the war situation there has been a general unrest among the student body here. . . . Many of our men have left the school work to enlist into the army or navy, while a greater number have volunteered their services in the mobilization camps with the Army Y.M.C.A." Owl said he hoped to go to an agricultural college in Massachusetts the following year but recognized "there are possibilities that I will be conscripted into some sort of patriotic service."[7]

Complicating Cherokee registration in North Carolina were the dispersed nature of the reservation population and also the uncertainty about the ages of some Indians. At least one Cherokee disputed agency claims that he was an adult and refused to register.[8] Nonetheless, the work proceeded without much difficulty, and on June 8 Henderson informed the commissioner of Indian affairs, Cato Sells, that 115 Cherokees had registered: "Their willingness far exceeded my expectations and I am proud to say many of them seemed eager to register . . . and not a one showed the least unwillingness in the matter." Assistant commissioner Edgar B. Meritt commended the Cherokees for their patriotism and said his office was "highly gratified" by the response of Indians throughout the nation.[9]

The initial quota of conscripts for Swain County was eighty-one. David Owl's number was well down the list of those drawn in the draft lottery of July 20, but his brother George, a student at Hampton, was not so fortunate and faced probable induction. Even more certain of service was Stephen Youngdeer, a former Carlisle student from Jackson County whose number was the sixteenth drawn nationally and fourth among registrants in his county. Several other Cherokees were also on that county's list of likely draftees. The *Jackson County Journal*, of Sylva, encouraged all such men to enlist quickly to demonstrate both their patriotism and the willingness of Jackson County to do its part. There was little chance of escaping service, it said, for only a few individuals with severe physical or family problems would be exempt. Among those following this advice was Stephen Youngdeer, who went to Asheville and enlisted in the army.[10]

George Owl preferred to await the draft, but his older sister Lula, a nursing graduate, entered the army's medical corps as a second lieutenant—the only Eastern Cherokee officer in the war. Brother David, though temporarily safe from conscription, was having second thoughts about its legality for Eastern Cherokees. He broached the matter in a letter to Henderson, noting that though the Indians enjoyed some legal rights in the state, they did not appear to be citizens. What practical consequences did this have regarding the draft? Owl continued: "My interest in all phases of Indian administration causes these interesting as well as perplexing questions to arise in my mind" and, he admitted, "of course I am seeking this information for my own personal use."[11]

Henderson's reply was disingenuous, suggesting that the Cherokees were citizens because they had voted from time to time. He ignored the fact, however, that since 1900 county officials had almost completely denied the franchise to Indians. Gratuitously he added, "There is a certain element among the Cherokees who like to be citizens when it is to their best interest to be so and wards of the government when it is to their best interest to be so." But he confessed he was not qualified to judge on the legal aspects of Cherokee citizenship and thought "that nothing less than a decision of the United States Court will fully clear up this matter." [12]

Like David Owl, many other American Indians had misgivings about the legal implications of registration and the draft. In Oklahoma, some refused to register and then rioted when officials forced the issue. On a few remote reservations in the Far West other Indians also created minor disturbances, which their white neighbors usually exaggerated. In New York State the League of Iroquois adopted a novel though logical approach to the situation. Insisting it was a sovereign nation, it separately declared war on Germany, after which Iroquois males enlisted in the American armed forces as allies. [13]

Some whites in the mountainous area of North Carolina were less circumspect than David Owl and openly, defiantly opposed selective service. Localism and a strong sense of independence had always characterized these mountaineers, and they resented the long arm of Uncle Sam plucking them away from their homes to fight a war few understood or cared about. By March 1918 an armed band of deserters roamed the mountains of Jackson, Swain, and Macon counties and threatened anyone who might come after them. Local authorities were embarrassed by this disloyalty and concerned that other disgruntled men facing induction might join the band. [14]

Cherokee objections to conscription never conveyed such threatening overtones and typically took the form of respectful inquiries and protests, occasionally backed up by lawyers. The quiet persistence of a few individuals led Indian commissioner Sells to concede that noncitizen Indians were not subject to conscription, but the status of the Eastern Band of course was uncertain. In January 1918 he replied to the questions of three Cherokee brothers in Graham County by saying their local draft board would decide on their citizenship. [15] By then thirty-three of the Eastern Band had either enlisted or been drafted, while another had left a northern school and joined a Canadian military unit. [16] But the question of Cherokee status remained troublesome, and Provost General Enoch H. Crowder requested clarification. Assistant Indian commissioner Meritt replied by citing two completely contradictory federal court decisions, the most recent of which, the 1897

Boyd case, had held the Eastern Cherokees to be noncitizen wards of the United States. Meritt avoided any definitive statement of responsibility by blithely concluding that "the question of citizenship is an individual one dependent upon the facts and circumstances in each case, and therefore I am unable to give you anything more definite on the subject."[17] Presumably the local boards would continue to decide.

As an agent of the Wilson administration, Superintendent Henderson understandably felt pressure to make the Eastern Cherokees appear eager to save the world for democracy. He was vigorous in getting them to register, even to the point of threatening arrest for noncompliance. And though he confessed his bewilderment over their citizenship in correspondence with acculturated tribal members, he was not frank about the exemption of non-citizens from conscription. Even had he been certain of Cherokee citizenship, he could have done more to assist the Indians in coping with conscription. Indeed, he later admitted that some non-English-speaking Cherokees may have appeared before draft boards for exemption hearings without benefit of interpreters.[18] To cite another case, had he counseled Stephen Youngdeer, who spoke English, it is possible the young man could have obtained an exemption as a necessary support of his parents and brothers.[19] In fairness to Henderson, his many obligations on Qualla Boundary probably precluded his handling such matters in all four counties where the Cherokees resided.

Like officials in many predominantly white communities, Henderson found the draft a convenient means of handling young men who might otherwise become troublemakers. According to him, a certain full-blood was a notorious moonshiner whose whiskey had caused "most of the drunken orgies in this locality during the past three years." The man was finally arrested and jailed about the same time he was drafted. Henderson "considered the case carefully and decided that it would be much better to have him go to the army where he could serve his country, retain his self respect and learn to obey than to go to the United States penitentiary for a year and a day."[20]

With the Indian Office having abrogated its responsibility by leaving decisions of citizenship to county boards, local authorities struggled with a dilemma of their own making. If they decided an individual was a citizen, he could be drafted to help fill the county's quota. However, a citizen presumably could vote and enjoy other privileges that had been systematically denied the Cherokees since the turn of the century (partly because of their penchant for voting Republican). One official, Robert L. Phillips of

Graham County, came up with a historically accurate assessment of the Indians' status and also a solution to the dilemma. Phillips, a Democrat, wrote the state adjutant general that in his opinion the Cherokees were noncitizen wards of the federal government who did not have such rights as voting or sitting on juries. Another argument against conscripting them, he said, was that many of those in Graham County (from the conservative Snowbird community) spoke no English and would require interpreters in the service. Perhaps, Phillips argued, it would be best to remove them from the selective service rolls and reduce the local quotas proportionately.[21]

These sentiments notwithstanding, the Eastern Cherokees continued to be drafted until the war ended. Among the draftees was David Owl, who, despite his inquiries regarding citizenship, was inducted in the spring of 1918 and served as a first sergeant and drill instructor at Camp Jackson, near Columbia, South Carolina. An excellent athlete, he was an outstanding pitcher for his division's championship baseball team.[22] Though most other Cherokee draftees did not question their induction, a few resembled certain whites by seeking exemptions. In Graham County three young men claimed they were noncitizens who could not comprehend English and acquired the services of an attorney to challenge the government's right to induct them.[23] Assistant Indian commissioner Meritt reiterated that county officials would decide the citizenship issue and vehemently argued that the War Department was already coping nicely with Indian servicemen who could not understand English. Besides, he said, agency records showed that two of the attorney's clients did speak English. Soon afterward the teacher at the Indian school in Graham County reported that the third client also spoke English, and very well; his family was simply trying to keep him out of the service.[24] All three were drafted.

The official service records of members of the Band reflected the vast confusion surrounding the Cherokees' legal status. In the section asking if they were United States citizens, some said yes, others said no, some wrote "ward," and George Owl, at least, responded with a question mark.[25] The war muddled the situation even more by placing officials of the Indian Office in what amounted to a conflict of interest. They well understood the complexity of the citizenship issue and its ramifications for conscription, but they were also part of the wartime administration and wanted desperately for Indians to be patriotic Americans. Though it might appear self-serving, they could even support military service as an agent of acculturation and assimilation.[26] But regardless of their own interests, they had an obligation to deal with the Eastern Cherokees honestly, even if it meant attempting to unravel the myriad threads of the citizenship issue. Thus the decision of the Indian office to leave the matter to local boards reflected expediency and virtual abandonment of its responsibility.

Perhaps 10,000 or more Native Americans served in the war, approximately three-fourths of whom enlisted (a reflection of the noncitizen status of many western Indians and their exemption from conscription). There were sixty-eight Eastern Cherokee servicemen, including a few who had enlisted before 1917. Service records are missing for at least two others who apparently failed to complete basic training. Thirty-six of the Cherokees were draftees, twenty-seven from Swain County.[27] This sizable number of conscripts obviously resulted from the Indian Office's relegating the complex matter of citizenship to local boards. The largest single group of Cherokee servicemen comprised draftees in Company I, Third Battalion, 321st Infantry Regiment, Eighty-first (or "Wildcat") Division. The 321st was organized at Camp Jackson in late summer of 1917. It appears that about seventeen Cherokees were in the regiment, most if not all in Company I. Most prominent among these was George Owl, whose command of English, comparative worldliness, and leadership abilities quickly earned him respect and the rank of sergeant. An outstanding athlete like his brother, he played on the division football team, where he caught the attention of senior officers. He was also solicitous about the welfare of his fellow Cherokee soldiers and communicated with Henderson and the Indian Office about their problems.[28]

Like countless other servicemen, the Eastern Cherokees were not always happy about leaving home or with the food and discipline at training camps. Yet they posed few problems, adjusted to the presence of whites, endured, and became good soldiers. Brigadier General George W. McIver, commander of the brigade that included the 321st, viewed his men as a relatively homogeneous group made up predominantly of white southern draftees who had inherited "the hardihood and military virtues of their pioneer ancestors." The Cherokees, of course, were an exception, but McIver had nothing but praise for them. "There was never anything like race feeling as far as they were concerned," he remembered. "They made good soldiers and served in perfect harmony with the white men who were their military associates." In particular he remembered George Owl, who "was looked upon as one of the conspicuous figures among the enlisted [*sic*] men of his regiment."[29] Guy Littlejohn of Company I confirmed this interracial harmony by writing from Camp Jackson that he and his fellow Cherokees were doing well and that he had made a number of friends among whites.[30] Some

Lumbee Indians of eastern North Carolina also served in the 321st without discrimination, though in at least one other command the Lumbees were treated as Negroes because of their uncertain lineage.[31]

In the meantime a significant change had occurred among the civilian population on the Cherokee reservation. No longer was the war an irrelevancy in their lives. Now, thanks to Henderson's efforts and the growing number of Cherokee servicemen, the North Carolina Indians avidly followed war dispatches and were determined to "do their part." They supported fund drives for the Red Cross with box lunches, one of which featured Governor Thomas W. Bickett as speaker, and at the 1918 fair they considered showing an appropriately anti-German film, *In the Wake of the Huns*.[32] That same year the tribal council voted unanimously to buy $1,000 in war saving stamps, and many individual Cherokees purchased additional stamps.[33]

After one national fund-raising drive, the *Jackson County Journal* referred to Qualla township as "the banner township in all western North Carolina" because it had subscribed its entire quota of $27,240. This performance was even more remarkable because Qualla reached its goal through grassroots participation, no individual pledging more than $600. The whole of Jackson County, in contrast, had pledged only 54 percent of its quota of $285,000, a source of considerable embarrassment to the newspaper.[34] The greatest display of Cherokee financial commitment to the war came just a month before the armistice, when the tribal council, as part of its "patriotic duty to help in this hour of need," voted thirteen to zero to buy $50,000 of Liberty bonds with tribal funds.[35] In all likelihood Henderson encouraged this action, but there is no reason to doubt the sincerity of the Indians' newfound patriotism.

Eastern Cherokees filled a variety of noncommissioned positions in the army, navy, marines, and army air corps. Most were in infantry units that embarked for Europe during the spring and summer of 1918. In July Stephen Youngdeer and Cain George, a fellow Cherokee, arrived with the Thirtieth Division near the French-Belgian border. They soon saw action, and Youngdeer was noted for volunteering to leave the trenches and go "over the top." According to a later account, he once told his comrades that he had come to kill Germans and would kill all he could. On August 31 he suffered severe leg wounds that were soon complicated by pneumonia, and he died on September 15 at age twenty-five.[36]

Ute Crow, a private in Company H of the Nineteenth Infantry Regiment, also saw combat and was credited with saving the life of his commanding officer, Captain J. H. Howell, of Waynesville. Crow spoke very little English and was reluctant in later years to discuss his exploits, but Howell related a story about how he was spared from a German bayonet when Crow grabbed the point of the weapon with his bare hands and wrested it away from the German soldier. According to another story, Crow also captured an enemy machine-gun nest single-handed.[37]

The 321st Infantry Regiment arrived in France with the rest of the Eighty-first Division in mid-August and soon moved to the front in the Vosges sector, near Saint Die, where Company I helped repulse a brief enemy sortie in which fourteen Germans were killed or captured. After several more deployments, the 321st moved into the front lines near Moranville on November 10. The Third Battalion, including Company I, came under a heavy barrage by German artillery but escaped with very light casualties.[38]

At 5:00 A.M. on November 11 American artillery pounded enemy positions opposite the 321st, presaging an attack that began at 6:00 A.M. Companies I and M were in the forefront of the Third Battalion's advance through a dense fog that probably helped keep casualties down. Almost immediately the troops encountered machine-gun fire, "but in each case the assaulting companies pushed rapidly forward and the enemy machine guns withdrew in haste." The battalion also went through "a perfect hail of high explosive shell, shrapnel, and gas shell, with an almost miraculously small loss." The advance continued for a distance of about three kilometers until 11:00 A.M., when the armistice ending the war went into effect.[39] After more than a year of training and anticipation, the 321st had tasted significant combat only in the final hours of World War I.

Total war casualties for the 321st were comparatively light. The unit had lost two officers and forty-two men killed in action, plus four more who later died of wounds. One hundred and eighty-three were wounded, including several Cherokees who had either been gassed or hit by gunfire or shrapnel. Among these were Blaine Hill, Arneach Toineeta, and Jack Taylor; Wilson Thompson, part of an artillery unit within the Eighty-first Division, was also wounded. Cherokee casualties in other outfits included Ute Crow, Cain George, Stancil Powell, and Nick Bradley, who dropped out of Carlisle, enlisted in Pennsylvania, and was wounded twice. Joe Kalonuheskie, of the 165th Infantry Regiment, died after the armistice of his wounds and pneumonia, the only Eastern Cherokee death from the war besides Stephen Youngdeer.[40]

When the 321st arrived back in the United States in June 1919, most Cherokee servicemen headed for the Carolina mountains.[41] Some, however, recognized the limited opportunities at home and were willing to consider military careers. Sergeant Simon Thompson, for example, stayed in the army for many years and saw exotic places around the world that Cherokee warriors of an earlier era could never have imagined. James Henderson encouraged Cherokees to consider the service as a career by noting that the reservation "is not very good for young men who desire to make a good living."[42] Robert S. Youngdeer, former principal chief of the Eastern Band and a career military man, believes some Cherokees found the service attractive because they were familiar with the semimilitary regimen of schools like Carlisle, Haskell, Hampton, and the Cherokee boarding school.[43] Perhaps, too, there was a lingering pride in the Cherokee warrior tradition. Whatever the reasons, World War I marks the beginning of a continuing Cherokee willingness to serve in the armed forces.

According to Indian commissioner Cato Sells, World War I also served as "civilizer" by forcing Indian servicemen to acquire knowledge, judgment, courage, and character. Their wartime experiences represented a uniquely practical education and gave them the ability to "'go over the top' anywhere."[44] An Indian Office brochure, *The American Indian in the World War*, further developed this argument and concluded that continued Indian advancement was inevitable because Native Americans now realized there was a place for them in the great commonwealth of America.[45] The Indian Office had thereby neatly—and paradoxically—accommodated its traditional goal of civilization with the exigencies of a world war.

Though Cato Sells and other officials clearly exaggerated the war's "civilizing" impact, it did expose the Eastern Cherokees to a world far more expansive than the familiar confines of their reservation. Indian servicemen had had daily contact with whites from many different states and educational levels. They had gone through basic training together and prepared to face death together. Cherokees knew firsthand the destructiveness of twentieth-century warfare but had also glimpsed some of the more admirable features of life in the United States and Europe. At least one Cherokee married a Frenchwoman and brought her home. Many wartime experiences were shared vicariously by friends and relatives and helped bring them all into a larger, more cosmopolitan web of relationships. Many Indians now perceived themselves as members of an American society that transcended the reservation. Cherokee veterans were justifiably proud of their service (they all received honorable discharges), while tribal civilians could take satisfaction in having consistently surpassed their white neighbors in fund-raising and other patriotic endeavors. A symbolic affirmation of this "Americanizing" process was the creation of the Steve Youngdeer American Legion Post, allegedly the only all-Indian post in the United States.

A more important aspect of Americanization, of course, was allotment, and the heady aftermath of the war seemed ideal for finally accomplishing it. Pressures had long been building for allotment—or severalty—despite its disastrous impact on many other tribes. Some of the more accultur-ated and influential Eastern Cherokees claimed they could not fully improve their property until they received a fee-simple title through severalty. They wanted to use their lands as other Americans did, without tribal restric-tions. Some Cherokees living off the reservation favored it so they could sell their share or use their title as collateral for loans. And for more than a decade individuals of dubious Cherokee blood had clamored for inclusion on the tribal roll in anticipation of sharing the fruits of allotment. Most of the reservation Cherokees, however, probably feared the effects of severalty or fatalistically accepted whatever was to happen.

On November 6, 1919, after more than two years of negotiations with the Indian Office, the tribal council approved fifteen to zero a resolution "providing for the final disposition" of the Eastern Band's affairs. The reso-lution noted the Band's growing interrelations with whites, the difficulty of determining tribal membership, the "chaotic" nature of individual property rights, and the undefined status of the Band. It therefore approved a transfer in trust to the United States of all reservation lands and other assets (in-cluding $178,000 on deposit) and asked Congress to accept this trust while preparing the Band for allotment. Implicit was the expectation that the gov-ernment would prepare a new tribal roll. The trust conveyance eliminated any lingering doubts whether the government could proceed while the Band owned all tribal lands under a state charter. The resolution also asked Congress to withhold from allotment certain mineral lands, quarries, and water sites that were to benefit all tribal members.[46] Shortly after the reso-lution's passage, western North Carolina's congressman Zebulon Weaver introduced a bill authorizing Congress to accept the trust conveyance and to proceed with the Band's allotment.[47] But it was not to be so simple, for severalty became inextricably entwined with the always confusing question of Cherokee citizenship.   * * *

One issue World War I had persistently illuminated was the matter of Chero-kee citizenship. By refusing to address this problem squarely, the Indian Office had given tacit consent to the apparently illegal conscription of thirty-six members of the Eastern Band, while others had enlisted only to avoid

44

induction. In 1919, as an afterthought and a reward for Native American patriotism, the government decreed that any noncitizen Indian veteran with an honorable discharge could obtain citizenship simply by applying.[48] By early 1920 no Eastern Cherokee veteran had submitted such an application.[49]

The citizenship issue was revealed in stark relief by an ugly controversy attending the 1920 elections. To the surprise of many whites, a number of Cherokees not only registered but voted that year, including many women who were taking advantage of the recently enacted Nineteenth Amendment. One explanation for this unexpected turnout, that young Cherokee women were educated enough to pass literacy tests, is unconvincing because, as James Henderson admitted, Indian literacy had never prevented local registrars from disqualifying Eastern Cherokees. More persuasive is the allegation that Republicans in Swain and Jackson counties encouraged Indian registration and completely surprised local Democrats, who expected the custom of Indian disfranchisement to continue. Henderson suggested as much in a candid letter to David Owl by alluding to "some unprincipled white men trying to exploit the Indian vote." Democrats later complained that Republicans had even intimidated local registrars into registering the Indians.[50] Still another factor may have been an increased Cherokee interest in politics after the war.

Whatever the cause, Cherokee votes had a direct and obvious effect in Jackson County, where Republican candidates won almost every office by very narrow margins. Democrats immediately protested the election results because of alleged Indian ineligibility and for other reasons. Republicans began to fear that the Democrat-controlled Jackson County Board of Elections would overturn the election results. Unruly Republican crowds in Sylva, the county seat, threatened to disrupt the board, which finally adjourned to the sanctuary of Asheville to continue its deliberations. There it finally decided to throw out all eighty-three Indian votes in Qualla township, seventy-nine of which were for Republicans, on the grounds that the Cherokees were noncitizen wards of the United States. This would give all but two of the county offices to Democrats. Carl Standingdeer, a Cherokee graduate of Carlisle who was present at the deliberations, protested that this amounted to taxation without representation.[51]

Jackson County Republicans promptly began proceedings in court, contending that the Cherokees were state citizens whose ballots were valid. Litigation over this issue continued in Jackson and other western North Carolina counties, with one suit getting as far as the United States District Court. There, in May 1924, Judge E. Yates Webb concluded that the Eastern Cherokees were noncitizen federal wards and therefore not entitled to vote.[52]

The following month, on June 2, Congress seemingly solved part of the problem by passing an Indian citizenship act, declaring all Indians born within the United States to be citizens. Before its passage approximately two-thirds of American Indians had already achieved that status. Some saw citizenship as a reward for Native American patriotism during World War I, while others had argued that long-term Indian progress was impossible without it. Significantly, the new act in no way infringed on voting requirements set by individual states. Citizenship, then, did not automatically bring enfranchisement, as the North Carolina Cherokees would discover. But even with such limitations, citizenship was seen as a powerful ally of allotment in bringing about the long-desired assimilation of Indians into American culture.[53]

In this case, however, citizenship and allotment worked at cross-purposes and ultimately made the Eastern Cherokees' status even more confusing. This was because the citizenship act was juxtaposed with another congressional act of June 4 "providing for the final disposition" of the Band's affairs in preparation for allotment. Zebulon Weaver and his supporters had been pushing this matter in Congress for more than four years and finally appeared on the verge of success that spring; as added support, a hand-picked delegation of mostly acculturated Eastern Cherokees arrived in Washington to lobby for the bill's passage. Among these was David Owl, whose uncle was current chief Sampson Owl. The younger Owl was on the staff at Haskell and had not lived on the reservation for years. Sibbald Smith, ever suspicious, believed the delegation had been carefully "coached."[54]

According to David Owl, "The process of seeing legislation through Congress is as slow as the flow of cold syrup and on the other hand requires the patience of Job." Yet such patience paid off, and on June 4, 1924, the bill providing for eventual Cherokee allotment was passed. Owl had already expressed the view that it would usher in a new era for his people. But passage of the bill had ironic consequences. Included in its detailed plans was a stipulation that a new tribal roll would be made of those eligible to share in dissolution of the Band's assets and—here was the joker—a provision that the Eastern Cherokees would become citizens *after* receiving and registering their allotments. This provision had been common in earlier allotment bills, but in this case it provoked controversy by being passed two days after the Indian citizenship act. The obvious question was whether the Eastern

Cherokees were citizens under the June 2 act or whether the later bill superseded it and delayed their citizenship until completion of allotment. North Carolina Attorney General James S. Manning concluded they were not yet citizens, while the Indian Office maintained they were. Because of legislative oversight—or, as some suggested, a Machiavellian maneuver by Zebulon Weaver, a Democrat—the allotment bill had muddied the citizenship issue even more. And it provided local registrars with additional justification for denying Indians the franchise.[55]

Another provision of the allotment bill reinforced white determination to prevent Cherokees from voting. It stipulated that within one year of the bill's enactment the lands of the Eastern Band would be withdrawn from the county tax rolls until after allotment and a twenty-five-year federal trusteeship (which could be reduced at the secretary of the interior's discretion). After the federal government formally assumed trusteeship of the Band's assets in July 1925, county officials were told not to tax Indian property. For the first time since the Eastern Band had acquired its lands in the nineteenth century, the Indians would not pay property taxes.[56] This federal action created consternation in Swain and Jackson counties. The Cherokees had about 54,000 acres there, in addition to almost 9,000 acres in some fifty tracts in Graham and Cherokee counties. The *Jackson County Journal* estimated that in that county alone $1 million worth of property was now exempt from taxation. For their part, Swain County officials stubbornly attempted to continue Indian taxation and in 1927 even "sold" part of Qualla Boundary for nonpayment; this eventually led to a decision by the circuit court of appeals that upheld federal withdrawal of Cherokee lands from taxation. But even while the case was pending, resentful county officials redoubled efforts to block Cherokee voting on grounds of either illiteracy or lack of citizenship.[57]

As stipulated in the allotment bill, the federal government also began preparing a new membership roll for the Eastern Band. The 1908 Churchill Roll had included many individuals of questionable Cherokee ancestry who hoped to share in sales of tribal timberlands and any future division of assets. Now, with allotment imminent, "Cherokees" magically appeared in every nook and cranny of western North Carolina and, indeed, across the United States. In the allotment bill Congress had specifically rejected a clause in the Band's corporate charter limiting membership to individuals with at least one-sixteenth Indian blood. The House Committee on Indian Affairs made it clear that Congress determined qualifications for tribal membership, not any state or even the tribe in question. In fact, some people were enrolled for Oklahoma allotments with as little as ¹⁄₂₅₆ part Indian blood. The committee decided that membership in the Band should include not only those on the reservation but others with a verifiable trace of Cherokee ancestry who lived anywhere within the historical domain of the tribe.[58]

This catholic interpretation of tribal membership had predictable consequences. Guion Miller, who had earlier prepared a controversial Cherokee payment roll, was one of several lawyers who encouraged and processed applications by potential enrollees in return for a fee and commission. By mid-1926 the number of applicants beyond those already enrolled was 11,525 and eventually rose to more than 12,000. The secretary of the interior appointed Fred A. Baker to sift through these applications, and his initial roll in November 1928 included 3,146 individuals. Immediately the tribal council challenged the eligibility of 1,229 who had a low quantum of Cherokee blood and whose inclusion would severely reduce the benefits to others on the roll. Because the government intended to provide each Cherokee with an allotment of thirty acres (including, if possible, his home and improvements), 3,146 enrollees would require more than 94,000 acres—more than half again as many acres as composed the entire reservation. Although the government would pay a monetary equivalent to those who did not receive land, this would also reduce benefits to bona fide members by coming from tribal funds.[59]

Meanwhile 2,982 unsuccessful applicants appealed for inclusion on the tribal roll, and after a series of hearings the Baker Roll was revised *upward* to include 3,157 individuals, many of whom had less than one-sixteenth Cherokee blood and lived apart from the tribe in western North Carolina, Georgia, and Tennessee. One estimate was that no more than 2,000 on the roll lived on the reservation, with perhaps 600 or so living elsewhere in North Carolina and 400 or more in other states. Most of those off the reservation in North Carolina were "for all practical purposes" whites, while most living beyond North Carolina were former Cherokee students who had ventured into the outside world. This inflation of the tribal roll made allotment much less attractive to reservation Cherokees and led to bitter disapproval of "white" or "five-dollar" Indians—the latter an allusion to fees collected by lawyers like Guion Miller for listing claimants of dubious Cherokee ancestry. What is curious is that enrollees tended to have either at least three-fourths or no more than one-fourth Cherokee blood. Relatively few were between those figures.[60]

In the midst of the enrollment controversy James Henderson was coming under fire from Indians and whites alike. Having held his position as super-

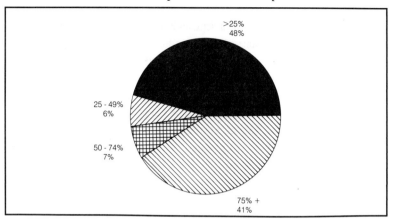

Baker Roll: degrees of inheritance (N = 3,155). Source: Patricia Quiggins, Department of Anthropology, University of Tennessee

intendent for fourteen years, longer than anyone before or since, he could hardly hope to remain unscathed amid such turmoil and dispute. He had made enemies, and after an investigation he was forced to resign in the spring of 1928. R. L. Spalsbury briefly succeeded him and then, in quick order, Ralph P. Stanion, L. W. Page, and Spalsbury again.[61] As the 1928 elections approached, Stanion denounced the continuing disfranchisement of Cherokees and threatened federal legal action should it occur again; imposing certain educational requirements was acceptable, he said, but not if unscrupulous registrars used it for across-the-board disfranchisement. Despite his forceful stand, county officials again prohibited Cherokee registration. The highly articulate if irascible Sibbald Smith vented his anger and frustration in a letter to Zebulon Weaver and castigated unnamed villains for their alleged role in confusing the matter of Cherokee citizenship back in 1924; he was careful, however, not to lay the blame at the sensitive Weaver's doorstep.[62]

Finally, on June 25, 1929, Congress passed another act that attempted to resolve any misunderstandings arising from the two 1924 bills. It stated that "it was not the purpose of Congress when passing the act of June 4, 1924 . . . to repeal, amend, modify, or abridge the provisions of the act of June 2, 1924" and explicitly reaffirmed Cherokee citizenship as of June 2. But it was to no avail, because local officials in North Carolina steadfastly refused to register Indians. In May 1930 Henry M. Owl, a brother of David and George Owl, filed an affidavit claiming he had been denied the right to register in Swain County. Because Owl had recently written an M.A. thesis in history at the University of North Carolina, the registrar could hardly claim he failed to meet literacy standards. Instead, he refused to register Owl and other Indians on the grounds of their alleged lack of citizenship—this nearly a year after Congress had forthrightly reaffirmed Cherokee citizenship.[63]

Obviously something had to be done. On June 19, 1930, Congress again emphatically confirmed full rights of citizenship for members of the Eastern Band, including the franchise if they otherwise met state requirements for voting. Local newspapers protested this "interference," worried about the effect six hundred to seven hundred Cherokee voters would have on local politics, and in a novel paraphrase of Patrick Henry complained that allowing Indians to vote amounted to "representation without taxation." The newspapers need not have worried. Despite Congress's explicit and repeated directives, county registrars continued to deny Cherokees the vote until after World War II.[64]

By the late 1920s national attention was increasingly focused on America's Indian "problem." It was apparent that many of the old assumptions about Native Americans and the proper policies for them were ill founded. The Indians were not disappearing. They were not becoming assimilated. They continued to be impoverished, undernourished, and poorly educated. They were still victimized by unscrupulous whites. And most apparent, allotment had proved a disaster. The decade of the twenties witnessed the creation of various Indian rights organizations, an increasing scholarly interest in Native American cultures, and the systematic investigation and reassessment of Indian policy. The voluminous Meriam Report of 1928 offered a wide-ranging critique of current Indian policies and the efficacy of previous allotment programs. In short, the very period that brought about a bill for allotment of the Eastern Band was laying the groundwork for a new policy that would disavow severalty.[65]

This reaction on the national level coincided neatly with growing consternation among the Eastern Cherokees over the picayune share each would receive should allotment be based on the Baker Roll. Perhaps it would be better to retain tribal landholding and control of funds on deposit. In November 1929 the Cherokee council again complained about the Baker Roll and asked the secretary of the interior and commissioner of Indian affairs what had been decided about the contested names. It then referred to "the persistent rumor going the rounds here that your department is opposed to the allotment of our lands and that in all likelihood this will not be done." It requested both a settlement of the enrollment issue and a statement from the Indian Office as to its intention regarding allotment. Chief John A.

Tahquette, Vice Chief Andrew Otter, and fourteen council members unanimously voted for the resolution.[66] The Cherokees were perceptive indeed. Herbert Hoover's administration was backing away from allotment.

Finally, on March 19, 1930, the tribal council passed a resolution calling for removal of 1,222 names from the roll and asking that no one be recognized as a tribal member with less than one-sixteenth Eastern Cherokee blood. It also requested the United States to continue holding the Band's lands in trust and averred that, for the time being at least, the Cherokees were absolutely opposed to allotment. Many Indians believed that the 1924 allotment act, especially the sections relating to enrollment, violated certain understandings the council had reached with federal officials back in 1919. The Indian Office tacitly agreed to reconsider the situation by sending Flora W. Seymour, a member of the Board of Indian Commissioners, to investigate. She concluded that the proposed allotment would result in each Indian's receiving less than two acres of "desirable agricultural lands" and objected to individuals with only a trace of Cherokee blood receiving a share of tribal assets.[67]

On December 4, 1930, secretary of the interior Ray Lyman Wilbur referred to these recent events and admitted that "allotments in severalty . . . have not in many respects worked to the best advantage of the Indians," and that perhaps some other plan could be devised for controlling tribal assets. One possibility for an unallotted tribe would be to form a corporation and "under proper supervision" invest it with those assets. He even suggested that the Eastern Band's status as a North Carolina corporation, under congressional jurisdiction, might "be an ideal situation with which to try out the incorporation plan."[68] The irony of extolling the Band's status as a possible model for other Indians apparently passed unnoticed. But Wilbur's suggestion was a prelude to some of the sweeping changes included in the Indian Reorganization Act of 1934.

In any case, allotment for the Eastern Band was dead. On March 4, 1931, Congress amended the 1924 act by "deferring" severalty until a more suitable policy could be devised. It also declared the Baker Roll definitive as of June 1924 but, heeding Cherokee complaints, specified a one-sixteenth blood quantum for any future members.[69] The council viewed the enrollment provision as a half-measure at best and continued to repudiate the Baker Roll. Likewise, it requested certain amendments to the tribal charter reflecting its paranoia over white Indians. One increased the blood quantum required for chief and vice chief from one-fourth to one-half, and another gave proportionately more representation to traditionalist and full-blood communities like Big Cove and Snowbird by reducing the number of councillors from fifteen to six—one from each town. Although representation was quickly changed to two councillors from each community—an arrangement that continues to the present—that too favored those with a significant degree of Cherokee ancestry. Another amendment allowed Cherokee women to vote in tribal elections.[70]

Cherokee reactions to the demise of allotment must have varied considerably. Many no doubt welcomed it, but the council's sentiments are harder to assess. It appears that since 1924 the main objection of various tribal leaders to allotment was the inflated Baker Roll. As late as 1932 the council requested, if necessary, a congressional appropriation of $150,000 to pay off the contested members, "whose presence on the roll . . . will delay the allotment of our lands and the final settlement of our affairs at least another generation."[71] But it was already too late. Tribal opposition to the Baker Roll had delayed severalty until the slowly germinating policy changes of the 1920s called into question the wisdom and efficacy of allotment. This had proved decisive in preventing that final step toward dissolving tribal assets and, perhaps, tribal identity. The Eastern Cherokees would remain a united though fractious people, citizens without rights of citizenship, landowners lacking property rights, a "people of paradox."[72] Some of the more acculturated would bitterly resent the failure of allotment and what they perceived as an enforced "return to the blanket." Nor would they find solace in the Indian policy of Franklin D. Roosevelt's New Deal.

4

Continuity and Change

IN THE EARLY twentieth century the Eastern Band teetered between the comfortable certitude of familiar folkways and the tantalizing possibilities of a changing America. In 1919 the tribal council approved an eventual allotment of the reservation in the belief that this would help make Cherokees like other Americans. Although allotment never came about, tribal leaders clearly believed it was time for their people to emerge from the comforting cocoon of tribalism. During the next decade or so events inexorably pushed them closer to the cultural mainstream. A declining lumber industry forced a search for alternative sources of income, the most promising of which—tourism—required closer contact with whites. At the same time, a national reevaluation of Indian policy brought new educational developments that successfully challenged traditional ways.

For most of the 1920s the Eastern Band continued to rely on the logging and milling industries, but there were slumps that brought about temporary unemployment and other hardships. During a recession early in 1921, agency superintendent James Henderson rejected a request for Indian contributions to relief efforts in the Middle East by noting that hard times had "brought considerable distress among the Cherokees," and they needed everything for themselves.[1] Yet lumber production was soon back to normal, and the early twenties marked the boisterous heyday of mills and logging camps where Indians could find employment, moonshine, and a shaky morality—a combination that worried Henderson. Throughout the Great Smoky Mountains lumbermen were enjoying one final glorious fling before most of the coves and valleys would fall silent.[2] This dynamism was not an unmitigated blessing, for it led to requests for rights-of-way across the reservation and a recurrence of timber trespass by both whites and Indians. Dry seasons like the fall of 1925 threatened the loss of tribal resources through forest fires, and sawdust and other mill wastes deadened stretches of streams where the tribe was attempting to establish fisheries.[3]

By the beginning of 1929, however, it was all over. The Ravensford and Smokemont mills had both closed, and employment for Indians elsewhere in the lumber industry was almost nonexistent. The Band continued to log portions of the reservation—indeed, the average annual cut of tribal timber during the 1930s exceeded that of the previous decade—but this did not compensate for the decline of off-reservation employment. Furthermore, growing prospects for an Appalachian national park in North Carolina and Tennessee sounded the death knell for a revived lumber business in the immediate area.[4] Like many of his predecessors, agent Ralph P. Stanion encouraged the Cherokees to reemphasize agriculture and stock raising, both of which had declined during the days of wage labor. County stock and fence laws, however, limited stock raising because the Indians could not afford to fence their animals to prevent them from ranging off the reservation and damaging crops. Whatever the difficulties, the Cherokee council agreed with Stanion on the need for changes and in 1929–30 appropriated money to promote agriculture.[5]

Another approach to unemployment was to encourage more Cherokees to find jobs in Detroit, Akron, Flint, Charlotte, and other cities with automobile-related industries. James Henderson also thought that Cherokee girls might follow in the footsteps of poor mountain whites and seek work in the new mills mushrooming throughout the Carolina Piedmont. But Ralph Stanion later said, without elaboration, that the textile mills were not "attractive" to Indians. Stanion was also pessimistic about possible self-employment on the reservation. His idea was to request funds from the federal government to enable qualified Cherokees to leave Qualla Boundary and obtain urban employment, a precursor of what would become the government's relocation policy of the 1950s.[6]

Even amid such hard times, there seemed to be a prescient awareness that tourism might someday offer the Eastern Cherokees the best chance of earning a living in their own homeland. By the early twentieth century visitors from all over the eastern United States were already flocking to the North Carolina mountains for a momentary respite from the pressures of urban life. Resort hotels had opened in Asheville and other nearby communities, and tourists increasingly wanted to visit Qualla Boundary, see "real" Indians, and perhaps buy a few handicrafts. By 1920 the annual tribal fair was a well-known regional institution, dedicated in large part to attracting visitors and marketing Indian wares.

More than anything else, the automobile promised to make Cherokee tourism a reality. By the 1920s America's growing infatuation with it bordered on obsession, as Henry Ford and other manufacturers annually turned out millions of inexpensive cars that offered a freedom of movement unimaginable to an earlier generation. The allure of the open road was irresistible. Social critics both lauded and bemoaned the automobile age, but most Americans had no such ambivalence. It was a love affair, a passionate mating of culture and machine. Who cared if one had to buy a car on credit?[7]

To sustain such a passion, of course, it was necessary to have roads— hundreds of thousands of miles of new highways. Federal highway acts of 1916 and 1921 officially committed America to a nationwide system of interconnecting paved roads to meet the demands of the new age. During the twenties a latticework of federal, state, and local highways spread in all directions, linking urban and rural areas and further nationalizing the American economy and culture.[8]

In Swain County, the Cherokee heartland, Model T Fords first appeared on the streets of Bryson City in 1914, and within another year bonds had been issued for a countywide system of highways. Within a decade a network of paved roads connected the counties of western North Carolina, and one could make the round-trip from Bryson City to Robbinsville in half a day, a trip formerly requiring an overnight stay. Even more important was the highway completed in 1925 between Bryson City and Asheville, reducing the driving time to a mere two hours. Four buses ran in each direction daily, bringing a rapid decline in railroad passenger traffic between the two towns.[9] In 1928 sociologist Ellen Black noted the effects of all this on Swain County: "The importance of the highways in practically every aspect of . . . life can scarcely be overestimated. The rapid changes which are self-evident are coextensive with their development." Among other things, more and more tourists were arriving by car, and "local products such as Indian baskets have doubled in price in the last five years."[10]

Unfortunately, road construction on the reservation lagged. By 1924 only ten of the seventy miles of road there were improved, and by the end of the decade the situation was not much better. The state maintained an all-weather route (Highway 107) between Bryson City, Bird Town, and Cherokee, as well as a short portion of the Big Cove road and an unimproved route from Cherokee up Soco Valley to Paint Town and Wolf Town. The route to Big Cove was described as a "fair mountain road," but automobiles sometimes became mired at the fords and had to be pulled out by oxen. Even though only about half a dozen tribal members owned automobiles, future development of the reservation obviously depended on better roads. Agents consistently reminded federal officials of this need and sometimes even proposed specific plans for state and federal cooperation on such projects.[11]

Automobiles and highways were also critical components of a growing campaign to create the Great Smoky Mountains National Park, which offered Cherokees hope for economic revitalization.[12] Qualla Boundary adjoined the eastern fringes of the proposed park, and Cherokee itself provided the most convenient access via the Oconaluftee valley. As early as August 1927, James Henderson saw Cherokee as a major gateway and argued for construction of a new state highway through the town into the parklands.[13]

* * *

Paralleling this new tourism was a growing popular and scholarly interest in the Eastern Cherokees, spurred in part by national attention to Indian problems. Letters seeking information about the Cherokees arrived regularly at the agency, and agents did their best to answer them. In 1919 Horace Kephart, a resident of Bryson City and author of *Our Southern Highlanders*, featured the Band and its history in a series of articles in *Outing* magazine. Relying heavily on James Mooney's *Myths of the Cherokee*, these articles were later reissued as *Cherokees of the Smoky Mountains*, a tourist-oriented pamphlet that has gone through several printings and still sells well. Kephart also occasionally reported on the Cherokees for North Carolina newspapers, which by the early 1930s regularly published features on them.[14]

This popular interest in the Eastern Cherokees was matched by a growing scholarly awareness. James Mooney was merely the first of a procession of anthropologists and other scholars who visited the reservation: Franz Boas, Frank G. Speck, Frans Olbrechts, L. H. Snyder, A. R. Kelly, William H. Gilbert, Leonard Bloom, John Witthoft, and others. Boas, Kelly, and Snyder studied Cherokee physical traits and blood types, while the others concentrated on tribal culture. Mooney himself died an untimely death in 1920, his reputation forever secure as the founding father of scholarly Cherokee studies, but Olbrechts found that when he arrived in Big Cove for fieldwork in 1926, his invocation of Mooney's name "served as the best introduction I could have desired. People who looked askance, and medicine men who looked sullen when first approached, changed as if touched by a magic wand as they heard his name and as I explained my connection with his work." [15]

Olbrechts and his colleagues attempted primarily to assess the persistence of traditional Cherokee culture on Qualla Boundary, especially in Big Cove, but it is difficult to determine to what extent they glimpsed actual fragments of the tribal past. Many ceremonies persisted in modified form, but as scholars admitted, most of the major ones Mooney witnessed in his first visits had largely disappeared, and in some cases the best sympathetic traditionalists could do was to reproduce vaguely remembered ceremonies that were perhaps subtly shaped by the evident anticipation of the anthropologists themselves. [16] Quite possibly visitors would have found more genuine manifestations of traditional culture in the more remote and less well-known Snowbird community in Graham County.

Regardless of the degree to which Cherokee life actually replicated that of an earlier period, it at least retained some of its old flavor. Log cabins continued to be the most common homes, and photographs from an extensive survey of 1922–23 show that such habitations were much like those of mountain whites, ranging from mere hovels to commodious, well-kept buildings. Except for five or six families occupying frame houses they had built themselves, Big Cove residents lived in one-room cabins that were at least a quarter of a mile apart, though Olbrechts said this did not prevent inhabitants "from knowing all that happens in the valley." [17]

William H. Gilbert of the University of Chicago was another investigator who found vestiges of traditional—or at least earlier—Cherokee culture on Qualla Boundary. Conducting extensive fieldwork in 1931–32, he confirmed many of the settlement patterns Olbrechts described and also looked closely at community institutions and kinship patterns. He found that a major feature of town life was the gadugi, a kind of cooperative that had evolved among the Cherokees during the preceding century and was designed to accomplish specific economic purposes. By the time of Gilbert's visit, the gadugi typically hired out its services and divided any profits among its members. In Big Cove about one-fourth of the residents, including women, belonged. Other town institutions included societies for conducting funerals and providing assistance to the poor, as well as ball teams that competed against those of other communities. [18]

By the early twentieth century the ballplay was a common feature of Cherokee efforts to attract white attention and money. It was always a major feature of the annual tribal fair, and nearby white communities often invited teams to compete before enthusiastic crowds on special occasions like the Fourth of July. Agents and acculturated Indians had mixed feelings about such invitations, welcoming the interest but sometimes fearing that the contests projected the wrong kind of image and delayed assimilation. James Henderson at first believed they encouraged "idleness" and prompted violence among drunken spectators, but he later considered the invitations on their own merits. In 1923, for example, he agreed to send a ballplay team to Washington D.C. for the Shriners' convention.[19]

What Henderson had perhaps come to realize was that the ballplay of the 1920s was only a pallid reflection of the earlier game. Conjurers still performed secret rites to support their favorite team or undermine an opponent, and an athlete might still "go to the water" and endure ritual scratching for purification or perhaps even observe certain dietary and sexual restraints before competing. Yet such practices were voluntary and probably more a cursory bow to tradition, a welcome break from the Cherokees' routinized life, than part of any deeply ingrained belief. And even though there was considerable enthusiasm for rough play, with occasional broken limbs, the contests were no longer the "little brother of war." Compared with college football, at least, Frank Kyselka believed the ballplay was a model of decorum. In 1910, when fatalities among collegiate athletes had become a national scandal, he expressed the belief that football's rule makers could learn "valuable points from a study of this Indian game."[20]

The same young men who competed in the Cherokee ball game on special occasions were likely to play baseball much more regularly. Before World War I, Jack Jackson and Stephen Youngdeer sometimes walked ten miles to Bryson City to play a game with whites, then trudged back home. Progressive Era reformers had already discovered that athletics, especially America's "national pastime," provided immigrant children with an effective rite of passage into our cultural mainstream. Likewise, the Indian Office encouraged baseball and other "American" games on reservations. As early as 1912 Frank Kyselka reported that Cherokee children were developing a keen interest in baseball, despite a lack of equipment. Earlier it had been difficult to interest them in this sport because the Cherokee ballplay "held their undivided attention."[21]

The example of nationally known Indian athletes also probably contributed to growing interest in mainstream sports. At a time when black players were excluded from major league baseball, Indians faced no such prejudice. Well-known players like Charles A. "Chief" Bender and John T. "Chief" Meyers showed that Native Americans were no mere curio pieces but part of a dynamic, inclusive society—or so some believed. And when Jim Thorpe of Carlisle became famous for his football exploits and victories in the 1912 Olympics, it redounded to the glory of his school, gladdened the hearts of assimilators, and stirred Americans of all colors. Similarly, Eastern Cherokees like Ben Powell and the Owl brothers became versatile, well-known competitors at school and in the armed forces. Powell played alongside Thorpe on some of the great Carlisle teams, while the Owls— David, George, Frell, Henry, and Thomas—were all superb athletes. Henry partly paid for his college education by playing professional football, and Thomas was so proficient that the principal of a Vermont high school went to considerable difficulty to certify his eligibility for competition.[22] Except for the tourist-oriented ballplay and a brief revival of interest in archery about 1930, Cherokees participated in white sports.[23]

While traditional Indian sports declined, Cherokee crafts enjoyed a resurgence as white tourists bought more and more baskets, pottery, blowguns, and other items. According to one informed source, the two years before 1929 brought a 50 percent increase in sales of Cherokee baskets and generated an income of about $10,000.[24] The variety of handicrafts reflected an uncertain lineage at best. Anthropologists speculated about whether they were truly Cherokee in origin or derived in part from other tribes and mountain whites. Catawba influences on pottery were clear and apparently dated from the mid-nineteenth century, when members of that tribe settled among the Band. An earlier Cherokee kind of pottery had largely disappeared by the 1920s. Woodworking and weaving both owed a large debt to whites, the latter almost disappearing among the Eastern Band during the heyday of wage labor. Cherokee basketry, in contrast, had clear tribal antecedents in dyeing techniques, the use of split white oak and river cane, and the double-weave pattern. This was the most widespread tribal craft of the early twentieth century, though whites sometimes compared Cherokee work unfavorably with that of western tribes.[25]

Throughout the 1920s, despite an attempt by the Indian Office to prohibit "useless and harmful" dances and ceremonies, Cherokees continued a few of their traditional dances in modified form. During the annual fair they regularly staged ballplay dances and even on occasion the green corn dance (or a version of it). Will West Long, the Big Cove traditionalist, frequently directed these and other dances for the edification of anthropologists and tourists alike. Frank G. Speck and Leonard Broom relied extensively on him for reenactments of the booger dance, whose meaning is still debated, where dancers wore elaborate carved masks. Other dances had more obvious import. The burial dance was staged by Big Cove traditionalists for seven consecutive nights at the home of the deceased to alleviate the bereaved family's grief and turn "their thoughts again to the normal affairs of life."[26]

Perhaps the best example of cultural continuity on the reservation was the daily use of the Cherokee language in most households, though increasing numbers of Indians could also speak English. Like all modern languages, spoken and written Cherokee was undergoing change. Olbrechts found two distinct dialects remaining on the reservation but said the differences between them were only slight. By the mid-1920s, moreover, certain "archaic, ritualistic expressions" found in early Cherokee documents were disappearing from usage.[27] Probably most distressing of all to traditionalists was the mounting success of white educators in teaching children to speak English. Years of punishing recalcitrant students for using their native tongue had finally taken their toll.

James Henderson was notably successful during the 1920s in upgrading education on the reservation, especially at the boarding school. Early in the decade a lack of sufficient federal funding resulted in outdated facilities and chronic overcrowding, and Henderson felt obliged to continue operating the grossly inadequate day schools in outlying parts of the reservation. When Inspector Peyton Carter visited in April 1922, he praised Henderson's diligence and abilities but noted that the boarding school's enrollment was well above its capacity of 200. Yet there were still 121 school-age children on the reservation not attending classes of any kind. Carter recommended three more classrooms and other improvements at the boarding school, but the Indian Office, while sympathetic, thought it might instead be necessary to eliminate grades seven and eight in order to provide a modicum of education for all Indians. Henderson replied that ideally the school should be expanded to a capacity of 300 and that dropping the two highest grades would be a mistake, since 35 Cherokees would thereby be deprived of education during the next term. The overcrowding, he explained, was due both to inadequate funding and to the tendency of Cherokee parents to send their children to the boarding school in hard times so they would be clothed and fed. This was an important obligation, and he believed his school had kept Cherokee children better fed than their white neighbors.[28]

Indeed, a look at the school menu over a seven-day period in May 1922 seems to confirm Henderson's contention. Students had a meat entree on five of those days, fish on another, and hash on the seventh. (Cherokee children preferred pork to any other meat and often frustrated efforts of school officials to feed them beef and mutton in disguised forms.) The usual accompaniments included potatoes and rice, stewed raisins or prunes, and a dessert of fresh strawberries or pudding. Breakfast mostly consisted of oatmeal and side dishes high in carbohydrates.[29] It is not clear whether this menu was typical of the Cherokees' daily fare.

Although shortcomings of the boarding school could be overcome by increased funding and expansion of facilities, Inspector Carter was much less optimistic about bringing the four day schools up to standard. The one at Bird Town, only two miles from the boarding school, was the most impressive, but its teacher lacked proper pedagogical skills and failed completely in his daily recitations. With thirty-three students, it had the largest enrollment of the day schools, but attendance was irregular and dropped to about 50 percent during the winter. The relatively heterogeneous population of the community caught Carter's attention, and several of the students appeared to have no Indian blood at all. About the only good thing Carter could say was that the school had a privy, a feature the others lacked. Despite the inspector's litany of inadequacies, some students could look back on their experiences there with nostalgia. Robert Bushyhead's memories of attending school in the 1920s limn an almost idyllic American student experience, tempered by the sometimes conflicting nature of traditional Cherokee life:

> The school building was a one-room schoolhouse with four grades and one teacher. We had double desks to utilize space, and the school was heated with a stove. We walked to school. The school furnished our paper and pencils. I remember that a railroad [the Appalachian line] went by the school, and a train came by at recess. The boys put pennies and nails on the rack, and the train flattened them. I was in a play the first Christmas I was at school, and my father rehearsed me for my part. I stood up on the stage and said, "There's only one boy in this world that I envy. Do you know who it is? Santa Claus's son!" When I was nine years old my family moved way back on a mountain and built a two-room log house. It was too far to walk to school, and I was placed in the boarding school then. Cherokee families were close-knit, and it was a tearing-away.[30]

Peyton Carter found the Big Cove school to be even more primitive than Bird Town's and certainly more isolated—twelve miles from the boarding school by logging train, assuming the sometimes uncooperative lumber company was willing to allow use by agency personnel. The school consisted of one old log building containing both the teacher's quarters and the schoolroom. There were no sanitary facilities or outbuildings of any kind.

The teacher, Arthur Dixon, taught grades one through three and exhibited "fair" pedagogical techniques but had only meager equipment. Even so stern a critic as Carter was captivated by the school's picturesque location, which he likened to that of a resort.[31]

The two day schools in Graham County, however, caught Carter's full wrath. The one at Snowbird Gap was an unpainted frame shack, "the most disreputable and unsatisfactory school that I have ever seen, except possibly the public day schools for Indian children maintained by Mississippi." Some of its windows were boarded up, and the inside walls were plastered with newspapers—most of which, the meticulous inspector noted, dated from June 1910. Carter found a few modern desks but little else, not even an outbuilding. The teacher, John F. Hyde, was unfamiliar with pedagogical methods and distorted attendance by not taking roll until 4:00 P.M., by which time all the lackadaisical students who planned to attend had arrived—and were ready to go home. (Hyde was aware that the Indian Office would close a school that did not average at least eight pupils.) Despite Hyde's claim that he had eleven students, Carter believed there were no more than four or five. "There was not a single redeeming feature about the school," he said, and it should not stay open a day longer than necessary.[32]

The other Graham County school, Little Snowbird, was much the same: few books, no maps, no privy, and wide cracks in the walls and ceiling. The teacher, S. S. Hooper, spoke Cherokee and had sterling qualities but knew "absolutely nothing about good methods of teaching" (perhaps too much to ask of a farmer who received only $60 for ten months of instructing Cherokee children). Like Hyde, he boosted attendance by taking roll at 4:00 P.M. Of the seven students present when Carter visited, only one could spell correctly, and she had no idea what any of the words meant. Nor could the pupils do simple arithmetic. Carter recommended closing the school at term's end.[33]

Henderson opposed closing the Graham County schools, contending that many great men had attended worse. If those two were closed, it would be very difficult to persuade local Cherokees to send their children away to the boarding school, and even if they did it was too crowded to accept them. But things quickly changed. By 1925 there was additional funding for the boarding school, its capacity had increased, and the Snowbird schools were no longer in operation. Despite talk by the Indian Office of reopening one, Henderson now advocated that Cherokee children in Graham County attend the boarding school because otherwise their home environment would cause them to unlearn at night what they had been taught during the day. He believed "no people ever needed being taken out of their old haunts so much as these people."[34]

Many Graham County parents disagreed and viewed pressures to send their children to school in Cherokee as an unwarranted disruption of family life. The Indian Office was sympathetic, for national criticism of boarding schools had produced a reemphasis on reservation day schools or, where possible, enrollment of Indians in public schools. The parents were able to take advantage of this situation. Despite Henderson's initial skepticism and opposition, they persuaded county officials to provide a teacher in return for some of the funds normally going to the federal schools. By decade's end the dream had been realized, and the county ran a small school for eighteen Snowbird children whose tuition was paid by the federal government. Their parents were well pleased with the arrangement, and that this was an exclusively Indian public school did not bother them at all. By late 1930 Graham County had constructed a new Cherokee school building six miles west of Robbinsville, and L. W. Page reported that the teacher was having "wonderful success not only in keeping the Indian children in school, but in winning the confidence and respect of the adult Indians." Thus the Snowbird Cherokees could provide an alternative approach to educating their youth, one that allowed a measure of autonomy and separateness not possible for other members of the Eastern Band.[35]

Other changes in Indian education were apparent by the end of the twenties. The Indian Office now mandated more emphasis on academic instruction and expected teachers to attend summer institutes and otherwise upgrade their credentials. The Cherokee boarding school boasted an increased enrollment, major renovations, new buildings, and for the first time a principal who concentrated solely on academics while the superintendent was freed to administer the reservation. Instead of dropping the seventh and eighth grades, as proposed earlier, the Indian Office added a ninth grade and made the institution a junior high school. Acculturated Cherokees and whites alike saw these as major accomplishments. Robert K. Thomas has argued that educational advances during this period also brought a widespread use of English on the reservation. There appeared to be a balance between the two languages, but few could doubt that the pendulum would soon swing toward English.[36] The rapid opening of the reservation to the automobile and tourism would ensure it. For those who believed that language is the foundation of traditional culture, the prospect must have been ominous indeed.

And yet despite the inroads of "civilization," many facets of traditional

Cherokee culture were apparent in daily reservation life, even if in modified form. Sometimes old and new were juxtaposed in unusual ways. Common-law marriages were still frequent, but they created peculiar difficulties when widows attempted to collect their husbands' benefits from the Veterans Administration. Sympathetic agents argued that these informal liaisons were as valid for many Cherokees as those sanctioned by church and state. In Big Cove, meanwhile, conservatives continued to believe that menstruating women possessed an inherent "nefarious influence" and that eating food they prepared, touching an object they used, or even being in their presence would have deleterious consequences. Although ancient taboos against such women had relaxed to the point where they no longer passed their periods isolated in small huts, Raymond D. Fogelson later discovered that Cherokee conjurers had found a "functional replacement" for the huts: where possible, they exiled their young wives to their grandparents during menstruation.[37]

Other physiological or medical taboos were observed on Qualla Boundary during the 1920s, and Olbrechts reported that at least a few traditionalists continued to believe white people—especially physicians—intentionally transmitted epidemic disease to Indians. Magic was the preferred way of passing on such maladies.[38] Perhaps this suspicion of white physicians explains the continuing willingness of many Cherokees to rely on traditional medicine. In 1908 DeWitt Harris claimed they were still "inclined to follow their native system of conjuring and native medicine," and a few years later a knowledgeable visiting physician said that in the time he had been on the reservation, "there have been few cases of illness among the Indians in which I have not, to a varying extent, been hampered in my treatment by the advices of the medicine man. A great many, I know, absolutely refuse to accept treatment from the white physician in any case." To the extent that they were willing to heed white advice, one doctor complained, they were more likely to buy patent medicines than to get a prescription and follow its instructions. Despite this lament, it appears most Eastern Cherokees were at least willing to consider white medicine as an alternative approach to injuries and disease. For example, one with a dislocated back went to a conjurer, who bound it up with moss and treated it with other Indian remedies. When this failed to ease the pain, the man readily came to the school physician.[39]

The distrust between conjurers and whites was symptomatic of the larger, unending struggle between Indian traditionalism and those whites—clerics, agents, or physicians—who favored "progress." Since the days when Europeans first came to the New World, many had believed the first step toward civilizing and converting Indians was to destroy the reputation of the local shamans and conjurers.[40] By the twentieth century, the latter were clearly on the defensive and usually found only in conservative communities. No real threat to white authority, they nevertheless remained an irritant, a symbolic reminder that the standards of civilization remained unmet. For their part, many conjurers had resigned themselves to their loss of authority, believing they were waging a "hopeless battle." They were likely simply to say that white medicine might be best for whites but traditional treatments were more efficacious for Indians.[41]

One can only imagine what traditionalists thought about the 1918 influenza pandemic that killed more than 21 million people worldwide and intruded into the farthest reaches of the Cherokee reservation, taking young and old and completely disrupting school. Influenza remained a potent threat during the next two years and periodically thereafter. Other infectious diseases like measles sometimes afflicted students at the boarding school, while tuberculosis, malnutrition, and "female problems" were also common on the reservation.[42] The situation had apparently improved, however, by the time Walter S. Stevens made a medical inspection in the summer of 1923. He reported that there were very few illnesses except occasional cases of enteritis among children (a result of poor diet, he believed). He also noted problems with hookworm ("quite prevalent"), pellagra, and goiter.[43]

As for health standards at the federal facilities in Cherokee, Stevens said both the dormitories at the boarding school were clean, though boys had to sleep two to a bed. The boys' toilets were in a separate building and sometimes caused problems, whereas the girls' were in the basement and in good working operation. Stevens said the twenty-four-bed hospital was "excellent" and staffed by a government physician, Dr. Russell D. Holt, a nurse, and an assistant. The Cherokees had considerable confidence in Holt, who had spent most of his twenty-six years of government service among them. For surgical matters, however, he usually called upon the specialized services of a Whittier doctor who was interested in the Cherokees. For the year ending June 30, 1923, the Cherokee hospital admitted 251 patients and discharged all but one, who died. Thus it appears that most Indians either did not obtain medical attention in their final illness or chose to die at home.[44] Likewise, Cherokee mothers preferred to give birth in familiar surroundings assisted by a midwife, and many still went to the water with conjurers during their fifth month of pregnancy. According to Stevens, the lack of hospital care for maternity cases was partly responsible for the high infant mortality rate on the reservation. By 1930, however, the tribal hospital handled eighteen maternity cases, representing almost half the births on the reservation.[45]

One continuing difficulty in Cherokee health care was the relative inaccessibility of parts of the reservation. Many Indians could not conveniently get to the small agency hospital, were perhaps ignorant of its existence, or were afraid to entrust themselves to such strange surroundings. Even by the late 1920s the agency doctor normally made his rounds by horse and buggy, although Walter Stevens, James Henderson, and others requested funds to provide him with a car. Assisting the doctor in his reservationwide work was field nurse Lula Owl Gloyne, the first Cherokee to hold a responsible health-care position on Qualla Boundary. She was highly successful in dealing with Indians who otherwise would have refused treatment.[46]

Two other problems in Cherokee health care received little attention in the official reports of Walter Stevens and other federal investigators. One was the continuing denial to Indians of services that were routinely extended to other residents of North Carolina. Because of the Cherokees' anomalous status, officials refused to admit them to state-operated hospitals, and mental patients were usually sent to the Indian bureau's institution in Canton, South Dakota.[47] Another health problem was alcohol, which continued to haunt the Eastern Cherokees even during the Prohibition decade. Moonshining was commonplace on the reservation and in surrounding mountain counties, despite the best efforts of Sibbald Smith, who for a time was a special agent entrusted with ferreting out stills. Forrest Carter, a successful Cherokee novelist, described in *The Education of Little Tree* how as a young boy he and his grandfather manufactured their moonshine in a narrow little cove and waged an unending campaign to outwit suspicious agents.[48] Whiskey making and other crimes, according to James Henderson, were most rampant in Big Cove, which he described as the most "backward" and "vicious" community on the reservation.[49]

By 1930 the Cherokee population was culturally and genealogically less homogeneous than it had been. Between 1910 and 1930 the percentage of full-bloods in the Eastern Band dropped from 66.4 to 38.7.[50] A partial explanation, of course, is that the tribal roll had recently been inflated by inclusion of many mixed-bloods. In addition, there were more descendants of Cherokee unions with rural whites dating back before the turn of the century. Some of these families had long lived on tribal lands, while others had moved to the reservation more recently. There was also a migration of some indisputably Indian families from off-reservation sites to Qualla Boundary. The Catt family, for example, was predominantly Cherokee but had long lived near Ducktown in southeastern Tennessee; then, after 1900, it relocated several times before settling on the 3,200 Acre Tract. Cherokees continued to move freely from town to town on the reservation, though those living in more traditionalist communities were less likely to do so.[51]

By the 1920s, Robert Thomas suggests, Cherokee families increasingly fell into one of three groups. There were the conservatives, who usually had a high quantum of Indian blood and, more important, defined themselves culturally as Cherokees and continued to place a heavy emphasis on using their native language. The second group, the "generalized" Indians, still thought of themselves as Cherokees but had internalized certain aspects of white American culture, especially the notion of "progress." Most of them had attended school at least briefly, and they were less likely to speak Cherokee because it seemed "to serve no purpose in the modern world." Occasionally they betrayed anxiety about being part of two different worlds. The third group Thomas characterizes as "rural white Indians," who were from families where whites (especially males) had intermarried within the preceding two generations and who had developed a pronounced white orientation. Their grandchildren were growing up shortly after the war and could seldom speak Cherokee—because of both their home environment and their experiences at the boarding school, where English was emphasized. They in turn often married whites, and the conservative and generalized Indians increasingly excluded them from tribal life. No doubt a major reason for this growing hostility was the inclusion of such individuals on the tribal roll. Strangely, these rural white Indian families seldom chose to move from these surroundings, and Thomas speculates that they had become an inner-directed kin group who paid little attention to their neighbors and continued to marry outside the tribe.[52]

Not surprisingly, it was the more traditional communities that attracted the most attention from anthropologists. But even in a place like Big Cove, according to William Gilbert, the material culture of residents was virtually "indistinguishable" from that of mountain whites. The culture that remained uniquely Cherokee was nonmaterial. The foremost example of this, of course, was the widespread continuation of two different dialects of the Cherokee language. Yet it was also apparent in the persistence of the ballplay, conjuring, various ceremonies and institutions, and clan affiliation. The last was largely invisible to outsiders, and even those having firsthand contact with the Cherokees were uncertain about its extent. Agent Frank Kyselka remarked in 1912 that he had been told by Indians and James Mooney (a recent visitor) that the clans were no longer maintained.[53] This apparently

1. Mary Wolfe, Big Cove, using a mortar and pestle in the 1940s. Courtesy of the Museum of the Cherokee Indian.

meant only that Cherokees no longer observed all the strictures of clan membership, because later anthropologists found clear evidence of a continuing clan identity. Gilbert estimated that in 1931–32 more than half the people on the reservation still had such affiliations, and in a majority of the families he surveyed spouses belonged to different clans. This conformed to the rules of exogamy but did not necessarily reflect a conscious adherence to them. And in a random sampling of conservative full-bloods in 1935–36, Leonard Bloom found that older Indians knew both their own clans (inherited from their mothers) and their fathers'. For those Indians who were in their twenties, however, only 20 percent could even identify their mothers' clans and only 10 percent understood how the matrilineal exogamous clan system worked. Later investigations confirmed Bloom's conclusion that the clan system was fading from the Cherokee experience.[54]

* * *

No one individual can adequately typify an entire period, but James Blythe in many ways exemplified the changes among the Eastern Band during the early years of the twentieth century. This mixed-blood had gained prominence as a young man in the 1880s, when the Quakers began their educational program on the reservation. Bilingual and well educated, he was proud of his Cherokee heritage and also solicitous for the well-being of his less acculturated tribesmen. He had been a faithful interpreter and informant when Mooney conducted his ethnological investigations in the 1880s and had a clear sense of helping to preserve his people's heritage. Yet he also had the idealism and rectitude of a Progressive Era reformer and was an advocate of tribal acculturation. The alleged moral shortcomings of his father-in-law, Principal Chief Nimrod Smith, had outraged him. Because he was ideologically sound in regard to acculturation, Blythe had even served briefly as the resident federal agent, the first Cherokee so honored.[55] Then, under a succession of other agents during the early twentieth century, he performed a variety of services ranging from clerk, agricultural expert, and forester to an investigator of would-be enrollees on the tribal roll.

Blythe was the progressive antidote to his older contemporary, Swimmer, the conjurer who also assisted Mooney and yet who steadfastly adhered to the old ways until his death in 1899. Agents viewed Blythe as an example of what a modern Cherokee could be. When he died in February 1920, James Henderson said that "he was the best informed Cherokee who has been connected with the Eastern Band." And yet he had successfully maintained contact with his past and had reassured those who were less certain of what the new era might bring. His funeral, Henderson observed, "was largely attended by the full bloods whose friend he was."[56] Like Swimmer, Blythe was a man torn between two worlds, but unlike Swimmer he did not reject either. His son Jarrett would in some ways prove even more remarkable.

Other transitional figures included the remarkable Owl family—mixed-

2. Owl family reunion in later years (from left: Lula, David, George, Henry, Frell, Thomas, Charlotte). Courtesy of the Museum of the Cherokee Indian.

bloods who, through their own initiative, acquired good educations and had satisfying careers both on and off the reservation. The oldest brother, David, was a baseball pitcher, served in the army, taught and coached at Haskell, testified in Washington in favor of allotment, and served as a minister among the Seneca Indians of New York—becoming, in effect, a symbol of pan-Indian acculturation. Yet Owl never lost his Cherokee identity and was strongly committed to preserving his tribal heritage. No man was more enthusiastic in recounting traditional stories, and he was always ready to share his knowledge of Cherokee lore, whether he happened to be living among the Pimas in Arizona or, later, tending his flock in New York. James Henderson once suggested that an inquisitive correspondent approach Owl for information on tribal legends, saying, "He is sometimes called the Uncle Remus of the Cherokees."[57] His siblings were equally noteworthy.

Will West Long is an even better example of the countervailing tendencies and directions within Cherokee society early in the century. One of the most prominent conservators of tribal lore, he was born in Big Cove about 1870 and was the son of a Cherokee Baptist preacher and a mother, Sally Terrapin, who belonged to a prominent traditionalist family. As was usual in earlier Cherokee society, Long's maternal uncle (and later his cousin and older half-brother) instructed him in tribal lore. At the age of sixteen he spent a few lonely months at Trinity College in Randolph County before escaping back to the reservation, hiding by day and traveling at night. Later he returned to Trinity for about a year, where he not only learned to read and write English but, with the assistance of an older Indian classmate, also mastered the Cherokee syllabary. After coming back to Qualla Boundary, the teenager farmed and began acquiring information from conjurers and other traditionalists.[58]

When James Mooney conducted fieldwork on the reservation in the late 1880s, he hired Long to interpret for him and to copy manuscripts written in Cherokee. The two became fast friends, and eventually, at Mooney's urging, the youth attended Hampton Institute. He then continued his work and studies for about ten years in Boston and other parts of New England, becoming thoroughly conversant with white ways. Yet despite the assumptions of Indian reformers, this exposure did not make Long into a red-skinned white man; instead, he was vaguely dissatisfied with his hectic life, and his thoughts increasingly turned to the North Carolina mountains and his family. Informed that his mother was dying, he returned to Qualla Boundary in 1904 and lived there the rest of his life.[59]

Back on the reservation, Long reacquired his faith in traditional Cherokee ways, began buying conjurors' notebooks, and earnestly entreated older men to share their knowledge of tribal lore. From time to time he would appear at Cherokee schools and captivate children with tales and legends from their tribal past. But he was a man of two Cherokee worlds, the modern as well as the traditional. Certainly few traditionalists of any tribe had such a thorough grounding in mainstream American education or had traveled and worked so extensively off the reservation. Even back in Big Cove Long remained acutely aware of the exigencies of the "real world." He continued to farm and became an articulate political leader, serving on the council for some thirty years and at one time opposing Cherokee allotment. He even married a woman of his own clan—unthinkable for traditionalists of an earlier era. He also became a small-scale capitalist, selling his expertise and services (for fair market value) to a long line of Mooney's professional successors. Such scholars were naturally attracted to a traditionalist community like Big Cove, and Will West Long was most instrumental in persuading suspicious residents to accommodate the visitors and even reenact a variety of ceremonies, dances, and rituals that had lain dormant since Mooney's earliest visits. Long himself was probably the Eastern Band's most prominent mask carver, a function continued by his son.[60]

When Frans Olbrechts arrived on the reservation in 1926, he quickly came to rely on Long. Yet while readily admitting this indebtedness, the

3. Will West Long, 1926 or 1927. Courtesy of the Museum of the Cherokee Indian.

scholar maligned Long in his published work by questioning his honesty and his standing with fellow Cherokees and even suggesting that Long was perceived as a threatening individual who cast spells on his enemies (a belief in witches was still common among conservatives). To "protect" his Indian informants, Olbrechts coyly referred to them by initials but then printed their individual photographs so that anyone could easily identify them. His comments on Long amount to defamation of character and reflect poorly on a scholar who had relied so extensively on his victim's hospitality and expertise.[61] Olbrecht's treatment of Long—and many of his other subjects—created a minor scholarly scandal among fellow anthropologists. It is remarkable that the slandered Long continued to assist later generations of investigators, who accorded him considerably more respect than did Olbrechts. When Long died in 1947, John Witthoft wrote an informative and touching tribute to him in the *American Anthropologist*.[62]

Unfortunately, the records of the Cherokee agency sometimes betray the same condescending and patronizing approach that Olbrechts employed. In an industrial survey of 1922–23, for example, officials included photographs of many Cherokee homes accompanied by biased and sometimes gratuitous commentary dealing with a particular Indian's intelligence, work habits, marital problems, sexual pecadilloes, child-rearing abilities, and money management. Some of the comments are almost libelous but were probably not unusual for employees of the Indian Office. White ethnocentrism—even racism—persisted into the supposedly more enlightened days of the Indian New Deal.[63]

* * *

Clearly the Eastern Cherokees were a people in transition, caught between old familiar ways and the mysteries and opportunities of modern America. More of their children attended school than before, but some parents and students were still skeptical about the benefits of education. And even after World War I, Cherokee pupils frequently appeared at school speaking only their native tongue. Most residents of places like Big Cove and Snowbird were still full-bloods who had little to do with the more acculturated tribal members. Factionalism, most apparent in arguments over enrollment and allotment, continued to plague them and presaged an even more bitter divisiveness to emerge in the 1930s. Traditional medicine, dances, games, and ceremonies persisted, albeit in modified form, and clan identification was still strong among the older generation.

In many other ways Cherokee life blended old and new. By 1913 there were ten Christian churches on the reservation, all but two with Indian preachers using their native language. Some of these individuals were traditional medicine men and ceremonial leaders who saw "no conflict in attending all night dances and attending church." Before long there would be other churches where services were in English and the preacher was likely to be a "generalized" Cherokee or what Robert Thomas calls a rural white Indian.[64] Religion also intruded into political life. The Cherokee charter specified that officeholders believe in future rewards and punishment, and the council sometimes granted special favors to reservation churches. Council meetings always opened with a Christian prayer—usually in the 1920s by Vice Chief Andrew Otter, a minister. By then the Baptist denomination was preeminent on the reservation because it had certain features, like baptism by immersion, that coalesced nicely with traditional Cherokee beliefs. Other likely factors were its informal organization, the total freedom of individual congregations, and the firm Baptist allegiance of most nearby whites, some of whom had intermarried with Cherokees. By the early 1930s the Baptists were also the only denomination with a white missionary residing on the reservation.[65] This growing sectarian influence affected not only religious belief but also other aspects of cultural behavior in post–World War II tribal society.

Whatever the echoes of the past on the Cherokee reservation, there were clear signs of a new age. Besides the growing emphasis on education, federal officials could point to improved health care, a fleeting exposure to wage labor, and modern conveniences like automobiles that, while not part of most Cherokee households, helped bring awareness of larger possibilities. The tensions and ambiguities inherent in the changing times would become even more apparent during the New Deal.

5

A New Park and
a New Deal

PROBABLY few Eastern Cherokees noticed the stock market crash of October 1929. Events on Wall Street outwardly had little bearing on their lives. Already the tribal economy was in a shambles, employment was almost nonexistent, and many Cherokees were hard pressed to provide for their families. For the Eastern Band, America's depression decade blended almost imperceptibly with the economic hard times attending the decline of western North Carolina's lumber industry. A few tribal members had migrated to industrial cities, gone into military service, or found employment on other reservations, but most preferred to survive as best they could at home.

One immediate response to the crisis was an attempt to revitalize Cherokee agriculture, which had stagnated during the years of wage labor. Few Indians had much knowledge of modern, systematic agricultural practices, though there were some notable exceptions, including full-bloods like Will Saunooke and Johnson Owl. Saunooke cultivated about twenty-five acres and regularly won prizes at the Cherokee fair, while Owl, a Bird Town resident and former Carlisle student, farmed some ninety-five acres—far more than the average Cherokee. Yet even Owl worked on the outside when he could. In 1930 he had a job in Pennsylvania and planned to return to Bird Town only at harvesttime. Otherwise the pattern was a familiar one, with the typical reservation family tending five to ten acres and using methods little different from those of the preceding century.[1]

Despite the limited amount of arable land, the Cherokee council voted in 1929 to spend $5,000 of tribal funds during each of the next five years to improve reservation agriculture. By 1932 a resident farm agent, A. M. Adams, had organized four farm districts on the reservation for agricultural self-improvement. The tribe furnished good-quality seed, farm tools, and livestock, and a special effort was made to provide steers for plowing long-abandoned fields on steep hillsides. Under a reimbursable plan, Adams was also buying milk cows, sheep, and hogs and providing instruction on their proper care. Families with children had priority in obtaining the cows. Expressing cautious optimism, agency superintendent R. L. Spalsbury believed that "farming should take a considerable rise within the next year, and every Indian on the reservation who is able to do so should raise enough for his family as well as some produce to sell."[2]

But these modest improvements in agriculture could not shield the Indians from the depression's impact, and typically they devised their own means of coping with hard times. Unlike urban Americans, most Cherokees could at least raise a few garden crops and call on traditional institutions of self-help. The gadugis continued to operate during the depression, as did other organizations within the communities. And for years the tribe had been regularly paying small sums of money—usually five dollars at a time—to those who were destitute.[3] These were mostly the elderly or infirm, but the Band stood ready to provide, without any stigma, at least nominal assistance to all needy members. To assist a fellow Indian or to receive such aid was acceptable and even expected. The Cherokees were self-reliant, but within the strong social context of the tribe. It was quite different for white Americans, whose culture stressed self-help and suspicion of government assistance. That attitude changed, of course, as most Americans came to realize that modern calamities like the depression demanded federal intervention.

Another way the Eastern Band furnished relief for its own members was through a stumpage fee on all legally cut timber on the reservation. Each month the tribal business committee issued permits allowing individuals to harvest small amounts of timber on their claims, usually a cord or less. In addition, the Band periodically sold larger quantities of timber on uninhabited tribal lands. The gigantic Champion Fibre Company at Canton bought much of the pulpwood, while nearby tanning plants provided a market for acid woods. During the depression Cherokee timber brought from $10 to $18 per thousand board feet, 10 percent of which was a stumpage fee used for tribal relief efforts. With the end of wage labor, the Eastern Band increased its annual cut of both individual and tribal timber. After a sharp dropoff in 1932 and 1933, the depths of the depression, the figures went up remarkably—from a low of 1.8 million board feet in 1936 to an average of more than 7.5 million a year during 1939–41. Stumpage fees reached a high of $9,126 in 1940, providing a vital source of tribal relief.[4]

Many Cherokees resented not being allowed to harvest timber on their possessory claims whenever and in whatever quantities they wished. As had often happened in the past, some simply ignored or evaded tribal prohibitions. Federal agents found it difficult to prevent this and, worse, were almost helpless against renewed timber trespass on unoccupied lands in remote sections of Graham and Cherokee counties. Certain lumber companies in that part of the state were willing to buy any timber offered at a reasonable price, no questions asked. Besides violating tribal law, this cutting obviously represented a loss of relief money from stumpage fees. Agents also warned against possible overcutting and fire hazards and as an example pointed to the "non-productive and unsightly" forests near Bird Town.[5]

Amid the more publicized human crises of the depression, Cherokee forests were inexorably undergoing one of the great ecological disasters of the twentieth century. The chestnut blight, introduced from Asia, was spreading across the eastern United States and by the early 1930s had already killed many trees on the reservation, where in a few areas chestnuts represented 60 percent of the timber. The full scope of the impending disaster was imperfectly understood, but all adult chestnuts were doomed. Those Cherokees who wished to cut timber were encouraged to concentrate on this species, both for home use and for commercial sale. The tribal government meanwhile stepped up its own harvesting of these trees, and this partly explains the remarkable increase in timber cutting during the decade. Another dimension of this tragedy was its impact on the lives of traditional Cherokees. The appearance, texture, and ambiance of a familiar environment was radically altered. No longer would chestnuts be a staple, a given of everyday life. Raymond D. Fogelson says the passing of the great trees left a "psychological void" among Cherokees.[6] For older Indians, especially, it must have seemed an inexplicable disaster.

Despite its relative self-sufficiency, the Eastern Band quickly discovered that it lacked adequate resources to provide assistance to all its destitute. Less than a month before Franklin D. Roosevelt defeated Herbert Hoover in the 1932 elections, agent Spalsbury estimated that about 200 out of 496 Cherokee families would likely need outside assistance during the coming winter. The Hoover administration had been notoriously reluctant to provide direct relief to citizens, so Spalsbury requested two thousand yards of cloth and a supply of flour from the American Red Cross. Although helpful, such small contributions were at best a palliative for the tribe.[7]

Tourism clearly offered the most promising economic opportunities for the Eastern Cherokees. The Great Smoky Mountains National Park was almost a reality when the depression began, and tribal officials understandably wanted its development to continue. In supporting the park, the Indians found themselves part of a curious mix of allies that included conservationists, promoters, and philanthropists. Since the 1890s the idea of an Appalachian park had been slowly germinating, until the advent of the automobile age awakened individuals in eastern Tennessee and western North Carolina to the possibility that such an attraction might lure visitors. By the 1920s they had organized an effective campaign to convince their states to condemn and buy mountain properties along the boundary. Conservationists, though wary of an unholy alliance with businessmen, approved. Backed by money from the Rockefeller family and buoyed by successful lobbying in Raleigh, Nashville, and Washington, park supporters pushed relentlessly forward, eventually acquiring even the holdings of large lumber companies. These lands were then conveyed to the United States as the nucleus of the park. The park was already in operation when Roosevelt was inaugurated early in 1933, though it was not formally established until the following year.[8]

Construction of modern roads across the park and reservation promised both jobs and tourist dollars. In 1931 agent L. W. Page called for completion of a partly constructed state highway from Bryson City through Cherokee to Newfound Gap in the Smokies, where it would connect with a road to Gatlinburg, Tennessee, at the park's western entrance. Realizing that contractors would likely hire whites before Indians on this project, Page also recommended state construction of a long-discussed reservation highway from Soco Gap to Cherokee; this would guarantee Indian employment and provide convenient access between Cherokee and the outlying communities of Paint Town and Wolf Town. With impending construction of a state highway from Waynesville to Soco, it would also boost tourism by offering an alternative route through the reservation to the park.[9]

The transmountain highway was completed in mid-1932, and R. L. Spalsbury believed the eagerly awaited convergence of the other roads at Cherokee made "prospects for . . . this place rather attractive. We have already had a number of requests for locations for hotels, garages, auto camps, etc. So far we have not encouraged any development of this sort but it is a problem that must be faced in the near future."[10] Unfortunately, construction of the new segment between Bryson City and Cherokee stopped when the Appalachian Railroad refused to surrender its right-of-way, and the Soco Gap highway was indefinitely delayed when it became embroiled in an ugly dispute involving Cherokee political factions and state and federal agencies.

* * *

Franklin D. Roosevelt brought a jaunty optimism to the presidency and a bold New Deal featuring myriad agencies for coping with the depression. Amid these sweeping changes was an "Indian New Deal" designed by John Collier, Roosevelt's commissioner of Indian affairs. A native southerner and former New York City social worker, Collier had been impressed by the richness and variety of the immigrants' cultural heritage and had become a proponent of cultural pluralism. No longer should our nation strive for a homogenized, uniform citizen emerging from the melting pot of America. Instead, national culture should be a blend, reflecting certain common values—respect for equality under the law, for example—and varied ethnic attributes. By the 1920s Collier had developed a fascination with the Puebloan tribes of the Southwest and emerged as an impassioned spokesman for Indian rights. Extrapolating from his earlier experiences with immigrants, he believed Indians could be a vital part of American culture while retaining much of their tribal identity. His familiarity with Puebloan folkways had also given him respect for communalism as an agent of cultural bonding and cooperative change. Communalism or tribalism, he thought, might operate as an effective restraint on rampant American individualism.

Good progressive that he was, Collier also wished to address the Indians' many social, economic, and educational problems. A persistent critic of the Indian Office, he had supported the systematic analysis of reservation problems conducted by Lewis Meriam and applauded many of the conclusions in Meriam's published 1928 report. Thus Collier's background suggested that his approach as Indian commissioner would reflect both the fervor of progressivism and an appreciation of ethnic and cultural diversity.[11]

The cornerstone of the Indian New Deal was the Wheeler-Howard Act of June 18, 1934, often called the Indian Reorganization Act (IRA). A decisive about-face from previous policy, it affirmed the validity of Indian cultures, formally abandoned the already discredited allotment policy, and promoted Indian progress within a modern tribal context. With the end of allotment the reservations would become sacrosanct communal societies. In some cases they would even be enlarged. Tribes were encouraged to write their own constitutions, organize as corporations, and apply for federal loans for economic development. Meanwhile the new administration would deemphasize off-reservation boarding schools and promote practical, socially responsible education among the Indians themselves. This included encouraging traditional crafts and skills as a means of preserving tribal culture and also earning money. Like many New Deal programs, then, the IRA combined old and new ideas with a bold willingness to experiment.[12]

One of the most remarkable features of the IRA was a provision allowing tribes to vote on whether they would accept the new law and thus be eligible for its benefits. Never before had Indians been encouraged to exercise their own judgment in policy matters relating to themselves, and a number of tribes disappointed Collier by voting against the IRA—in part for the novelty of saying no to the federal government and partly because of questions about how the new policy would actually be implemented. Initially, however, the Eastern Band had only mild objections. It was willing to incorporate under federal law, despite satisfaction with its state charter, but wanted certain practices to continue: state law enforcement on the reservation, tribal operation of a new handicraft guild, and heirship rights to possessory claims. Otherwise, agent Spalsbury noted, the concept of corporate self-government struck a responsive chord: "These Indians have been operating under a similar organization for many years and believe in it."[13] In May 1934 the tribal council approved the pending Wheeler-Howard bill, and on December 20 the entire tribe likewise endorsed the recently passed act by a vote of 705 to 101. Counting absentee ballots, 806 out of an estimated 1,114 eligible voters went to the polls, better than 72 percent. Support was lopsided in all six communities as well as among the 60 absentee voters. Harold W. Foght, the current Cherokee agent, reported satisfaction "with the way the Indians turned out and voted, particularly as the mountain roads were in bad condition after several days of rain and snow."[14] He anticipated quick adoption of a new tribal constitution and charter of incorporation to replace the existing 1889 state charter.

To many Eastern Cherokees, the most important facet of the Indian New Deal was the creation of new jobs on the reservation. Tribal unemployment had become particularly acute in the last months of Hoover's administration, and about the only income came from the agency's own limited road building.[15] Fortunately, many of Roosevelt's famous "alphabet agencies" provided employment and relief to Indians as well as other Americans. One of John Collier's first steps as Indian commissioner was to establish the Indian Emergency Conservation Work Program (IECW), an adjunct of the Civilian Conservation Corps (CCC). Often called the Indian CCC, the IECW was, at Collier's insistence, "Indian-built, Indian-maintained, and Indian-used" and devoted exclusively to relief measures on reservations. It was quite prominent on Qualla Boundary and provided employment in reforestation, fire and erosion control, road building, and similar programs. More than 500 Eastern Cherokees applied for the 100 full-time positions, and to benefit the maximum number of Indians Harold Foght set up two shifts, each working two weeks a month. Later it became necessary to limit even further the hours any one individual could work. Other New Deal agencies like the Works Progress Administration (WPA) and the Public Works Administration (PWA) also allocated funds to the Department of the Interior for similar job programs on reservations. Even with all this, employment lagged badly. Late in 1936 only 135 out of about 650 eligible Eastern Cherokees had jobs—mostly on roads, the IECW, and a new hospital project. Yet the efforts at relief continued, and between 1933 and 1941 various New Deal agencies pumped a total of about $595,000 into the North Carolina reservation. Nationwide, the Indian CCC alone spent some $72 million among American Indians.[16]

With passage of the Johnson-O'Malley Act in 1934, Collier's Indian Bureau encouraged state and local agencies to share in providing many Indian services. The state of North Carolina, for example, contracted with the United States Public Health Service and the Department of the Interior to furnish additional medical care for the Eastern Band. By 1938 the state had a district health unit operating out of Waynesville and a resident field nurse on the reservation who visited even the most remote Cherokee homes. For the first time almost every Cherokee child received a medical examination and necessary immunizations, while prenatal care and treatment for venereal disease became readily available for adults. As in the past, state and county officials also continued to provide most tribal law enforcement, though sheriffs were sensitive to the fact that Indians paid no taxes. Less successful were federal efforts to interest white public school systems in admitting Cherokee pupils under the Johnson-O'Malley Act. As agents often pointed out, prejudice against Indians was simply too strong in Bryson City and Sylva.[17]

Taking advantage of the IRA's desire to maintain and even enlarge reservations, the Eastern Band made an effort during the 1930s to acquire more tillable land to accommodate its inflated membership rolls. Some Indians talked about selling the more remote tracts in Graham and Cherokee counties and using the proceeds to buy better—and more defensible—property closer to Qualla Boundary. And on several occasions the tribe offered mar-ginal though scenic property to the Great Smoky Mountains National Park in exchange for farmland, especially around Ravensford. The tribe was never able to make the exchanges it wanted, but it did eventually pay $25,000 for the 884-acre Boundary Tree Tract as a site for tribal tourist industries. While bargaining with the park service, the Cherokees also attempted to use New Deal agencies to acquire some 23,000 acres south of Qualla Boundary and in Graham County. Arrangements were nearly complete when, according to Harold Foght, the government dealt "a great blow" to Cherokee aspirations by deciding against it.[18]

One revolutionary phase of the Indian New Deal of particular impor-tance to the Eastern Band was its encouragement of Native American tra-ditions, crafts, religion, and self-identity. In contrast to the early 1920s, when the Indian Office warned Indians to cease their "useless and harmful" dances and ceremonies, Collier explicitly encouraged Indian religious free-dom and preservation of tribal cultures. To the disgust of many missionaries and longtime reformers, he issued a circular in January 1934 directing the Indian Service to show an "affirmative, appreciative attitude toward Indian cultural values." Furthermore, "No interference with Indian religious life or ceremonial expression will hereafter be tolerated. The cultural liberty of Indians is in all respects to be considered equal to that of any non-Indian group." Tribal arts and crafts should be "prized, nourished and honored."[19]

Responding to this new directive, Harold Foght advocated teaching Indian history in Cherokee schools and creating a museum to exhibit craft work from other Indian schools in the United States. This "would lend an understanding and inspiration to the children that would be difficult to get in any other way."[20] As for Cherokee religion and traditions, he later ex-plained, "We are thus going out of our way to have meetings with the older Indians who are rapidly dying off to have them transmit in permanent form what they still retain from the ancient national epic of creation, their guid-ing supernatural spirit and the world hereafter as reward for noble deed and worthy living." Then, in a comment accurately reflecting the new ideol-ogy, he added, "Unfortunately, the Cherokees have not been a conservative religious group holding onto their ancient religion."[21]

Cherokee crafts had been a matter of keen interest to Indian agents, tour-ists, and others well before the depression. Across the mountains in Gatlin-burg, Tennessee, the predecessor of the Arrowmont School fostered tradi-tional mountain crafts, an emphasis blending nicely with the new awareness of Indian culture. By spring 1932 R. L. Spalsbury was trying to organize a crafts guild among the Eastern Cherokees so they could become an auxiliary of the Southern Mountain Hand Craft Guild in Gatlinburg. Spalsbury confidently predicted that the new transmountain road from Knoxville and Gatlinburg would bring more tourists to Qualla Boundary and create greater demand for Cherokee crafts; the new Indian guild and its affiliation with the larger organization would help meet these demands. Unlike before, when Indians often bartered crafts for supplies at local stores, the new arrangement would allow them to bring their wares to the guild storehouse, where they would receive cash. The guild would then sell the crafts at enough of a markup to pay expenses and allow for future expansion. Using funds borrowed from the tribe, the guild was finally organized in the summer of 1933 and operated out of a storeroom in the new council house then nearing completion.[22] It was the predecessor of the crafts guild that today handles much of the Cherokee artistic output.

Spalsbury and Harold Foght followed up these early efforts to promote Cherokee handicrafts. There were crafts classes in the tribal schools, an attempt to anticipate tourist demands, and frequent inquiries from the Indian Office regarding the state of Cherokee artistic creativity.[23] Goingback Chiltoskey, a woodcarver and one of the most famous artists of the Eastern Band, received much of his instruction and encouragement during this period. Likewise, Roosevelt's New Deal gave a moral and financial boost to artists throughout America. On the other hand, the employment programs of the Indian New Deal sometimes detracted from Cherokee crafts. The government employed instructors in basketry and pottery part time at the boarding school but then lured them away with higher-paying opportunities elsewhere. Spalsbury advocated raising the instructors' salaries from twenty-five to fifty cents an hour, with at least fifteen hours of work a week.[24] Yet New Deal programs continued to work at cross purposes. As Harold Foght noted in summer 1934, "I find that only a limited number of the reservation Indians are engaged in basketry and weaving, and very few in pottery making. This is probably due in part to the fact that the men have had remunerative work on Government projects in recent years."[25]

Nourishing Indian handicrafts was simply one part of a larger program to transform Cherokee into a tourist center. As early as 1932 R. L. Spalsbury was anticipating future needs by advocating development of a plan for leasing attractive business sites in town and at Soco Gap.[26] One problem was the number of whites already operating businesses under arrangements made with individual Indians before the government assumed trusteeship over the reservation. By spring 1933 the tribal council had decided that 10 percent of the consideration for all business leases would go into the tribal treasury to help with relief, and Spalsbury was requiring white businessmen to obtain traders' licenses from his office.[27]

Completion of a modern highway system into Cherokee was of course critical, and by late 1935 the Appalachian Railroad had finally liquidated its holdings and surrendered its right-of-way for the new and more direct highway linking Bryson City and Cherokee.[28] Whenever the long-discussed highway from Soco Gap was completed, Cherokee would also be a convenient gateway for motorists approaching from the east. In anticipation of these developments, the council voted to appropriate $50,000 of tribal funds to undertake an "industrial development" program in Cherokee. Basically it entailed tearing down some of the old shacks and constructing new tourist-related facilities, including a hotel, trading post, craft shop, and service station. The council intended to oversee all phases of construction, the leasing of concessions, and landscaping. One objective was to drive out of business R. L. McLean, a white trader who operated a large general store and trading post on a small parcel of land in the heart of the business district; this had never been part of the reservation. Harold Foght said that McLean had long been "a thorn in the flesh" of other traders, whom he regularly outsmarted. The Indians at first were willing to start legal proceedings to force McLean to sell out, but Principal Chief Jarrett Blythe soon decided that if the tribe could open a new cooperative store as part of its industrial program, McLean would sell of his own volition. Little did Blythe realize that his program would soon come under attack by some fellow Cherokees as undemocratic and even subversive.[29]

* * *

Whatever the accomplishments of the Indian New Deal, some Eastern Cherokees became disenchanted because it fostered tribalism at the expense of individualism, decisively eliminated the prospect of allotment, and appeared to be a "return to the blanket." They found themselves joining a rising chorus of opposition to Collier's programs among many acculturated Indians throughout the United States. Ironically, these dissenters found support among some poorly educated or conservative Indians who saw the Indian Reorganization Act not as an affirmation of tribal ways but as a suspicious new tactic adopted by an always devious federal government. What emerged on many reservations, then, was an alliance of convenience between certain acculturated and traditionalist Indians to resist the IRA.[30]

On the Eastern Band's reservation all that was required was an individual to crystallize such latent fears and resentment. Fred Blythe Bauer was the individual.

Bauer was born in December 1896, the son of Rachel Blythe Bauer, a Cherokee mixed-blood, and Adolphus Gustavus Bauer, a northern-born white architect who designed a number of important state buildings after moving to Raleigh. When his mother died just two weeks after his birth, Bauer was sent by his distraught father to Qualla Boundary to live with James and Josephine Blythe, who adopted him. Blythe was Rachel Bauer's brother, and his wife was the daughter of former principal chief Nimrod Jarrett Smith. Fred Bauer grew up with his cousin Jarrett Blythe (who was ten years older), attended Carlisle, and during World War I served with the army air corps in France. Afterward he taught and coached at various Indian institutions around the country.[31]

By the early 1930s Bauer and his wife Catherine were employed at the school in Mount Pleasant, Michigan, and when it closed they returned to Qualla Boundary, where their intelligence and forceful personalities quickly ensured their prominence. R. L. Spalsbury was delighted to provide a teaching position on the reservation for Catherine, and her husband worked on a variety of relief projects, including construction of reservation highways. Before long, however, the couple became open and persistent critics of the Indian New Deal. Fred Bauer had always been a progressive who, culturally at least, was a "white Indian." To him full and unconditional Indian citizenship meant a good education, allotment of reservation lands, distribution of tribal assets, private initiative in business and government, and an end to Indian Office bureaucracy and paternalism. Anything less was un-American and unacceptable. In his eyes Collier's romantic notions of tribalism were not only un-American but communistic.[32] Not surprisingly, Bauer quickly enlisted allies among other white Indians and suspicious conservatives willing to believe the worst about federal Indian policies. Of necessity they found themselves frequently at odds with the principal chief, who steadfastly backed most New Deal programs. That man was none other than Bauer's cousin and adoptive brother, Jarrett Blythe. It was a scenario befitting a Greek tragedy.

The catalyst for Bauer's campaign against Collier and the Indian New Deal was the new educational program on the Cherokee reservation. In September 1932, before Roosevelt's election, agent R. L. Spalsbury had posed a basic question: "What is the proper educational program for this reservation?" He had an answer. In line with the Meriam report and other critiques of Indian education, he called for "a complete reorganization" that would reduce the role of the boarding school at Cherokee and emphasize "close contacts between the school and the home" by means of day schools. Somewhat paradoxically, he finally concluded this could best be accomplished by improving the local road system, closing the two existing day schools, converting the boarding school into a consolidated day facility, and busing in students who lived in Bird Town, Big Cove, and the Jackson County communities along Soco Creek. "This has all the merits of a consolidated school in any community," Spalsbury said. "It provides close daily contacts between the school and the home. It permits the children to maintain their home contacts while getting their education and suggests that the school might extend its influence easily by reason of these contacts to the improvement of the home life of the adults." It would also be cheaper than the current boarding system and would free several dormitories for other uses. For an indefinite period, however, Spalsbury admitted it would be necessary to retain boarding facilities for a few orphans, refugees from broken homes, and pupils from remote tracts in Graham and Cherokee counties. Whatever the merits of his proposals, the lame-duck Hoover administration had no intention of undertaking such costly changes on the Cherokee reservation. Instead, it authorized construction of a new day school in Soco Valley.[33]

John Collier's regime likewise rejected the notion of a large consolidated Cherokee school and opted for expanding and improving existing day schools and making them more responsive to community needs. Spalsbury quickly proved himself a disciple of the new administration by defining tribal education in the broadest possible terms. Sketching the preliminary outlines of an idealized program for the Eastern Band, he said, "Our program of education will be wider than the classroom. It will take in the home, the fields, the forests, the churches, the tribal organization, and every individual entitled to participate in the tribe. Community wide in its ramifications, it will aim to better and improve the economic, social, sanitary and spiritual condition of these people." As he admitted, "This is a large order." Schoolwork would reflect the Cherokees' own environment and would not require such things as foreign languages or "higher mathematics." Spalsbury hoped to add grades eleven and twelve to the boarding-school curriculum during the next two years and, assuming the school could hire the necessary instructors, to teach both written and spoken Cherokee at those levels. As the agent put it, "On the background of [Cherokee] racial inheritance we should build a structure of knowledge, skill and attitudes dovetailing into their environment so that they will be able to make the best use of it without waste."[34]

Spalsbury saw the "adult phase" of the new program "centering around the home and the family. These are the two primary social units that must be strengthened and developed." But the agent had only a vague idea of how this might be accomplished, and he acknowledged that everyone connected with the Indian New Deal would "have to attack and develop" the problem. One thing he knew for certain:

> Rugged individualism must give way to social cooperation. The social element is dominant. An individual can only develop in organized society. If this means anything, it means that the social organization of the community must receive major attention. The Cherokees have some most commendable features in their social life which should be preserved and extended. Their community club organizations for mutual help in times of trouble or need are examples of this. As their social stability rests on the strength of the home and family, every effort should be made to improve their economic and moral condition. Health and sanitation are important elements to be stressed throughout.[35]

Spalsbury's successor, Harold Foght, was equally diligent but more practical in attempting to set up an educational system that conformed to the broad-gauged objectives of the Indian New Deal. He emphasized prevocational and vocational instruction in agriculture, forestry, and the mechanical arts. Basically he ignored curriculum formats and requirements in other North Carolina schools, thinking it "wasteful and positively foolish . . . to ape" them. An ominous foreshadowing of future events occurred when students at the boarding school and some Cherokee parents protested, to which Foght replied that they simply did not understand "the real situation." He was preparing Cherokee children for the realities of reservation life, but if there should be "a young Indian boy or girl who shows outstanding gift in certain cultural or professional fields, we would recommend such students for transfer from Cherokee to white high schools willing to accept Indian students."[36]

Foght quickly found himself bewildered and beleaguered by a rising tide of opposition to the new school programs. In part it was a matter of his own "stern" personality, in part a reaction to the aggressive, radical nature of Collier's entire administration. The welter of anxieties and uncertainties relating to the Indian New Deal had suddenly coalesced and focused on the issue of education. And it was on this issue that Foght first directly confronted Fred and Catherine Bauer. Catherine had proved a very good substitute teacher in the spring of 1934, and Foght had had no qualms about recommending her for a full-time position at the new Soco Day School.[37] By spring 1935, however, she and one or two other reservation teachers openly opposed the educational program. Her husband and a number of white Indians were meanwhile holding meetings and, according to Foght, making "insidious insinuations and false statements" and inducing many parents to sign a petition against the new programs. The exasperated agent dealt with his most immediate problem by firing Catherine Bauer, claiming she had been insubordinate and had "joined in the movement to discredit the new system of education." He asked the acting director of education within the Indian Office to investigate the matter himself, adding that "the Tribal Council, from the Chief down, is standing by us and look upon the whole matter as impertinent interference on the part of a few discontents."[38]

Bauer meanwhile had gone at his own expense to Washington, conferred with Collier, and received no satisfaction. Back in Cherokee, he and others organized a "Cherokee Indian Rights Association," which held a strike against tribal schools; some parents were persuaded to protest the IRA educational program by withdrawing their children from classes. Amid the furor, the tribal council appointed a committee to look into the situation, and it prepared a report generally supporting Foght's educational program.[39] For those favoring an education emphasizing assimilation rather than tribalism, Bauer made the case most cogently in a congressional hearing a few years later: "Suppose you, a white, born in a white community, see only white people, attend white schools, have only white associates. After you attain manhood you are suddenly dropped down in China, India, or Africa, with people of a different race, language, and social customs. Do you think you would be accepted without question into the social, economic, and political life of that community? And be happy there?"[40] Cherokee children, Bauer argued, should attend public schools with white children to be better prepared for the "real world." The problem, as Bauer no doubt realized, was that schools in Swain and Jackson counties did not admit students who were phenotypically Indian. Withdrawal of the Cherokee reservation and the new national park from Swain County tax rolls had drastically reduced the local tax base, and quite apart from any racial animosity, county officials were not inclined to provide public services for the Cherokees.[41]

A prominent ally of the Bauers was William Pearson McCoy, a white

Indian from Bird Town who operated a small restaurant in Cherokee, where authorities seized two slot machines in summer 1934. Foght labeled him and Fred Bauer "the chronic trouble maker[s] of this reservation" and indeed they were to be persistent enemies of the Indian Office for years to come.[42] But the list of Foght's critics went considerably beyond those two and included certain discontented parents and even a few teachers. Outsiders also had unkind things to say. A Tulsa woman, Mrs. R. M. Hill, appeared on the reservation during Foght's initial troubles with the Bauers and, according to the agent, seemed to be a religious crank who wanted the school day to begin and end with prayer. She also "launched upon a tirade against the teaching of Bolshevism and certain communistic practices in our schools, all of which was so preposterous that it was difficult for me to refrain from taking the whole matter in a jocular vein." Mrs. Hill's chief target was a teacher of industrial geography who had discussed the Soviet Union and had a pupil prepare a report on its economic system based on a book from the teacher's own library. A bit defensively, Foght acknowledged that "Communism and Bolshevism have no place in the report or in the book, but the word 'Russia' was evidently sufficient to set our objectors on edge. Anyhow, they had filled this woman with a lot of nonsense."[43]

Charges that the IRA was promoting communism were reiterated by Fred Bauer and the American Indian Federation (AIF), an organization he had joined and whose assistance he solicited in the spring of 1935. The AIF was a national association of Indians of diverse backgrounds and viewpoints who happened to agree on three basic objectives: removal of John Collier from office; repeal of the IRA; and most important, abolition of the Office of Indian Affairs. Founded in Oklahoma in 1934 in response to the IRA, it was headed by Joseph Bruner, a wealthy, acculturated Creek who came from a traditionalist background. The "brains" of the AIF was its energetic publicist and Washington lobbyist Alice Lee Jemison, a Seneca who was also part Cherokee. Like Bauer, many AIF members perceived Collier and the Indian bureau as obstacles to Indian individualism and modernity. The IRA, they believed, fostered a bureaucracy and paternalism that stifled initiative and self-reliance. They argued forcefully for the Indian's "emancipation" and complete integration into white society. Others opposed the Indian New Deal because it seemed to violate treaty rights that guaranteed preservation of their identity as tribal Indians.[44] A favorite attention-getting ploy of the AIF was a right-wing rhetoric that accused Collier and his program of being atheistic, communist inspired, and pawns of the American Civil Liberties Union.[45]

In June 1935 the AIF asked the Senate Committee on Indian Affairs to investigate the situation in Cherokee and distributed a circular titled "Collierism and Communism in North Carolina" to every member of Congress. Eventually, at hearings before the committee in April 1936, the AIF charged that the "present Indian Bureau program involves 'atheism, communism and un-Americanism in the administration of Indian Affairs both at Cherokee and in general.'" Harold Foght and others at Cherokee were supposedly trying to destroy private ownership of property, promote collectivism, deny free speech, substitute social science for Christianity in the schools, and "subversively" teach sex.[46]

Though the Senate committee proved unresponsive, the AIF continued its efforts to uproot the IRA on the Cherokee reservation. In January 1937 Alice Lee Jemison wrote North Carolina's Senator Josiah Bailey that "the regime at Cherokee" had become "autocratic and tyranical" as well as vindictive: "Those who have opposed their program at Cherokee have been denied work of any kind and every possible barrier has been thrown in their [way] to prevent them from earning a livelihood through individual enterprise."[47] When Bailey asked Collier to respond, the Indian commissioner said Jemison's allegations were "arbitrary fictions in most cases. They are so wild and bizarre that an answer to them carries one into the realm of detective stories."[48] On February 15 and 17 the Senate committee held additional hearings on the Cherokee case and focused on allegations about communist teachings in Cherokee schools, the IRA's support of native conjurers at the expense of modern medicine, and agency assaults on Christian belief. Similar accusations were made at hearings in 1938, 1939, and 1940, and Jemison claimed she spoke for about three hundred disgruntled Cherokees.[49]

Amid these charges and countercharges, Fred Bauer was daily becoming more influential. Nowhere was this more apparent than in a tribal election of August 1935 on a proposed new constitution under the Indian Reorganization Act. Bauer and his allies waged what Foght characterized as "a campaign of falsehood and misrepresentation" that resulted in a decisive defeat of the constitution, 484 to 382. In Cherokee there were 74 votes for the constitution and 79 against; in Bird Town 54 for and 121 against; Paint Town 22 for and 92 opposed; Wolf Town 54 pro constitution and 129 con; Big Cove 97 for and 32 against; Graham County (Snowbird) 78 for and 2 against; and 2 absentee ballots in favor and 29 in opposition. Foght thought it significant that Graham County and Big Cove, "the two precincts inhabited by the full-blood Indians were the only two to vote right. . . . They seem still able to think for themselves. Birdtown, which is the stronghold of the white Indians gave a better vote for the Constitution than did either Paintttown or Wolfetown, which ordinarily line up right on a proposition."[50]

Foght had no trouble explaining why there had been such a remarkable turnabout after the overwhelming tribal support shown for the IRA less than a year before. In an obvious reference to the Bauer–Pearson McCoy group, he said "the real cause was after all a campaign of falsehood and misrepresentation that has been carried on by a certain faction well known to you for a long time. The only astonishing thing to me is that the propaganda used could so utterly mislead people who ordinarily do their own thinking." Despite his embarrassment, Foght said many Cherokees hoped for another election, "as it will not be long before these people will see the mistake they have made."[51] But he was wrong. The Eastern Cherokees never adopted a new constitution and instead continued to operate under their amended 1889 state charter.

Just a few days after rejection of the constitution, Foght and the Collier program received another blow when Fred Bauer was elected vice chief of the Eastern Band. As an added insult, Pearson McCoy became a new councilman. The only real consolation to Foght was the reelection of Principal Chief Jarrett Blythe, a staunch IRA supporter. (Like many other Americans, the Eastern Cherokees have never shown much consistency in voting for their leaders.) Bauer's enemies attempted to block his swearing in because tribal law required the vice chief to have at least one-half Cherokee blood, and the Baker Roll listed him as three-eighths. The most persuasive evidence, however, suggests that Bauer was only one-quarter Cherokee. Part of the confusion over his ancestry resulted from the romantic tales surrounding his mother's marriage to Augustus Bauer, their supposed ostracism by Raleigh society, and Rachel's untimely death. According to stories circulating in the 1930s, she had been a full-blood Indian "princess." Perhaps these tales explain why several witnesses assured the tribal council that Rachel Bauer's son was a half-blood and therefore legally qualified for office. The council acquiesced, and the candidate quickly assumed his position as vice chief.[52]

Bauer immediately made his presence felt by convincing the council to rescind the resolution of the preceding year appropriating $50,000 for construction of new tourist facilities. Foght almost sputtered with rage, but he was helpless to prevent reduction of the construction program to a face-saving standby basis.[53] Bauer's obstructionism then took a different turn as he launched a campaign to halt plans for a new "park-to-park" highway across the reservation. This scenic mountain route, the Blue Ridge Parkway, would eventually stretch 469 miles from the Shenandoah National Park southwest of Washington, D.C., to the Great Smoky Mountains National Park. Late in 1934, after considerable controversy and lobbying, secretary of the interior Harold L. Ickes selected Cherokee as the terminus for the Smokies.[54]

Originally the reservation section of the parkway was to be the long-needed state highway from Soco Gap to Cherokee, for which North Carolina had obtained a right-of-way sixty feet wide. The state then planned to reconvey the property to the United States. To the Cherokees' amazement, however, the National Park Service insisted on a much wider route along Soco Creek that would gobble up valuable farmland and potential business sites. It would also virtually wipe out the main street of Cherokee and necessitate moving back existing commercial buildings to the Oconaluftee's floodplain.[55] Tribal access to the parkway, moreover, would be limited. Amid such revelations the Cherokees decided against the park demands, which Foght called "little less than confiscatory." Secretary Ickes pointed out the obvious benefits of such a road but said he would not force it on the Indians, who continued to hope the state would undertake construction of its own highway along the original right-of-way.[56] To this extent, at least, Foght and Blythe found themselves in rare agreement with Bauer. For a while it seemed the parkway would not cross the reservation at all.[57]

By early 1937, however, negotiators had worked out a compromise proposal involving a land exchange between the tribe and the national park. The Cherokees would give the park some marginal acreage in return for long-coveted parkland near Ravensford. Then, in exchange for their properties along the necessary right-of-way, as well as North Carolina's promise of just compensation for damages, the affected Cherokees would receive part of the Ravensford lands. A bill allowing such an exchange was duly introduced in Congress, while Foght lined up a majority of councilmen to approve the plan. Then, to his shock and indignation, three of his staunchest supporters changed their minds during a Sunday adjournment and helped defeat the measure, six to five. Foght believed they had been threatened by the Bauer faction. Furious, he alluded to Bauer's lack of sufficient Cherokee blood to hold office, then asked, "Now would the Office of Indian Affairs sanction an attempt to displace him at this time, or shall the majority continue to suffer these unwarranted proceedings directed by him and two others[?]"[58]

In an apparent effort to overcome Bauer's opposition, the House amended the pending bill to authorize the land exchanges if approved by secret ballot in a tribal election within sixty days of the bill's enactment. It was passed in August 1937, much to Chief Blythe's chagrin. He gave three reasons for opposing it. First, the Indians did not understand the act "and have been misinformed in regard to same"; second, because of past injustices the Cherokees were suspicious "of any proposition put to them by the Indian Office"; and third, section 2 of the bill stipulated that the results of the election would be final, "and since it is my belief that it will surely lose at this time, I do not think it wise to hold the election." The election never took place, probably saving the parkway from outright rejection by the Cherokees.[59] Obviously Blythe recognized the potency of Bauer's opposition.

Finally, a new compromise emerged in 1938. Under this plan North Carolina would build a highway through Soco Valley, while the parkway would follow the mountain ridges surrounding Qualla Boundary and then descend to Ravensford, where it would connect with the road through the national park. This would give the Eastern Cherokees virtually everything they wanted: a new highway through Soco providing direct access to the park and leaving Indian tourist businesses intact, and a new parkway offering unobstructed views of mountain grandeur as well as alternative access to the park and reservation. Clyde M. Blair, Foght's successor as agent, canvassed all council members, including Fred Bauer, and expected unanimous approval. But much to his surprise, the council rejected the proposal, nine to two. The only explanation given Blair was that some Cherokees feared the state would later turn control of the Soco highway over to the park service. In all likelihood Bauer was responsible for this misimpression. Both Blair and Chief Blythe were frustrated and disappointed.[60]

George Stephens, publisher of the *Asheville Citizen*, was even more distressed, fearing Cherokee intransigence might mean loss of a parkway that promised millions of dollars for the regional economy. He believed that both Fred and Catherine Bauer had "inherited the ancient grudge of the Indians against the white man" and that their arguments had befuddled the average Cherokee. Furthermore, it was his understanding that the Bauers intended to ask North Carolina newspapers to publish articles they had written attacking the Indian Office. Stephens thought such diatribes would "so stir up the Cherokees that it will be impossible to ever get any cooperative action from the Indians on the Blue Ridge Parkway." He asked Curtis B. Johnson of the *Charlotte Observer* to delay publication of any such articles "until present negotiations are definitely settled." Johnson agreed to cooperate.[61]

Congressman Zebulon Weaver was even more determined to have the parkway. He introduced a bill that would, if necessary, appropriate tribal lands for the project. The secretary of the interior would select lands for the parkway right-of-way in consultation with the tribal council but was not bound by its wishes. He would then convey those lands to North Carolina. In congressional hearings in July 1939, Weaver insisted he had no intention of harming the Eastern Band. "All I desire is to bring this road down there to them where more than a million people will pass over and through there during the year. Except for this roadway, they are isolated." Spokesmen for North Carolina said they were willing to pay the Band a total of $40,000 or $30 an acre, whichever was greater, for the compromise right-of-way; testimony demonstrated that this was much more than the land was worth. Under Weaver's bill, the Cherokees were allowed to use part of this money to buy more productive lands from the national park.

True to their sometimes exasperating tradition of playing both sides of an issue, the Band had delegated both Chief Blythe and Vice Chief Bauer to represent them. The former, predictably, favored the proposed compromise as "a very generous offer." Bauer, now a candidate for chief in the upcoming tribal elections, had a platform of not alienating any tribal lands and proposed a parkway route that would be entirely outside the reservation. When asked why two Cherokee representatives should have such different views, Bauer said Chief Blythe was a central figure in the tribe's "relief setup" whose "bread and butter comes from the Government pay check." But neither the testimony of Bauer nor that of Alice Lee Jemison could stop the parkway. The bill finally passed the House in early August without specifying a route. Then it awaited Senate action, leaving the Band a choice of taking immediate steps toward approving the compromise offer or running the risk that the secretary of the interior would select a route less attractive to the tribe.[62]

This situation played into the hands of Jarrett Blythe, who was running against Bauer for reelection as principal chief. Blythe was probably the most popular political figure ever to hold office on the Cherokee reservation, a man Clyde Blair characterized as "very level-headed" and intelligent, "who has the best interest of the Indians at heart and who thoroughly understands the relationship between the Federal Government and the tribe." Against another opponent and in other circumstances, Fred Bauer might have been a more viable candidate. As Blair had conceded in 1938, Bauer exercised "a strong influence with the Council due largely to the fact that he is emotional, dramatic, clever and capable of very persuasive speech."[63] But that had been

4. Jarrett Blythe, principal chief 1931–47, 1955–59, 1963–67. Courtesy of the Cherokee Historical Association.

a year earlier, when things were going Bauer's way. Now it was clear the parkway would be built on reservation land, with or without Cherokee approval—and possibly on terms far less generous than the compromise proposal. Blythe clearly favored the compromise, and the prospect of receiving a large sum of money for largely uninhabited, unproductive lands along that route must have swayed many Cherokees. Nor did it make matters easier for Bauer that he had recently coauthored a booklet published by

William Dudley Pelly, head of the Silver Shirts of America, a pro-Nazi and virulently anticommunist and anti-Semitic organization. The booklet's title revealed its thesis: *Indians Aren't Red: The Inside Story of Administration Attempts to Make Communists of the North Carolina Cherokees.* Although Clyde Blair doubted it would have much impact on the Indians, he reported that Congressman Weaver was asking for an investigation of Pelly's publishing company.[64]

Whatever Bauer's problems, in all likelihood Jarrett Blythe would have beaten him—and anyone else—easily. One astute observer believed Bauer could have run against Blythe 150 times without winning. It was no contest. Not counting the Graham County returns, Blythe polled 707 votes in the September 1939 elections to 161 for his adoptive brother. Equally important, almost all of the new council members supported Blythe and the compromise right-of-way. Bauer's days of significant tribal authority were over, though his machinations and vocal opposition to the Indian Office would continue for another thirty years.[65]

Besides losing the election, Bauer and his followers also failed in their efforts to promote a Cherokee education reflecting mainstream American culture. By 1939 the school system, although modernized in terms of its facilities and certain administrative procedures, unabashedly geared its education to reservation life rather than outside opportunities. The boarding school now had grades eleven and twelve but emphasized vocational education and Cherokee arts and crafts. More than previous administrations, the Collier regime had also attempted to provide elementary education for all reservation children without disrupting family ties. Access to expanded and modernized day schools at Big Cove, Bird Town, Soco, and Snowbird was much easier than in earlier days, and many children now attended classes who otherwise would have been overlooked. This in turn helped reduce the number of boarders at the central school to 140, while another 260 students—mostly older children—were bused in each day. For the present, at least, the Indian Office realized that few Cherokees would be allowed to attend public schools with whites. During the preceding decade, out of $2,351,000 of nonrelief federal money spent on the Band through the Bureau of Indian Affairs, more than $1,255,000 had been for education.[66]

To Clyde Blair and other Indian Office employees, Bauer's eclipse and the unquestioned leadership of Jarrett Blythe must have brought enormous relief. Blair found the new tribal council to be diligent, cooperative, and willing to follow the advice of the chief. At the first meeting Blythe made it clear that he saw resolution of the right-of-way issue as a priority, and the council proved agreeable. In February 1940 it unanimously ratified what was essentially the compromise plan and, as a bonus to the Indian Office, denied that Alice Lee Jemison or any other outsider represented the Band. Congress promptly approved the new parkway route, and the Cherokees eventually had their Soco Valley highway as well.[67]

Whatever one thinks of Bauer, his opposition to the initial parkway plans clearly had the support of a tribal majority, as well as Chief Blythe and agents Foght and Blair. Such a proposal would have strangled tribal business enterprise in both the Soco Valley and the town of Cherokee. For better or worse, the compromise allowed the present strip development of commercial enterprise along reservation highways. When the real tourist boom began after World War II, the Cherokees would be prepared. The most enduring legacy of the New Deal among the Eastern Cherokees was the groundwork it laid for that boom.

6

Pursuing the Wily
Tourist

LURING white tourists to the Cherokee reservation had been an objective of the Indian Office since creation of the annual tribal fair in 1914. With the advent of the automobile age in the 1920s, the number of visitors to Qualla Boundary increased significantly, stimulating a modest revival of Cherokee crafts. But creation of the Great Smoky Mountains National Park guaranteed that tourism would become a vital force in Indian life—if not immediately, then when the depression ended. It was serendipity that the park became reality at the same time that John Collier was appointed Indian commissioner, because his commitment to Indian crafts and culture helped prepare Cherokees for this expected tourist onslaught. Many park visitors, it was believed, would also want to see "real" Indians, buy their wares, and perhaps be photographed with one. Agent R. L. Spalsbury understood and touted this symbiotic relationship of the park and the Eastern Band. Not only was the park a boon to the Indians, but the Cherokee presence "is a valuable asset to the Park. They will be a big drawing card for it."[1]

With renewed national interest in Native Americans, Cherokee agents encouraged tribal members to participate in a variety of special events that might call attention to the Eastern Band. Flair was more important than historical or anthropological accuracy. A good example was a 1935 Asheville parade led by Goingback Chiltoskey, mounted on a beautiful horse and wearing the spectacular regalia of a Sioux warrior (though as he now cheerfully admits, "I hadn't never been on a horse"). Behind him in the procession came a detachment of Indian archers and "blow gun shooters," assorted dancers and ballplayers, medicine men, "tom-tom beaters," women with papooses, and a float featuring an old-time Cherokee homestead complete with log house, corn grinder, basket weaver, pottery makers, and two nubile "princesses." Thanks to this Hollywood approach, the Cherokees won the first prize of a loving cup. Harold Foght saw the extravaganza not only as good publicity but as a necessary step toward the new programs of Collier's administration: "Pageantry of this kind has already quickened in many of the Indians a love for the historic past and will go a long ways to help us in the new education." [2] Throughout the 1930s Cherokee dancers performed in countless festivals, ballplayers traveled widely to demonstrate their prowess, and tribal beauty queens competed in regional pageants and contests. [3]

Encouraging Cherokee arts and crafts was another way to reinforce a sense of tribal distinctiveness and also attract tourists. Even though some of the handicrafts of the 1930s were of dubious aboriginal authenticity, the Indian Office nonetheless offered special instructional programs and allied the Band with regional crafts guilds to help in marketing tribal wares. Yet as Harold Foght admitted in 1934, "The basketry, weaving and pottery here— which are largely borrowed from mountain whites and Catawba Indians— lack the colorfulness and other attractiveness of the Southwestern Indian craftsmen. Likewise, the variety of articles produced is very limited." Tourists, he said, had been especially disappointed by the pottery. Tom Underwood, longtime craft-shop proprietor and connoisseur of Indian art, agrees that with few exceptions the work of that period was not very good, but he believes New Deal encouragement was critical for the eventual maturation of Cherokee craftsmanship. [4]

Even more important for the long-term growth of tourism was creation of an outdoor drama to enthrall visitors with a theatrical—and distorted— version of the Cherokee past. In January 1934, at almost the same time Collier issued his circular affirming the validity of traditional tribal cultures, R. L. Spalsbury was collecting information for "enacting a pageant of Cherokee history here, which . . . we hope to make an annual feature during the height of the tourist season." [5] This objective took tangible form under Spalsbury's successor, Harold Foght, who apparently staged a minor show in 1934 and then, before the 1935 tribal fair, announced the Indians would dispense with "all the cheap white ballyhoo" and instead, on four evenings, present a pageant called "Spirit of the Great Smokies." In it the Indians hoped to reveal "something of the Cherokee ancient religious life" and other features of Indian life "which we cannot afford to lose." He said that a special group of Indians from the Chilocco school would assist them with "some of the more difficult phases of the pageant artistry."[6]

Apparently the production went well enough, but it supposedly entailed so much work that agency personnel decided to make it a biennial rather than an annual event. In all likelihood an equally important factor was a bitter attack on Foght's control over the drama by the Bauer faction. Regardless of the reason, the subsequent interlude was enough to whet Foght's appetite for a more ambitious show. In spring 1937 he wrote Collier that "there is a growing enthusiasm for a repetition of the pageant given two years ago." This time the agent expected it to be shown once a week for eight weeks during the summer tourist season. He noted that in the previous year some 600,000 people had passed through the park, many also visiting the reservation. There was every reason to expect even more during the 1937 season. Certain Knoxville citizens had organized the Tsali Cherokee Foundation (in honor of an early tribal hero), which would help publicize the pageant and even assist in paying for costumes. Foght admitted that "it has frankly been my dream that we might set up a kind of pageantry here that may in time become known throughout the United States, something like the Messiah Festival among the Swedish Americans at Lindsborg, Kansas, or even the Passion Play of Oberammergau [Germany]."[7]

The 1937 pageant was historical in nature and covered the period from Spanish exploration to the present. Featuring more than 350 Cherokees in costume, it had a total of six performances in July and August. Probably the most interesting role was that of the tribal martyr Tsali, played by Cherokee traditionalist Moses Owl. Margaret Spielman, a member of the staff at Haskell Institute, directed. Immediately after the last performance, Foght announced that "Spirit of the Great Smokies" had a total paid attendance of 5,541 and total income of $2,231—$600 of which was used to repay the Tsali Foundation for its costuming expenditures. Although this was a decent showing, the pageant fell victim to the bitter tribal strife and was even attacked in congressional hearings by the Bauer-McCoy faction.[8] It was not to be revived again until thirteen years later, with a different name, different direction, and a different degree of success.

Other tentative steps to meet tourist needs were also being taken on the reservation. Agents were working out procedures for leasing Cherokee commercial properties to white entrepreneurs, organizing a tribal crafts guild, and issuing traders' licenses. Transportation on Qualla Boundary remained a problem, and by 1934 about half a dozen white taxi drivers of varying dependability were available.[9] The Appalachian Railroad meanwhile had discontinued passenger service to Cherokee—and in fact was about to go out of business. An improved, all-weather route was under construction from Cherokee via Bird Town to the state highway running through Bryson City, but progress was frustratingly slow because completion depended on using part of the railroad right-of-way. Agents meanwhile advocated constructing other roads linking the reservation with the new park and nearby communities. The town of Cherokee, they realized, must take advantage of its position as the eastern gateway to the park. Despite opposition from Fred Bauer, Pearson McCoy, and their coterie, the Cherokee council was attempting to create a tribally owned complex of tourist facilities and to make favorable exchanges of land with the park.[10]

Individual Cherokees also hoped to take advantage of the anticipated hordes of automobile adventurers. There were small-scale entrepreneurs selling beads and trinkets from tiny stands sometimes no more than eight feet square, as well as at least one operating from an ox-drawn wagon that attracted "quite a few tourists."[11] Other Cherokees were more ambitious, and as early as 1936 Jesse Lambert was planning to lease his property in remote Big Cove to a pair of experienced resort managers who intended to open an auto camp of rustic cabins for visitors wishing to escape the everyday world. Harold Foght was enthusiastic about the venture but said the prospective tenants wanted a renewable lease before investing their money. At that time a ten-year lease was the maximum approved by the Indian Office. Because of this, the Big Cove tourist camp was delayed indefinitely.[12] Foght believed this sort of problem was one reason the town of Cherokee was lagging so far behind Gatlinburg in the pursuit of tourists. Malcontents like Pearson McCoy took this argument even further, viewing Indian Office paternalism and bungling as a nearly insuperable obstacle to effective competition with Gatlinburg's free enterprise.[13]

Even the unfavorable leasing regulations did not prevent the opening of Cherokee's first motel early in 1937, when Mrs. Delia Cooper Queen rented part of her possessory tract for a craft shop, restaurant, and tourists' camp of eight modern cabins. This development, called Newfound Lodge, was on a prime site next to the highway about one mile above the boarding school, and Foght described the lessees (the Robert Halls) as wealthy Ashevilleans who would maintain the "right kind of place."[14] Lois Farthing, Mrs. Queen's daughter, recalls that her white father chose to farm rather than run a motel and had built the cabins partly in self-defense. Drivers were sometimes afraid to challenge the mountain road in late afternoon and wanted to spend the night at the Queens' house, just outside the park.

Mrs. Farthing remembers, "We had a little dining room here with our first cabins and a gift shop. We leased it out for 10 years to the Robert Halls. They sold only Indian crafts from here—they didn't sell much."[15] After World War II, Farthing was to expand upon these modest beginnings and become one of Cherokee's most successful entrepreneurs.

Despite the depression, the number of tourists visiting the reservation increased steadily during the late 1930s. In August 1939, for example, an estimated 169,000 people visited the national park, many also stopping in Cherokee. According to Pearson McCoy, business had boomed during the preceding year, with native crafts alone bringing in about $30,000; there were also newer and better shops.[16] Even as events in Europe and Asia darkened America's immediate future, visitors came. By the end of 1940 Clyde Blair, the new BIA superintendent, reported such an increase in tourism that the multitude of contractual obligations required another clerk at the agency. With continuing operation of the CCC and other New Deal programs, and with steadily increasing opportunities in new defense-related industries, more Cherokees than ever before found at least part-time employment.[17]

Unfortunately, tourist income was not evenly distributed on the Cherokee reservation. Indians living in Graham and Cherokee counties were too far removed from the park to share directly in its benefits. About the only return they received from the increased tourism was a proportionate share in reservation license and leasing fees. Apparently most survived by subsistence agriculture, odd jobs, and whatever they could earn from cutting timber (legally or illegally). Not until the end of the decade did significant numbers find jobs constructing nearby Tennessee Valley Authority dams. Understandably, there was some resentment in those counties toward Qualla Boundary and especially the town of Cherokee. When the council voted in November 1934 to appropriate $50,000 for construction of tribal tourist facilities in Cherokee, the lone dissenting vote was from a Graham County councillor who, according to Harold Foght, "always votes against every enterprise which seems to offer the main reservation more than the outlying sections."[18]

Tourism also became enmeshed in other aspects of tribal factionalism, as acculturated and nonacculturated Indians often disagreed over how best to develop the industry. Pearson McCoy, rabid foe of tribalism and communism, extolled the growth of business in Cherokee as a triumph of private enterprise and believed that only the Indian Office's subversive policies could undermine continued growth.[19] What he conveniently ignored was the enormous impact of both the National Park Service and the Indian Office in promoting tourism. On the other hand, many nonacculturated Indians, while not necessarily denigrating private initiative, resented those individuals who appeared to be too successful. Leaders like Chief Jarrett Blythe seemed ambivalent. They encouraged private development yet attempted to force at least one successful white entrepreneur out of business. At the same time, they continued to sponsor cooperative and tribal development of certain businesses and properties, an effort incurring the ire of anticommunists like the Bauers and McCoy. In 1935 the Bauer-McCoy faction temporarily gained the upper hand and persuaded the council to rescind its earlier approval of tribally owned businesses in Cherokee.[20]

Bauer's triumph was short-lived, however. A few years later, when he was out of office, Blythe and most councilmembers were again planning tribal enterprises. With impending construction of the Blue Ridge Parkway they hoped to develop Soco Bald, the highest point on the reservation, and also argued with the National Park Service over rights to acreage at Soco Gap. More important was an effort to acquire the Boundary Tree Tract and construct tribally owned tourist facilities there, apparently an updated version of the plans squelched in 1935. Blythe and others had been interested in this tract of nearly 900 acres for several years because of its favorable position adjoining both the park and the park highway. Attempts to acquire it by a trade had been unsuccessful, but by the early 1940s the council was planning to buy it, an objective likely to antagonize some private businessmen and idealogues like the Bauers and McCoy.[21]

Another facet of the split between more and less acculturated Cherokees was the rapid acquisition by the former of better-located tourist properties, a situation encouraged by the Band's unique system of landholding. Although the federal government held the reservation in trust, any enrolled member could arrange purchases and trades with other members. Most acculturated and nonacculturated Indians alike supported this system, and Clyde Blair recognized "the strong feeling of ownership these people have for their individual holdings."[22] As he later explained, the Indians did not view their lands "as a temporary assignment on which to live. They . . . think of them as do white people with deeds, as being theirs and that no one can take the land away from them." This situation had almost inevitable consequences: "Under this plan certain individuals have accumulated more than their share of property, and . . . others have very little or none."[23] The divergence between tribal haves and have-nots was becoming increasingly apparent, adding another element to factionalism and mounting tensions. That some of the most successful property holders had been added to the Baker Roll despite a low Cherokee blood quantum also rankled many Indians.

Details of the new tourism continued to be troublesome. Because business leases were for a maximum of only ten years, the tribal council found it difficult to attract long-term businesses willing to make sizable capital investments. What was needed was a twenty-five-year lease, but this required approval by the Office of Indian Affairs. This was of particular importance because the tribe contemplated buying and developing the Boundary Tree Tract and expected to lease the new businesses there to white entrepreneurs.[24] As might be expected, an array of problems and special cases concerning leases arose during those early years. For example, regulations stipulated that 10 percent of the lease consideration go to the tribe when the original lessor was not a member of the Band. But could a Cherokee avoid paying this by "leasing" his possessory claim to a relative who was also a member and then having that individual "sublease" the property to a white businessman? Or should Cherokees who had improved their property before leasing it be expected to pay more to the tribe for the increased rent that was, after all, a product of their own labor and expense? A perplexed Clyde Blair sometimes asked for advice from the Indian Office on such matters.[25]

A bit more ominous in its implications was a disagreement with the ever-troublesome Pearson McCoy, who operated "a sort of cooperative trading post" in Bird Town where he sold Indian crafts on a percentage basis. Cherokees also received part of the gate receipts for performing dances and games for tourists at his nearby "pow-wow" grounds. As a longtime advocate of detribalization and full citizenship, McCoy noted that the tribe operated under a state charter and contended that he did not need a trader's license because he was, in effect, licensed by the state. He also claimed that he collected and paid state sales taxes. On this issue, at least, Blair had no doubts as to the proper course. He explained to McCoy that it was not necessary to pay the state tax while doing business on a federally recognized reservation, but the trader was adamant and later made it clear he believed Qualla Boundary was not a reservation at all but a collection of privately owned lands illegally held in trust by the United States.[26]

* * *

Like many Americans, the Eastern Cherokees were more concerned with surviving the depression than with the ominous situation in Europe, where Hitler's aggression threatened another world war. Jobs, not guns, were required. Yet for America at least, wars have usually meant full employment and economic growth. When England and France finally declared war on Nazi Germany in September 1939, American industry was about to awaken from its decade-long slumber. President Roosevelt made no secret of his support for the Allies, and despite this nation's official neutrality our industrial and military resources were increasingly at their disposal. Although the United States did not formally become involved until Japan's attack on Pearl Harbor in December 1941, American industry was already on a quasi-wartime basis and young men were being drafted into military service. With America's entry into the war, jobs became plentiful. The depression was over.

For the Eastern Cherokees the industrial and military buildup between 1939 and 1941 created alternatives to employment in tourism and Indian CCC camps. Some found work in defense-related industries like naval shipyards, while others eagerly sought jobs constructing dams for the Tennessee Valley Authority (TVA). The Indians apparently encountered no discrimination and enjoyed the full cooperation of state and local employment agencies. In July 1941, in response to an Indian Office inquiry about employment and training in defense industries, Clyde Blair reported that some members of the Indian CCC and other New Deal programs were receiving training in such fields as auto mechanics, maintaining and repairing telephone lines, driving trucks, operating Caterpillar tractors, and using jackhammers. Another twenty-six Cherokees had recently worked on construction projects at Fort Bragg, a giant military base in eastern North Carolina. Although this was a good start, Blair said private companies had yet to hire Cherokees in any numbers because of their lack of transportation to the projects, their reluctance to leave their families, and the expense and trouble of joining labor unions.[27]

Probably the most attractive opportunity for many able-bodied Cherokee males was working on TVA's Fontana Dam, only about thirty miles away. This enormous power-producing facility would dam the Little Tennessee River and create a lake along the southern boundary of the Great Smoky Mountains National Park. As construction began immediately after Pearl Harbor, many Indians applied for jobs. By summer 1942 an estimated 260 Eastern Cherokees were working at Fontana "for very good pay." It was hard, dangerous work, and at least one Indian was killed at the site.[28]

This sudden abundance of jobs was not an unmitigated blessing. Even as the war created new defense-related industries, the Indian New Deal of necessity was cutting back on its programs, and it eventually eliminated almost all of them. For Cherokees who were restricted to the reservation, this must have imposed a severe handicap. In addition, off-reservation jobs and military service took away a large percentage of adult males, depriving Cherokee families of necessary assistance. This no doubt made it difficult for women, children, and elderly males, especially during the frigid winters. But once again the Eastern Band stood ready to provide whatever help it could, paying for relief out of tribal funds. "The old and needy are taken care of in that way," Clyde Blair said. "Each month a box of groceries is sent to those in need and the Tribal Council . . . and the Chief prepare the lists."[29] Meanwhile, the lack of manpower was particularly acute at the agency and the boarding school. The older and stronger Cherokee students, Blair said in September 1942, "with a spirit of patriotism, desire for adventure and a need for money have gradually gone away." Fifty-three had enlisted, and others had taken outside jobs. Many of the agency personnel had also gone into the service, forcing Blair to hire irregular labor for the essential heavy work around the school and its farm.[30]

To nobody's surprise, World War II also brought a sharp decline in tourism. No longer could Americans take to the highways whenever they pleased. No longer could they enjoy a comfortable two-week vacation and head for national parks. No longer would they be a daily presence on the Cherokee reservation. Winning the war took priority over everything, and gasoline and rubber were commodities too vital to use for the family automobile. As early as June 1942 the dropoff was apparent. "The tourist business is very greatly reduced this year due to the tire and gasoline rationing," Blair admitted. "Some of the traders are so much discouraged that they feel it may be necessary to close down."[31]

By this time many Eastern Cherokees were joining the thousands of Indians entering military service. Because Congress had extended citizenship to all Indians in 1924, it was no longer possible for groups like the Eastern Band to claim that conscription did not apply to them. With imposition of the first American peacetime draft in September 1940, Cherokee males dutifully registered, though one wrote secretary of the interior Harold Ickes that without further information he would refuse to comply. All went well, however, as 271 Cherokee males between the ages of twenty-one and thirty-five registered on October 16; non-Indian registrants on the reservation swelled the total to 331. Soon 100 percent of all eligible Cherokees had complied, and within a month 23 had already enlisted.[32]

In some ways the Cherokees were more assertive of their rights than in 1917. With perfect logic, many believed that a citizen expected to face possible death in war should also have the right to vote. Several, including

World War I veterans Fred Bauer and Jack Jackson, attempted to register to vote in Swain and Jackson counties and, predictably, were turned down by registrars. It made no difference when Clyde Blair intervened by citing Cherokee citizenship and the applicants' ability to meet all other state voting requirements. It is safe to say that Bauer knew the North Carolina constitution better than any of the registrars. To such a literate and articulate advocate of Americanism, rejection must have been an intolerable affront. Even the normally acquiescent tribal council was outraged and argued that the Cherokees' inability to vote in North Carolina denied them "equal rights and fair treatment" by the county draft boards.[33] In a resolution of November 5, 1940, it asserted that "any organization or group that would deprive a people of as sacred a right as the right of suffrage would not hesitate to deprive them of other constitutional rights including the three inalienable rights—life, liberty and the pursuit of happiness, if the opportunity to do so presents itself." Taking pains to affirm both the Cherokees' loyalty and their outraged sense of justice, the council continued:

> It is not that we wish to shield our young men and prevent their being inducted into the Service. It is not that our young men wish to shirk any duty which may come their way under the draft. . . . And we say here and now, if we may do so without seeming to boast, that there is not a more patriotic people to be found anywhere in this country of ours than the Cherokees of North Carolina. . . . We feel that the ends of justice will be better served so far as this reservation is concerned if a fair and impartial draft board is set up here, separate and apart from these county boards. We feel sure that a board thus set up would act understandingly and in a sympathetic manner in the induction of our young men into the service.[34]

It is interesting that the resolution did not also insist on voter registration, but after World War II Cherokee veterans would attend to that long-neglected matter.

In forwarding the tribal resolution, Clyde Blair expressed strong support for creation of a separate draft board and said, "The Indians here are determined not to make up the quota for the white people in Jackson and Swain Counties. . . . They do not have confidence in the fairness of these white people in their dealings with them."[35] Nor did Blair. The Indian Office responded that it could not create such a draft board but suggested the Eastern Band appeal to the governor, who exercised such authority. "We are in sympathy with the Indians in their statements and basis for a separate board," assistant Indian commissioner William Zimmerman wrote, "and would be disposed to support the Indians in their appeal to the Governor if such action is decided upon." One possible alternative was to ask the governor to appoint Blair to an advisory board for registration "so that the Indians may have greater assurance that there is some person interested in them and will look after their interests."[36] By May 1941 only two Cherokees had been conscripted while twenty-six had enlisted; then, in June alone, seventeen more enlisted, and by the time of Pearl Harbor there were forty-five enlistees and twelve draftees.[37]

For a while after Pearl Harbor, the number of Cherokee servicemen remained stable except for a few more conscripts, but by July 1942 there were fifty-seven enlistees and thirty-six draftees. Many of those who enlisted were too young for the draft, and the *Asheville Citizen* reported that Cherokee parents showed no hesitancy in giving their underage sons permission to serve.[38] The number of enlistees continued to exceed conscripts until 1943, and by war's end 123 Eastern Cherokees had enlisted and 198 had been drafted; a total of 586 had registered. Military service was the first time many had left the reservation for any extended period. Nationwide over 25,000 Indians served during the war—a higher percentage of their population, according to John Collier, than for any other ethnic group in America.[39]

In its eagerness to support the war effort, the Department of the Interior helped perpetuate old and sometimes demeaning stereotypes about Indians. Harold Ickes spoke of the "inherited talents" of Indians for fighting, and in a 1944 article in *Collier's* said the Indian soldier possessed "endurance, rhythm, a feeling for timing, co-ordination, sense perception, an uncanny ability to get over any sort of terrain at night, and, better than all else, an enthusiasm for fighting. He takes a rough job and makes a game of it. Rigors of combat hold no terrors for him; severe discipline and hard duties do not deter him."[40] Many whites subscribed to Ickes's views, believing that Indians were natural warriors especially well suited to scouting and stealth. By war's end it was common knowledge that one of the marines who raised the American flag on Iwo Jima was Ira Hayes, a Pima, and that Navajo radio operators had befuddled enemy decoders by relaying messages in their native tongue. Popular movies dealing with the war often featured "all-American platoons" that had at least one token Indian (unlike blacks, Indians did not serve in segregated units). Indians themselves contributed to these images by reviving warrior societies, making honorary chiefs of such luminaries as Franklin D. Roosevelt, Douglas MacArthur, and even Joseph Stalin, and in the case of the League of Iroquois, declaring war on

Italy and Japan (the League simply renewed its unrepealed 1917 declaration of war against Germany). Indian dancers and singers also performed in support of the war effort.[41]

Eastern Cherokees were in every branch of the service and saw action in all theaters of the war. Robert Youngdeer, for example, was part of a special marine reconnaissance team (perhaps because he was Indian) and fought in campaigns at Tulagi, Guadalcanal, and other Pacific islands. Joseph George enlisted in the army in the late 1930s and eventually wound up in France. According to federal records, twelve members of the Band died in service— six in the Pacific, five in Europe, and one in the United States. Seven more, including Youngdeer, were wounded. Besides Purple Hearts, Cherokees received two Distinguished Flying Crosses and two Silver Stars. (During the Korean War a few years later, Charles George, an Eastern Cherokee, was posthumously awarded the congressional Medal of Honor for saving several comrades by throwing himself on an enemy grenade.)[42]

Cherokees reported little or no discrimination against them during World War II, though Jeff Thompson recalls that recruiters in western North Carolina initially rejected him because he was an Indian.[43] More serious was the classification in 1943 of six Eastern Cherokees as Negroes, prompting them to refuse induction. The situation was not surprising, given the questionable lineage of some members of the Band. Fortunately, the United States District Court in Raleigh reviewed the evidence and affirmed their Indianness. The six Cherokees "joined the Army as Indians and were thus integrated in white units." Throughout the armed forces Indians mingled peaceably with whites and took no offense at usually being called "chief."[44]

As had happened in World War I, Cherokees also distinguished themselves on the home front. Soon after the United States entered the war, the council reaffirmed Cherokee patriotism by voting to invest $150,000 in war bonds or other such obligations issued by the federal government. Because this money was already drawing interest on deposit in the United States Treasury and was designated for other purposes, the Indian Bureau refused to allow purchase of the bonds. The council also voted $500 for the reservation's American Red Cross chapter to provide assistance to Cherokee servicemen. Individual Indians purchased bonds and stamps, raised victory gardens, and collected scrap metal. Others became part of what John Collier called "the greatest exodus of Indians" ever from reservations, an estimated 40,000 who found factory work during the war.[45] And like many other Americans in defense industries, all of the more than 200 Cherokees working at Fontana Dam agreed to a 10 percent pay deduction to buy war bonds. Other tribes showed similar dedication to victory. In 1944 Collier estimated that the total Indian financial commitment to winning the war amounted to about $50 million.[46]

Jarrett Blythe was the glue that held the tribe together during the war years. Too old to fight or to work in factories, he exercised a consistent, dedicated leadership on the reservation, supervising the dwindling New Deal programs and offering a comforting sense of continuity. No role was too small for him to play. To Blair's delight, the chief chaired a committee that convinced every family on the reservation to raise a victory garden. "This is a challenge to any other Indian Reservation in the United States to show an equal record," the agent boasted. Not since Nimrod J. Smith in the 1880s and 1890s had there been such an activist principal chief. Most of Blythe's predecessors during the early twentieth century had been content merely to preside over the periodic council meetings, but the Indian New Deal placed a premium on a different kind of leadership. Blythe mastered this new style, subtly undercutting vocal opponents like the Bauers and Pearson McCoy. Like Roosevelt, he was the consummate political survivor and was elected chief more often than any Cherokee before or since— six times. Any unsavory connotations aside, he was like an urban ward heeler. He got things done. He is remembered as "one of the most all inclusive, purposeful men you'd find."[47] By the war years his constituents had "attained such confidence in his ability and integrity that they are not satisfied until they see him."[48] And it was Blythe who, despite some Cherokee objections, finally achieved tribal purchase of the Boundary Tree Tract early in 1943. His ambitious plans for this property would contribute to tribal prosperity when tourism revived after the war.

* * *

The Indian veterans who returned to North Carolina in 1945 and 1946 were much more self-confident and assertive than the young men who had gone off to war. They found new jobs on a reservation where tourism was quickly reviving, raised families, and continued their education under the GI Bill of Rights. By 1947 about 140 Cherokees were enrolled in Veterans Administration–sponsored agricultural training programs.[49] The veterans also made it clear that they would no longer tolerate second-class citizenship. Having fought totalitarianism abroad, they were more sensitive to injustice at home. Nowhere was this more apparent than on the issue of voting. As early as the fall of 1945 the Steve Youngdeer Post of the American

Legion discussed the matter and appointed a six-man committee to spear-head efforts to secure the franchise. Heading the committee was post commander Jack Jackson, and another member was Joe Jennings, Clyde Blair's recent successor as agent. The committee wrote the chairmen of the Swain and Jackson county election boards, pointing out that Cherokees had long been denied their legal rights as voters and requesting hearings before those boards. This and a second letter were ignored. Nor did private conversations with several members of the election boards produce any results. The committee then appealed for assistance to the Bryson City post of the American Legion, which unanimously voted to support Cherokee efforts to win the franchise.[50]

In May 1946 Jennings accompanied five Cherokee veterans to Qualla Precinct in Jackson County; all were "able to read and write" the North Carolina constitution and otherwise qualified to vote. The registrar refused to register them, however, saying he was simply following instructions. That same day Jennings accompanied two other fully qualified Cherokee veterans to Ela Precinct in Swain County, where the female registrar went through the charade of asking one to read from a law book and then interpret the passage. John Gloyne, a veteran of five World War II campaigns (and later a trustee of Western Carolina University), gave what Jennings considered "a very sensible interpretation," but the official was not satisfied and refused to register him. The Cherokee election committee then appealed to several state officials, including Governor R. Gregg Cherry and Attorney General Harry McMullen, both of whom were sympathetic. Yet nothing was done, and the Cherokees were still unable to register for the state primary elections.[51]

Frustrated and angry, members of the Steve Youngdeer post hired Frank Parker, an Asheville lawyer, and informed United States Attorney General Tom Clark of their grievances. Two F B I agents arrived and spent a few days interviewing both Indians and local election officials. Mary Ulmer meanwhile was compiling information from past elections, showing conclusively that very few Cherokees had ever been allowed to register. Upon another request from the Legion, the Swain County Board of Elections held a hearing at which the Legion committee appeared with Parker. The Cherokees insisted on their right to vote, asked for dismissal of the current registrar, and requested that the county set up a new precinct more convenient to most Swain County Indians. The county board refused to accede to these requests, and the Jackson County board refused even to schedule a hearing.[52]

But the Indian veterans were not to be denied. When the tribal fair was held during the first week of October, volunteers passed out several thousand handbills describing the Indians' grievances. Meanwhile district officers of the American Legion were actively lobbying with state political leaders and Legion officers, while most area newspapers also supported the Indian cause. All these pressures finally had an effect. Shortly after the fair, Swain and Jackson county officials notified the Eastern Cherokees that they would be allowed to register. The Legion post then provided transportation for any qualified Cherokee who lived at a distance from the precincts. At Qualla Precinct a new registrar treated the Indians "in every respect just as the white registrants." At Ela Precinct the earlier registrar was still in charge and required all Indian applicants to read a paragraph, write it from dictation, and sign his name. "Her manner was unpleasant," Jennings said, "but she did permit nearly all of the Indians to register." The agent believed there would be no future electoral problems, but if there were "the Legion Post is ready to renew its fight for the franchise of all the Cherokees."[53] Fortunately, that was not necessary.

For the Eastern Band, at least, it appears there was no troubling economic readjustment after the war. Even before Japan's surrender, Cherokee crafts were again thriving, and the demand was greater "than we can possibly supply." Along with about twenty-five schools, cooperatives, and other organizations, the Band belonged to the Southern Highland Guild. By mid-1946 the tribal guild operated a store that had sales of about $40 a day even before the tourist season was in full swing.[54] This was the forerunner of today's highly successful Qualla Arts and Crafts Mutual, Incorporated. In addition, there was renewed interest in tribal timber resources and a host of related issues like cutting permits, stumpage fees, procedures for letting contracts, and demands that Indian truckers have preference in hauling tribal timber to market. The American Legion post again played an active role, advocating such things as modernizing the Cherokee business community, hiring a local police force, and collecting additional licensing fees to provide other necessities.[55]

The council meanwhile deferred action on applications from Cherokees who wanted to settle on the recently acquired Boundary Tree Tract. It was clear that Chief Blythe and the council intended to push ahead with plans for an ambitious tribal enterprise there consisting of tourist accommodations, a filling station, restaurant, and craft shop. By February 1946 the council was considering a resolution to seek a loan of $150,000 from the BIA's revolving credit fund to begin development of the tract; $120,000 would go for constructing the tribally owned enterprise, and the remaining $30,000 would be lent by the tribe to individual members or groups of members who wished to develop their own businesses. Predictably, Fred Bauer strongly opposed the resolution and claimed the council lacked authority under the tribal charter to undertake such a project. But his objections were clearly more fundamental, rooted in his deep aversion to anything resembling "socialism." It is a measure of his diminished prestige that the council respectfully read his letter of protest, then quickly voted to request the loans. One of only two dissenting councilmen was John C. McCoy, Pearson McCoy's kinsman.[56] Still the attacks continued, Catherine Bauer complaining to western North Carolina's state representative Dan Tompkins that Boundary Tree was a communistic enterprise. By this time the Bauers and other critics of the Indian Office were actively supporting the growing congressional clamor for "emancipating" Indians by terminating their federal services.[57]

Newly self-confident, the Eastern Cherokees resisted termination and continued planning for Boundary Tree. Although the Band received its loan, the Senate suddenly delayed matters by turning an attentive ear to the complaints of the Bauers and Pearson McCoy. Joe Jennings and Jarrett Blythe were alarmed because construction materials had already been purchased and hauled to the Boundary Tree Tract. Further delay would simply add to the costs and confusion. Their opponents' clamor against Boundary Tree, Jennings said, was simply another way of attacking both the tribal and federal governments. The thrust of his argument was clear: "real" Cherokees—the "little people" of the reservation—favored Boundary Tree, while most opponents were selfish individuals with little or no Indian blood who had unfairly gained inclusion on the Baker Roll. Blythe and Jennings invited a Senate investigation, confident it would remove the taint of communism and allow the project to resume.[58]

The complaints of anticommunists had only temporary effect, and construction on Boundary Tree soon began in earnest. By midsummer 1948 the tribe had nearly finished an attractive stone building that was leased for ten years to the Standard Oil Company as a filling station. Nearby were six recently completed tourist rooms with hardwood floors and tile baths, with twelve more rooms to be available by Labor Day. A lodge and restaurant were expected to open the next year.[59] Boundary Tree was a milestone in Cherokee economic life, marking a wholehearted commitment to tourism and a willingness, despite noisy opposition, to risk tribal assets when private venture capital was not readily available. Today it is still the first group of buildings motorists encounter when entering the reservation from the park. And unlike many newer and bigger businesses catering to tourists, its unobtrusive and attractive architecture blends nicely with the natural environment.

* * *

All these tourist-related developments on Qualla Boundary were merely a prelude to the main event, the revival of a historical pageant catering to tourists. The modest success of "The Spirit of the Smokies" in 1935 and 1937 had hinted at what might be possible, but that first pageant had died amid factional squabbling. There had been vague talk in 1941 of Clyde Blair's consulting with the creators of the famous "Lost Colony" pageant, and an Asheville resident supposedly wanted to stage a drama on Tsali, but events at Pearl Harbor ended such discussion.[60] In the postwar period, however, plans for a new Cherokee pageant quickly blossomed because of several interrelated factors: America's unprecedented new prosperity, a revived national obsession with the automobile, and the easy accessibility of the Great Smoky Mountains National Park. Add authentic Indians to this mixture, and the result was an attractive tourist "package."

If the Cherokees themselves lacked the necessary business experience to undertake such a worthy project, there were plenty of whites in western North Carolina willing to help. The first step came in 1947, when Western North Carolina Associated Communities—a consortium of eleven counties—decided to sponsor a drama that would depict Cherokee history and traditions. The new production would be of unprecedented scope and glitter, a monument both to efficient planning and to the postwar "can do" spirit of enterprise. To manage the pageant, Associated Communities incorporated the Cherokee Historical Association (CHA), a nonprofit organization dedicated to preserving Cherokee culture and history. The University of North Carolina at Chapel Hill agreed to undertake the technical aspects of the project. According to John Parris, the first public relations director of the show, "No one man or any dozen men" could claim credit for establishing the drama; it was "a project born of area cooperation—one of the finest examples of such cooperation in the country." Each of the eleven counties raised anywhere from $1,000 to $6,000 for construction of the theater, and the state of North Carolina contributed another $35,000 for the production. Cherokee traders, government employees, and others on the reservation also made donations. The Indian Office agreed to construct a road to the theater site as well as a parking lot. The tribe would spend up to $5,000 for possessory rights to suitable lands that would be conveyed to the CHA for its theater. Jarrett Blythe's strong support for the pageant was also crucial.[61]

As Parris readily acknowledged, the CHA believed its drama would "raise the economic level of the Cherokee," an objective the council eagerly embraced when it approved the plans in March 1948. It was the general opinion, it said, that the pageant "will contribute appreciably to raising the economic standard of the Cherokee people."[62] No doubt white businessmen in Associated Communities well understood that increased tourism on the reservation would inevitably benefit their counties as well. And no doubt they realized the Cherokees could offer tourists something they could not—a chance to see "real" Indians, or at least what passed for Indians in the eyes of most whites.

The CHA was clearly a white-dominated organization. Harry E. Buchanan was chairman and Joe Jennings, the Cherokee agent, was treasurer. Jennings was one of the most enthusiastic proponents of the pageant and a necessary liaison between the association and the Band. Molly Arneach, the association's secretary, was the only member of the Band holding an administrative position. As for the pageant itself, the most important person by far was Mr. Carol White, who would serve as general manager for many years. Although whites and Indians alike questioned both the composition and the intent of the association—and indeed still do—there is little doubt that such a regional organization of experienced businessmen and promoters was essential to undertake so ambitious a project.[63]

Even with these men leading the CHA, plans for the pageant dragged on for months. Despite early hopes of staging the production during the summer of 1949, valuable time was consumed by money and production problems, launching a publicity campaign, and writing a suitable script. By early 1949 it became apparent the production would be delayed another year.[64] One of the most pressing needs was to construct a suitable theater. The original plan was simply to have a raised stage in the middle of a large level area, but Sam Selden, director of "Lost Colony," decided otherwise. He was overwhelmed by the mountains around Cherokee and envisioned something more suitable to such grandeur. The story is that while taking a short stroll he came upon a lovely site for a hillside amphitheater and insisted that his dream become reality. Ross Caldwell, a local businessman and former engineer, worked almost two years without pay to make the site into the beautiful Mountainside Theater. Cherokee masons and other laborers did much of the construction. The result was a tiered theater of nearly 2,900 seats that still enchants audiences with its intimacy and mountain ambiance. With three stages, the largest eighty by twenty-five feet, the theater could easily accommodate the scores of actors and extras necessary for the pageant.[65]

5. Downtown Cherokee, 1949. Courtesy of the Museum of the Cherokee Indian.

Directing the play was Harry Davis of the University of North Carolina Playmakers, one of the South's most respected institutions of dramatic education. Dramatist Kermit Hunter wrote the script as part of his academic work at the university and basically followed the broad outlines of the 1935 and 1937 shows. Jack Frederick Kilpatrick, an Oklahoma Cherokee (and later an author on Cherokee history), wrote the musical score. Costuming, lighting, singing, dancing, and other aspects of the production all received careful attention, abetted by ample financial backing.[66] Finally, after an intensive publicity campaign, "Unto These Hills" made its debut before some 2,400 spectators on the evening of Saturday, July 1, 1950. With fourteen scenes, more than one hundred actors, and an acoustically perfect amphitheater, it was impressive in every respect. About twenty-five Indians were in the cast, a few in important roles. Arsene Thompson, for example, played Elias Boudinot, famous Cherokee editor of the 1830s and signer of the infamous Treaty of New Echota.[67]

The *Knoxville News-Sentinel* applauded the show's professionalism and believed it would gross a million dollars if staged on Broadway. In what proved to be classic understatement, it said the pageant "is certain to pay dividends."[68] With performances Wednesday through Saturday, "Unto These Hills" was staged fifty-three times through Labor Day and drew a total of 107,140 viewers—an average of 2,022 per performance.[69] Tom

Underwood supervised a cleanup crew that first season and recalls that the play drew fewer than a thousand spectators an evening until early August, when "the thing just broke wide open" and began drawing full houses.[70] An ecstatic Joe Jennings said the pageant "surpassed even our fondest hopes." The $25,000 owed by the CHA at the beginning of the season was paid in full, "and we should have at least $30,000 with which to open the season next year."[71] By that time there was a small historical museum in town, and the CHA was planning to construct an authentic Cherokee village depicting tribal life of the mid-eighteenth century.[72] Tourism had come to Cherokee in a big way.

The overwhelming triumph of "Unto These Hills" dictated that the CHA leave inviolate Kermit Hunter's script and its themes of early Cherokee history: the first contact with Spanish explorers; the Smokies as sacred homeland; dispossession by land-hungry whites; betrayal by President Andrew Jackson (a supposed friend); the tragedy of removal and the Trail of Tears; Tsali's supposed "sacrifice" so that a Cherokee remnant could remain in their beloved mountains; and finally reunification, reconciliation, and reaffirmation of the brotherhood of man. As is common in such pageants, historical nuances succumbed to broad generalizations and stereotypical characterization. Hunter's denigration of Jackson so infuriated the ladies of the Hermitage Association, which administers Jackson's estate, that they and Governor Gordon Browning of Tennessee protested—in vain.[73] Even more questionable were the characterizations of Indians like Sequoyah, Tecumseh, Drowning Bear, and unfortunately Tsali, who as an unassuming and obscure man would probably find his theatrical sainthood embarrassing.[74] Good history the pageant is not, but it is highly engrossing entertainment. Its formulaic script is a proven winner. "Unto These Hills," along with the national park, would transform the Cherokee reservation and economy.

Probably amid the excitement of opening night nobody really appreciated that the pageant carried certain ironic overtones. And yet even at that moment its theme of government betrayal was arising anew in the form of efforts to terminate federal programs to the Eastern Band and certain other tribes. Even as Cherokees reveled in the success of a pageant extolling their uniqueness, legislators were again assuming that Cherokees were losing that distinctiveness and becoming assimilated into the larger American society. And they intended to hasten the process.

7

Testing the Federal Relationship

MORE SO than most Indian tribes, the Eastern Band of Cherokees has had a long and complicated relationship with the federal government. By the New Deal era some members of the Band were challenging that relationship on two fronts: the government's failure to allot tribal lands as stipulated in the trust conveyance of 1925, and the about-face in policy represented by John Collier's Indian New Deal. The first was purely a local matter between the Band and the government, while the second was part of a national reaction by whites and Indians alike against a policy they perceived as a "return to the blanket." Among the Eastern Cherokees the most prominent critic of the federal relationship during the 1930s was Fred Bauer, but he had important allies, including the American Indian Federation.

As Bauer gained influence during the mid-1930s, the Eastern Band inevitably became one of several tribes figuring prominently in congressional hearings attacking Collier and the Bureau of Indian Affairs. In October 1938, while Bauer was vice chief and at the height of his popularity, the council resolved nine to one that the trust conveyance had been made solely in anticipation of allotment's taking place; that in 1935 the Band had voted down a proposed new constitution under the IRA and decided to continue under its 1889 state charter; that Qualla Boundary was not a federal reservation at all but had instead been purchased by the Indians themselves; and finally that the Eastern Cherokees were not even a tribe but a corporation, "to whom none of the laws applicable to Indian Reservations apply." The council therefore concluded that the "temporary wardship" established by the trust conveyance did not give the BIA "supervision and final Decision" over tribal affairs and that the bureau had "no legal power to destroy the vested rights" of the Band's members.[1]

This resolution was clearly the handiwork of Bauer and reflected perfectly the arguments he was to articulate for the next thirty years. Probably the only reason Chief Jarrett Blythe signed the measure was that it enjoyed overwhelming support with the current council and opposing it would serve no purpose. Besides, he doubtless understood that the resolution was simply another salvo in his opponents' campaign against the Indian Office and not likely to have much effect on the war. (Indeed, federal courts later rejected the resolution's main contentions regarding Cherokee status.)[2]

The next step in this unrelenting campaign against the paternalism of Collier's Indian New Deal came in 1939, when Bauer persuaded the tribal council to ask for a reconsideration of the Indian Reorganization Act as it applied to the Eastern Band. The Cherokees had approved the IRA in December 1934, before Bauer had become influential, and he hoped to revoke its application to the Band. In February 1940 the Senate passed S 2103, an omnibus measure that denied the IRA's application to the Eastern Band and several other tribes. It was accompanied by a report containing a series of charges against the Indian Office, including allegations of unfair tactics to win the Band's approval of the IRA.[3] By this time, as it happened, Bauer had already lost the political initiative to Chief Blythe and a newly elected council.

Even before Senate ratification of S 2103, Blythe had sent a telegram saying the Band had never formally repudiated its election approving the IRA. He also claimed that the actions of the council in February 1939 did not represent the wishes of the Cherokee people and the current council. Indeed, they now reaffirmed their desire for the IRA to remain in effect for them. A few months later Blythe darkly alluded to the Bauer faction's work against the IRA by saying that "ulterior and selfish motives have been at work at Cherokee."[4] In hearings of June 1940 before the House Committee on Indian Affairs, Collier effectively used information from Blythe to argue against passage of S 2103. The ubiquitous Alice Lee Jemison spoke on behalf of the American Indian Federation and the Bauer faction, but to little avail. The House did not pass S 2103, sparing Collier a humiliating repudiation. Yet his critics still had every intention of driving him from office and destroying the IRA.[5]

World War II helped bring about what Collier's opponents could not accomplish in 1940. Increasingly, Congress reduced Indian New Deal appropriations and even exiled the Indian Office to Chicago to make room in Washington for agencies more directly connected with the war effort. Senator Elmer Thomas (Oklahoma), a longtime critic, continued to take potshots at Collier and even submitted a report advocating the abolition of the Indian Bureau. Jed Johnson, chairman of the House Subcommittee on Interior Appropriations, whittled away at Collier's funding until by 1945 the bureau's budget was actually less than for fiscal year 1932.[6] Frustrated, Collier resigned in January 1945. Like his superior Franklin D. Roosevelt, he was a man who inspired strong emotions from friends and enemies alike, attitudes reflected in microcosm on the Cherokee reservation. To the Bauers and Pearson McCoy, Collier was a subversive who undermined traditional American values. But to Mary Ulmer, a teacher on Qualla Boundary, Collier was "crazy—right along with Jesus Christ and Einstein, and a few of the others. Crazy, but in a nice way."[7]

* * *

With the end of World War II and Collier's departure from office, many Americans—whites and Indians alike—believed that Indian affairs should go back to the old assimilationist assumptions before the New Deal. American Indians had served well in the war and deserved something better than second-class citizenship. They should be freed from the stifling paternalism of the Indian Office, "emancipated" to enjoy all the benefits of American life. Surely people who had adjusted so well to military service and a world war were capable of looking after themselves. Surely they would want to enjoy that freedom and share its prerogatives. And indeed, it was this new kind of assertiveness that led so many Cherokee veterans to insist on their right to vote. But as events were to demonstrate, one could not assume from such assertiveness that Indians favored termination of the federal connection.

American Indian policy also reflected in part some of the postwar paranoia concerning the Soviet Union and the specter of communism. Critics had long decried John Collier's programs as socialistic, and now, amid the tensions of the Cold War, many Americans idealized an individualistic society standing in dramatic counterpoint to the collectivism of the enemy. Tribalism and the maintenance of a number of separate cultures within American society seemed unpatriotic as well as expensive. Many saw the Indian Office as a collection of entrenched bureaucrats wedded to un-American programs and determined to protect their own jobs.[8]

One aspect of this campaign for emancipation was a flurry of bills allowing returning Indian veterans to exercise full control over their property despite any previous tribal or Indian Office restrictions. Senators Harlan J. Bushfield (South Dakota) and William Langer (North Dakota) introduced nearly identical bills for this purpose in the first session of the Seventy-ninth Congress. At hearings in June 1946, D'Arcy McNickle, speaking for the Indian Office, argued against these bills but stressed that his bureau was in basic sympathy with the senators' objectives: "To provide a mechanism by which competent Indians, who no longer wish to remain under the guardianship of the Federal Government and also wish to sever their connections with their tribes, may accomplish their purpose."[9] In the immediate postwar period, then, policymakers in the Indian Office were already backtracking on the assumptions and programs of the Collier era. Political discretion demanded as much at a time when some were clamoring for termination of the office itself. In January 1947 the Senate Committee on Indian Affairs reported that "the Bureau had ceased to be of utility," and Senator Dennis Chavez (New Mexico) forthrightly advocated its abolition.[10]

Not surprisingly, Fred and Catherine Bauer and Pearson McCoy immediately endorsed Chavez's proposal. Mrs. Bauer, however, believed the North Carolina congressional delegation would be more interested in continuing tribal projects like "Boundary Tree communistic tourist village etc." than "any real human progress for able individual Indians, and what this could mean to our counties in having Indians as full-fledged citizens."[11] Pearson McCoy was sardonic and succinct in asking Senator Clyde R. Hoey to support Chavez's proposal:

We wish the Indian Beaureau Abolished as far as the Cherokee Indians of N. C. are concerned. We wish to injoy our oppertunities that our fine roads, and the Great Smokey Mt. National Park, has made possible for us[.] We wish to lease and develop our Tourist Trade, We want Tourist Courts, Hotells, and everything a free interprise[.] We in other words Senator would like for Congress to transfer the Indian Beaureau over to Gatlinburg, Tenn. And keep it there till we could catch up with those people.

McCoy said the Cherokees were not wards but citizens, and he believed the Indian Office was denying them their constitutional rights.[12]

Early in February, less than two weeks after these attacks, acting commissioner of Indian affairs William Zimmerman issued a report assessing the readiness of various tribes for termination and cited four major criteria in making such a decision: the tribe's degree of acculturation; its economic resources and condition; the tribe's willingness to be relieved of federal control; and the willingness of the state government to assume responsibility. His report listed three categories, the first being those tribes ready for immediate termination, the second including those that should be ready within two to ten years, and the third consisting of tribes that would not be prepared until some indefinite time in the future.[13]

Zimmerman placed the Eastern Band in group two—mostly, it appears, on the basis of its acculturation. Using questionable tables based on census data from 1930, the Indian Office, in its magisterial wisdom, concluded that the Band retained 31.28 percent of its Indian culture. Each state with federal Indian populations was listed in this acculturation index, and North Carolina, with only the Eastern Cherokees, ranked tenth in terms of how highly acculturated its Indians were. Kansas ranked first, with its several small groups supposedly retaining only 16.22 percent of their Indian culture. New Mexico ranked last, with its Indians retaining 69.30 percent. It appears from the listing of various tribes in the three categories of readiness that if the North Carolina Cherokees had retained a few percentage points less of their Indian culture they might well have been placed in group one, those supposedly ready for immediate termination.[14]

Despite Zimmerman's assessment of Cherokee readiness, the Bauer-McCoy faction had already convinced some North Carolina politicians that the Eastern Band was indeed prepared for emancipation. In January 1947 Dan Tompkins, the state representative for Jackson county, introduced a bill in Raleigh to memorialize Congress to abolish Indian Office control over the Eastern Band. He argued that such a step was "simple justice to a great people" and denounced the Indian Bureau's "dictatorship."[15] About the only Cherokee leader echoing these sentiments was councilman John C. McCoy, Pearson McCoy's kinsman. Tompkins's bill passed the North Carolina House unanimously, prompting federal officials to invite Cherokees to hearings in Raleigh before the state senate education committee, which was considering the bill. Some hard-liners like the McCoys refused because they denied any jurisdiction by the Indian Office and expressed confidence in their state representatives.[16]

Ten defenders of the BIA, including Jarrett Blythe, had no such qualms about attending. Wisely avoiding an ideological stance, the wily chief first thanked Tompkins for his interest in the tribe. He went on to note, however, that the federal government spent about $300,000 a year to provide health care and education for the Eastern Cherokees. His tribe would have no objection to Tompkins's bill if North Carolina was willing to provide the same quality of services. In testimony that must have made federal officials blink with surprise, Freeman Bradley, representing the Steve Youngdeer American Legion Post, praised the government for its treatment of the Band and claimed that without its protection local discrimination against Indians would become even worse. The hearings appear to have been orchestrated by Senate committee member Frank Parker, who had helped the Band in the voting controversy and would later become its full-time attorney. He was primarily responsible for killing Tompkins's bill in committee.[17]

This setback merely encouraged Fred Bauer to redouble his attacks on the Indian Bureau. Early the next month he protested to the chairman of the United States House Appropriations Committee about what he considered an illegal federal takeover of Cherokee lands when the government assumed responsibility for the Band in 1868. He dusted off a United States District Court decision of 1942 in which Judge E. Yates Webb argued that the Band's lands were not a reservation. Bauer ignored the fact that the Circuit Court of Appeals had overturned Webb's argument in 1943. He also asserted that the Indian Office had reneged on its promise to allot Cherokee lands "because they want to control all enterprise at the North Carolina entrance to the Great Smoky Park." Shrewdly, he introduced a little Cold War rhetoric: "Bureau policies for the past thirteen years have been communistic, and their schemes have seriously curtailed private enterprise, and will eventually make it nonexistent at Cherokee. We are denied hundreds of thousands of dollars annual revenue through the Bureau's refusal to permit business enterprises that are begging to be allowed here at the Park entrance."[18] After attacking the Boundary Tree project as "a Government controlled cooperative," he claimed it was inconsistent to spend millions of dollars under the Truman Doctrine to fight communism abroad while spending money at home to promote communism "among a helpless minority of First Americans." He called for quick integration of Cherokee students into the public schools and an end within one year of all appropriations for the local Indian agency.[19]

This letter no doubt was the main reason work on Boundary Tree was held up that spring while agent Joe Jennings attempted to explain the situation to acting Indian commissioner Zimmerman. After attacking Bauer and Pearson McCoy by name, Jennings noted that most opponents of Boundary Tree were white Indians who had gained inclusion on the Baker Roll over tribal protests. Under the Band's unique system of landholding, these relatively acculturated individuals had acquired some of the best lands and tourist sites. Jennings said the white Indians felt insecure and favored abolition of the Indian Office and its controls because they would presumably receive titles in fee simple. He also pointed to a residue of ill will among local whites, who favored termination so they could tax Indian lands. Predatory real estate speculators were likewise lurking about, eager to pounce on choice Cherokee business sites when government trusteeship ended.[20]

When told that Cherokees had signed petitions against the Indian Office, Jennings replied that the names of some had been used without their knowledge. Others had been swayed by promises of receiving $3,000 each if the reservation was divided following federal withdrawal, while a few had been told they would be deported to Oklahoma or lose certain business rights on the reservation if they did not sign.[21] Although work on Boundary Tree soon resumed, Jennings was clearly on the defensive, which may well explain his major role in helping to create the pageant "Unto These Hills." This kind of tourist extravaganza would give both whites and Indians a vested interest in maintaining a Cherokee tribal identity.

The Cherokee council was not a passive spectator during these maneuverings. Although strongly favorable to continuing its relationship with the federal government, it occasionally took tentative steps toward modifying or slightly changing that arrangement. In October 1946, for example, it considered a resolution endorsing the bills introduced in the Seventy-ninth Congress removing restrictions on the property of Indian veterans with honorable discharges. The resolution would require the council to petition Congress to enact such legislation. After reading the letters of several Cherokee veterans who supported the legislation, and after a motion to table the resolution was defeated, the council passed it. For better or worse, Congress never enacted the bills, no doubt to the relief of certain councilmembers.[22]

The most striking evidence of how threatening the council found any radical alteration of federal ties came in October 1947 at its first regular meeting following the latest Bauer-McCoy crusade against the Indian Office. The attacks on Boundary Tree were no doubt another irritant. Although Bauer's Cherokee ancestry was sufficient for enrollment, the council noted the disputed status of many of his followers who were "continually stirring up trouble," denouncing federal actions, and asserting their desire for freedom from the BIA. The council therefore resolved to ask Congress to enact legislation allowing the Band to revise its roll by eliminating such individuals and requested that the government use nontribal funds to pay each challenged person a sum equal to one share of tribal assets. The council agreed to pay each one for any improvements on tribal lands. A major proviso was that no challenged members would receive such compensation if they had not recently lived on the reservation.[23]

The council was even more forthright a little over a week later when it resolved that a majority of the Eastern Band "desire to continue under the bureau." It asked Congress to pass legislation allowing any bona fide members of the band with less than one-fourth Eastern Cherokee blood to withdraw and sever their relationship with the Band whenever they wished, with each receiving an individual share of tribal assets as well as compensation for improvements.[24] Clearly the council preferred to maintain a tribal identity within the existing federal network and to encourage discontented members of minimal Cherokee ancestry to withdraw. That was probably the major consideration, but in all likelihood some councilmen also perceived the status quo as a means of retaining jobs and political influence. To this extent, at least, Bauer and other critics were probably correct. Whatever the reasons, by the end of 1947 it was apparent that at least two of acting Indian commissioner Zimmerman's four criteria for termination were lacking in the case of the Eastern Band: consent of the tribe and consent of its state of residence. Certain other tribes, however, faced more immediate danger. Within a short time a series of bills was introduced in Congress for terminating their trust status or reducing some of their BIA programs.

Another facet of Indian "emancipation" was the creation by Congress in 1946 of the Indian Claims Commission. For many years various tribes had been arguing that the United States should compensate them for past injustices, but the only way they could seek redress was through direct congressional intervention. Under the new legislation, a three-person claims commission would review legal briefs and other evidence presented by tribes within five years of the commission's creation. It would then have up to five additional years to make a binding judgment on the merits of each case. Its congressional sponsors believed it would streamline tribal litigation, pay off old federal obligations in an honorable fashion, and perhaps "financially liberate Native Americans from dependency on federal programs implemented during the Collier years."[25] The Indian Claims Commission was thus seen as a necessary step by those politicians who favored terminating federal services to tribes. In effect, supporters believed creation of the commission meant the final reckoning of federal responsibilities to American Indians. Judgment Day was at hand.

Like many tribes, the Eastern Cherokees saw the claims commission not as a prelude to termination but as a long-needed means of satisfying old grievances. In August 1951, inspired by large sums paid to several western tribes, notably the Utes, the Band filed three claims before the commission, seeking compensation for some 40 million acres taken from the Cherokees by the United States government between the 1785 Treaty of Hopewell and the 1835 Treaty of New Echota, which provided for final removal of the Cherokee Nation to present-day Oklahoma. These claims were in addition to similar ones filed by the Oklahoma Cherokees. Both groups also argued that various subsequent accounting and procedural errors by the government had cost the Indians millions of dollars. The Band found that dealing with the claims commission was an exasperating, time-consuming process. The number of tribal claims was so great—852 within the first five years—that Congress several times extended the life of the commission and expanded its membership to five. But eventually the rewards for the Eastern Band would prove worth the effort.[26]

* * *

After this groundwork for termination, President Harry Truman's appointment of Dillon S. Myer as commissioner of Indian affairs early in 1950 seemed eminently logical. The fifty-eight-year-old Myer was a bold, competent administrator who as director of the War Relocation Authority in World War II had supervised the detention of more than 119,000 Japanese Americans. Between 1942 and 1946 he had done his best to disperse the detainees to new homes in many parts of the United States, provide them with economic opportunities, and incorporate them into the cultural mainstream. He then successfully closed down the Relocation Authority. Myer's supporters saw a clear analogy between his record with Japanese Americans and what needed to be done for Native Americans. By the time of his appointment as commissioner, there was a general consensus among policymakers in favor of Indian "self-determination," which for Myer at least meant ending wardship and the regulation of Indian lives by the federal government. He had been given "a free hand to put the Indian Bureau 'out of business as quickly as possible'" and wanted to integrate Native Americans into the cultural mainstream.[27] Many Indian leaders also supported "self-determination" but, it soon became apparent, defined that as more Indian freedom of action without complete withdrawal of federal assistance.

Myer aggressively pushed his program of Indian emancipation, replacing Collier holdovers with people of his own thinking, encouraging Indians to attend public schools or off-reservation boarding schools, and in certain cases allowing tribes to exercise more control over their money and resources. One of his most ambitious steps was creating a Voluntary Relocation Program modeled on that established for Japanese Americans by the War Relocation Authority. The new program promoted voluntary relocation of young Indians in urban centers as a means of offering them more opportunities for employment. The government would provide transportation for their families, their first month's living expenses, counseling, and even training. Whereas many Indians saw relocation as a means of escaping poverty, others viewed it as simply another effort to break up the reservations, abrogate federal treaty responsibilities, and destroy Native American culture. By the mid-1950s relocation had been expanded to include adult Indian vocational training and job placement. Between the end of World War II and 1957 an estimated 100,000 Indians left their reservations, about three-fourths relocating without federal assistance.[28]

This was the beginning of an urban migration that continues to this day. Unfortunately, many Indians were forced by economic circumstance to settle in mushrooming Indian ghettos in cities like Los Angeles and Chicago. The Lumbees of Robeson County, North Carolina, migrated to eastern cities, especially Baltimore, where they created their own neighborhoods and from which they often returned to North Carolina.[29] No such pattern emerged for the Eastern Cherokees, and the success of relocating them is difficult to assess. Anthropologists working on the reservation in the late 1950s reported that relocation had generally failed and that many Cherokees had returned home, a conclusion disputed by Lucy Brown, the tribal relocation officer.[30] This disagreement may reflect different outcomes for those relocated under the aegis of the federal government and those who left the reservation on their own. Certainly by the 1950s more and more Eastern Cherokees were taking outside jobs and entering military service. Even if many did return, it does not necessarily signify an inability to cope with the outside world; it may simply have been a matter of personal preference. In fact, the reappearance on the Cherokee reservation of individuals who have enjoyed satisfying careers elsewhere is commonplace.[31]

Besides advocating relocation, Commissioner Myer was systematically taking other steps toward termination. In 1952, at the request of the House of Representatives, he collected voluminous information on the functions of the BIA and also distributed questionnaires among his field personnel regarding tribal readiness for termination.[32] Joe Jennings reported that many Eastern Cherokees feared termination would leave them at the mercy of local whites. Resentment against Indians was especially high in Swain County, he said, because tribal lands had been withdrawn from the tax rolls when the government assumed trusteeship in 1925. Cherokees had additional objections to termination, including distribution of tribal assets on the basis of the hated Baker Roll and loss of federal funding for education and health care.[33]

Education was a particularly troublesome issue. Both Swain and Jackson counties were among the poorest in the state, and public schools there did not offer the same opportunities that Cherokees enjoyed on the reservation. Because of federal support, the expenditure per Cherokee student in 1951–52 was almost three times that for students enrolled in North Carolina public schools. Likewise, health services for Cherokees were "at a far higher standard in terms of quantity and probably of quality than those available to the general population of the area."[34] State officials had already informed Joe Jennings that even in the best of circumstances it would be at least six years before North Carolina could assume educational responsibility for the Indians. In the meantime the federal government would have to agree to construct modern schools on the reservation so the counties would not have to incur added financial burdens.[35]

Jennings also said that individual Cherokees held possessory rights to all but about 8,000 of the more than 56,000 acres on the reservation. In his opinion at least 80 percent of the entire reservation should be left in forest, and this obviously required considerable planning and cooperation among both Indians and federal agencies. After noting the lack of good agricultural land, Jennings sounded what was to be a recurrent theme in arguments against precipitous termination: "If the tourist business is properly exploited the possibilities are such that it should provide nearly all of the Cherokees with a good living. These same possibilities make the Cherokees very vulnerable if withdrawal should come without proper safeguards set up by the State and Federal Governments." Many whites realized the reservation was a major economic attraction and were therefore interested "in working out a plan whereby the Indian can retain the reservation intact in Indian ownership," but in the meantime federal services should continue while Cherokees developed the ability to handle their own affairs.[36]

Jennings's assessment figured prominently in the subsequent recommendations of the BIA's Minneapolis area office, which supervised the Cherokee agency. It placed each tribe in its jurisdiction in one of four groups, the first being those most prepared for termination. The Eastern Cherokees, along with the Menominees of Wisconsin and the Red Lake Chippewas of Minnesota, were in group four, the least prepared. These were not final assessments, however, and the Menominees were soon judged ready for termination. As for the Cherokees, the opinion was that their valuable timber resources, complicated system of landholding, and valuable tourist-related real estate necessitated special precautions before ending trust responsibilities.[37] The office believed the Cherokees were still unable to administer their resources because they lacked tribal leadership and the necessary infrastructure. The report concluded with a call for a thorough study by specialists of "the entire complicated and complex Cherokee situation."[38]

For those Indians fearing termination, the change of national administrations in 1952 offered little solace. There seemed to be a ground swell of political sentiment to "emancipate" as many tribes as possible. President Dwight D. Eisenhower's commissioner of Indian affairs, Glenn L. Emmons, was a prominent businessman who intended to continue Myer's policies. Congress was similarly inclined and in July 1953 passed House Concurrent Resolution 108, which called for abolition of several Indian offices and termination of trust responsibilities for certain specified tribes. Emmons enthusiastically supported HCR 108 and suggested a number of additional suitable tribes. During the next decade Indian Office cooperation with politicians like Senator Arthur V. Watkins (Utah) led Congress to pass termination laws for more than one hundred Indian groups, ranging from small communities and rancherias to large tribes. For several, notably the Klamaths of Oregon and the Menominees of Wisconsin, termination proved disastrous.[39]

The North Carolina Cherokees, though not included among tribes listed in HCR 108, were also affected by the rising terminationist sentiment. In August 1953 Congress passed Public Law 280, which transferred civil and criminal jurisdiction over most tribes in five states to the respective local governments and allowed any other states to assume similar jurisdiction over their own Indian reservations.[40] Assistant secretary of the interior Orme Lewis sent a copy of PL 280 to North Carolina's governor William B. Umstead and noted the provision allowing such state assumption of jurisdiction. When Umstead requested a legal opinion, state assistant attorney general Ralph Moody argued that North Carolina did not need to follow up on PL 280 because of the Band's special circumstances. He admitted that the federal government exercised "certain powers of protection and guardianship," but he knew from personal experience that the Band's unique status had resulted in North Carolina's criminal laws' applying "to all offenses committed within the Indian Reservation." Implementation of PL 280 was therefore unnecessary, "for we have practically the same thing without it"— a claim distorting both law and historical circumstances.[41]

On the local front, meanwhile, advocates and opponents of Cherokee termination continued their noisy warfare. John McCoy complained to the *Asheville Citizen-Times* about an "Iron Curtain" of federal paternalism that limited individual control of landholdings, to which E. S. Saunooke replied that "if there were no restrictions our land would soon be sold piece by piece, and what would become of the Eastern Band of Cherokees?"[42] Momentum seemed to favor the terminationists, as the BIA undertook extensive negotiations with state and local officials about accepting responsibility for certain federal services to the Eastern Band. Also active in the planning were tribal leaders and officials of the Cherokee Historical Association and its parent organization, Western North Carolina Associated Communities. The CHA and WNCAC came up with a twenty-five-year program of tourist-related development that, much to the disgust of Fred Bauer, would attempt to preserve the "unique quality" of Cherokee life.[43]

The current chief was Osley Bird Saunooke, a colorful mammoth of a man (up to 370 pounds), veteran of 5,217 professional wrestling matches, and former world super heavyweight champion for fourteen years. When informed that the government intended to shut down the Cherokee hospital effective June 30, 1954, he managed to get an extension of at least one year while efforts were made to find a private sponsor—"preferably a religious denomination." The United States Public Health Service temporarily took over the hospital in July 1955 as the search for outside contractors continued. Saunooke, whose chiefly duties required him to be "everything from a Philadelphia lawyer to an undertaker," also claimed credit for an arrangement exempting the reservation from the state sales tax and allowing the Band to impose—and keep—an identical levy that would enable it to assume more responsibility for sanitation and police and fire protection. For such accomplishments he was honored in August 1954 as "Tarheel of the Week" by the Raleigh *News and Observer*.[44]

Despite these modest gains in tribal self-sufficiency, there remained the troublesome matter of Cherokee education. On July 1, 1954, the BIA reduced the status of Cherokee Central School from a boarding school to a day facility and then attempted to persuade state and local authorities to assume total responsibility for Indian education. In October 1954 Hildegard Thompson, chief of the BIA's Education Branch, met with state and local educators in Raleigh about the possibility of such a transfer. The major problem was access to public schools in Swain County. Officials in Bryson City, the county seat, admitted that a few Indian children were already enrolled, but these were predominantly white individuals from acculturated families. There was considerable opposition to accepting phenotypical

Cherokees in school because of past frictions, the Band's tax immunity, and resentment over the recent landmark supreme court decision of *Brown v. Board of Education of Topeka,* which declared segregated public schools unconstitutional.[45]

North Carolina officials were even more nervous about *Brown* because of widespread southern opposition to integration of blacks. The Cherokee situation was fraught with dangers, not only because Indians were sometimes viewed as people of color under state law, but because federal efforts to get them into the schools appeared to be one more case of outside meddling in racial matters. According to Thompson, another concern over the Cherokee situation was the possible implication for the state's Lumbee Indians, who had long been segregated from white society.[46]

Thompson made several recommendations: First, rather than create a separate school district out of the reservation, the BIA should work toward eventual integration of the reservation into the existing school districts of Swain and Jackson counties, moving at a pace consistent with changing white attitudes in the region. The BIA should not attempt to push the integration of Cherokee pupils into the school systems until North Carolina had worked out problems arising from the *Brown* decision, and nothing should be done to provoke the state legislature into taking any action. The situation was extremely volatile. What the bureau could do in the meantime was to continue the high school in Cherokee and provide facilities there for a consolidated Swain County elementary school. It could also work on changing white attitudes in Bryson City by emphasizing the economic benefits of the Band to the area, directing as much business as possible to the town, and quietly attempting to enroll more Indians there.[47]

Thompson's recommendations basically determined the course of action taken, and the BIA tiptoed diplomatically around the school desegregation issue. Southern race relations and the simmering impact of the *Brown* decision, while perhaps not decisive, certainly delayed prospects for full termination of federal services. Meanwhile, without undue publicity, Cherokee enrollment in public schools began to climb. During fiscal year 1955 Indian enrollment in Swain County schools totaled 54 pupils, half of whom had at least three-fourths Cherokee blood, while 38 children attended school in Jackson County. Four more were enrolled in Graham County. However, the overwhelming majority of Cherokee children—798—still attended federal day schools. The state of North Carolina, moreover, failed to allot enough money for about 50 Cherokees to attend the Whittier school because it argued they were strictly a federal responsibility.[48]

The BIA's caution on the educational front was offset by an administrative blunder that attracted considerable negative publicity. On November 12, 1954, the *Asheville Citizen* announced in a front-page headline that effective December 1 Joe Jennings's job would be eliminated and he would be transferred. The *Citizen* called the decision "the most recent and most far-reaching move to date in the government program aiming for the liquidation of the Indian Reservation system throughout the United States" and said officers of the CHA and WNCAC were asking first for a public hearing. hearing.

In an editorial entitled "Another Trail of Tears?" the paper attacked the removal, which came "in the midst of an orderly and well-timed liquidation of the Indian Agency's responsibilities at Cherokee." Certainly the paper did not quarrel with an eventual transfer of responsibilities to the state. Ultimately the Indians "must be integrated into the life of the nation. This, indeed, is in process. But slowly, considerately, efficiently—not abruptly: that has been the aim." As an example it pointed to the recent transfer of the tribal hospital to the United States Public Health Service while negotiations continued to transfer it to private sponsorship. North Carolina was gradually assuming more responsibility for roads, while the tribe itself was providing more and more community services. Swain County, the paper stated, was financially unable to assume the costs of Cherokee education, and the state was uncertain about its responsibilities in that regard. What was to happen with the end of federal supervision? It commended Jennings, the CHA, and the WNCAC for their contributions to Cherokee well-being, then snidely predicted that "a government clerk" in Washington would shut down the North Carolina agency. Finally, the editorial concluded,

> The future, as it looks, is unalterably dark. Liquidation apparently is to proceed with a bang, and to the echo of broken promises and the hollow re-echo of vast uncertainties—about the position of the Historical Association, the Indians' land and school and hospital facilities, the status, indeed, of the Tribal Council itself.
>
> This is a critical hour for Western North Carolina. The challenge of unfathomable actions in a strange time must be met. *The Cherokees must not be dispatched on a second Trail of Tears!*[49]

Immediately there was a storm of protest against Jennings's removal. Editorial comment from other cities echoed that of the *Asheville Citizen*, while tribal councillors, choosing their words carefully, denounced abolition of the superintendency without appearing too sympathetic to Jennings himself. (In fact, some Cherokees were highly critical of the agent.)[50] Harry

Buchanan, chairman of the CHA, claimed the removal was a "breach of faith." After meeting with associate Indian commissioner H. Rex Lee and an administrative assistant to Commissioner Emmons, he was convinced they would not delay Jennings's transfer but said he had received assurances that "there was no intention to lower the status of the Agency or its benefits to the Indians." Buchanan suspected otherwise and asked Governor Luther H. Hodges to protest directly to Emmons and secretary of the interior Douglas McKay. He claimed that congressmen and senators from other states had already registered their opposition (perhaps as a favor to Jennings's brother, Tennessee congressman John Jennings, Jr.).[51]

Bill Sharpe, publisher of a Raleigh magazine, complained to Senator W. Kerr Scott that the BIA action would harm the Indians, western North Carolina, and the entire state. He made it clear he feared economic dislocations attending a likely reduction in the role of the CHA and believed the Indians were incapable of managing "Unto These Hills" themselves:

> I have been visiting the reservation several times a year since 1937, and have watched the atmosphere change from one of hopelessness and indifference, to one of promise and activity. The tremendous growth of tourist industries in that area was accelerated by the program of the Cherokee Historical Association, and it appeared that at last the Indians were on the way to an economy in which they could participate, could thrive, and perhaps gain ultimate independence.
>
> With this activity, of course, came many complications. New elements entered into the relationships between Indians and whites, between reservation and neighbors, between tribe and outside agencies. The Indians, while benefiting from the changes were less able than ever to understand or cope with the resulting intricacies.
>
> Some of them even after the first season, became convinced that they could operate UNTO THESE HILLS alone. Like uninformed persons everywhere, they did not see the many factors behind their improvement. It has taken the utmost tact, skill and sympathy to bring the Indians to their present encouraging status.

Getting to the point, he said removing Jennings would endanger this progress, likely lead to "withdrawal of the outside assistance which has made all this possible," and return the Cherokees to "the miserable and hopeless and planless regime" of a few years before. The communities and people of western North Carolina and the CHA "have done more for the Indians' independence than all the efforts of the federal government in 100 years."

That the tribe had cooperated in these common endeavors was due to Joe Jennings. He concluded by saying,

> Realizing that sooner or later the Cherokees must be cut loose and must stand on their feet, yet I believe this move now is like towing a drowning man half way to the bank and then going off and leaving him in deep water. The move should be delayed, and study given to a situation which I am sure is unique among the tribes.
>
> All of North Carolina has a deep interest in and stake in the Indians, both economically and morally.[52]

This barrage of criticism forced Indian commissioner Emmons into a partial retreat. Joe Jennings would still be transferred—to Washington, D.C., rather than South Dakota—but Emmons insisted the BIA never intended to abolish the Cherokee agency. It was merely withdrawing the agency from the Minneapolis area office and bringing it under direct supervision from Washington. Emmons agreed that any termination of the agency must be "on a gradual, planned and orderly basis" and insisted that for the present no such program was envisioned. Richard D. Butts, the new Cherokee agent appointed in March 1955, likewise reassured the tribe on this point.[53] One wonders whether the whole affair was merely an administrative move (in part to eliminate the controversial Joe Jennings) or a trial balloon to test public sentiment regarding Cherokee termination.

In the meantime the CHA was mending its fences with certain disgruntled Indians, including Chief Saunooke, and late in December 1954 it announced a comprehensive program of protecting Cherokee lands, health benefits, and educational facilities. Chairman Harry Buchanan said his association's objective was "to represent the thinking of the Cherokee and to help the Cherokee get all that they deserve. If federal policies are to be put into effect that the Cherokee don't want," he continued, "we will go to bat for the Cherokee and fight for you." The CHA's program called for continued corporate landownership by the Indians; an effort to find a suitable nonprofit organization to operate the hospital; federal construction and state operation of a consolidated regional school; continued maintenance of reservation roads by the state after the federal government brought them up to standards; assistance in maintaining extension, soil conservation, and forestry services after transferring those responsibilities to state agencies; and continued cooperation in working toward Cherokee community objectives.[54] The tribal council's own program, adopted in March 1955, incorporated most of the CHA's objectives. In addition, it stressed revision of the tribal roll, registration of all possessory claims, and improvement of tribal housing.[55]

Revising the roll was a crucial part of the tribe's blueprint for confronting possible termination because of the large number of contested white Indians on the old Baker Roll. Frank W. Swan, a white who was a longtime Cherokee friend, said that practically everyone except five-dollar Indians wanted a new roll requiring at least one-sixteenth Cherokee blood.[56] Dewey Tahquette, an acculturated fuller-blood who favored termination, also insisted on eliminating many of the contested names or else "our 'real Indians,' as before would be *losers again*."[57]

In September 1955 Congressman James A. Haley (Florida) held a congressional hearing in Cherokee that probed Indian attitudes toward tribal affairs and, especially, termination. Fred Bauer and a few others predictably called for ending the federal relationship and granting fee-simple titles, but many other Cherokees at all levels of acculturation were opposed. These included Chief Saunooke and George Owl as well as many conservatives. Haley's call for a show of hands revealed that forty-five to fifty Indians wanted to maintain the present trust status while nine favored its abrogation. A few Bryson City whites were also present and testified that Swain County could not afford to take over Cherokee education without considerable federal assistance.[58]

Cherokee opponents of termination began to breathe more easily during the next few years as the BIA, facing mounting national opposition, began to downplay termination. Instead, both Indian commissioner Emmons and secretary of the interior Fred E. Seaton emphasized Indian economic development on and off the reservations as a necessary prelude to *voluntary* termination in the *indefinite* future.[59]

The point about tribal preparation and consent was reaffirmed in the town of Cherokee by Congressman Wayne N. Aspinall (Colorado) in September 1962. The occasion was the nineteenth annual convention of the National Congress of American Indians, a longtime foe of termination. This was the first time its convention had been held east of the Mississippi, and it had additional meaning for the Eastern Band because Chief Saunooke was elected vice president, the first eastern Indian so honored. Aspinall was the powerful chairman of the House Committee on Interior and Insular Affairs, which dealt with Indian matters, and he prompted cheers from the delegates by declaring, "As long as I am chairman of the committee no Indian tribe in the United States will be terminated until it is ready for termination."[60] It was symbolic validation of the path already taken by the Eastern Cherokees, a path of greater self-sufficiency within the context of continued federal assistance. This is what the Cherokees meant by "self-determination," and long before it became official policy they had been remarkably successful in achieving it.

8

Growth, Acculturation, and Self-Determination

THE EASTERN Band was more fortunate than most Indian tribes because of its proximity to the nation's most popular national park and the consequent flow of visitors. The immediate success of "Unto These Hills" and other tourist-related businesses increasingly provided the tribe with a viable—albeit seasonal—economic base. Tourism also gave the Cherokees a vested interest in resisting complete assimilation into the larger American society and termination of their federal relationship. With their increasing self-sufficiency, they moved toward greater self-determination within a matrix of federally sponsored support programs.

The Cherokee Historical Association was a major force in promoting tourism, creating both new jobs on the reservation and a degree of envy and suspicion on the part of some Indians. The association favored hiring Indians in its enterprises only if they were reliable and not prone to absenteeism.[1] Chief Osley Saunooke, among others, complained about the "few measly jobs" the association provided. Yet in 1951–52 the CHA either spent or allocated more than $90,000 for the Eastern Band (amounting to about $31 per member), including $64,000 in wages, $7,000 in timber purchases, $5,000 for developing arts and crafts, and $3,000 in scholarships.[2] During the same period the state assisted the CHA in developing another major tourist attraction—Oconaluftee Indian Village, a historically accurate re-creation of a Cherokee town as it appeared in the mid-eighteenth century. Situated next to Mountainside Theater, it featured thatched Indian homes, a council house, and an assortment of tribal craftsmen. In February 1952 the CHA also purchased the Museum of the Cherokee Indian, a collection of some fifty thousand artifacts owned by Mr. and Mrs. Samuel E. Beck, who had operated a private museum in Cherokee since 1948. From the outset, the CHA intended someday to build a modern building to house the impressive collection.[3]

The national park and the CHA were the major reasons for a tourist bonanza totaling about 2.5 million visitors by 1956, but individual Cherokees also generated considerable business. By mid-1956, fifty-nine of the ninety-six licensed trading businesses on the reservation were owned and operated by tribal members. Total annual gross income for all such businesses amounted to $1 million.[4]

Congress meanwhile had also taken steps to assist Cherokee economic development by passing, in September 1950, an act permitting twenty-five-year leases of certain unoccupied tribal lands within four hundred yards of state and federal highways on the reservation. Monroe Redden, western North Carolina's congressman, predicted it would open the reservation "for swift and immediate improvements."[5] Tribal leaders had long favored such a leasing arrangement, but Chief Saunooke noted that leases of individual possessory claims were still limited to five years (ten, if renewed)—a definite disadvantage to prospective investors. In August 1955 Congress obligingly increased the term of all leases on Indian reservations to twenty-five years, with a renewable option for another twenty-five years.[6]

Despite its impact, tourism was not seen as a panacea by Indian leaders. Both Saunooke and Jarrett Blythe agreed with commissioner of Indian affairs Glenn Emmons that self-determination required long-term economic development such as factories to provide year-round employment. Here again the Eastern Cherokees had an advantage over most tribes by being within a day's drive of major markets in the East and Midwest. The first significant step in nonseasonal employment came in the spring of 1956 when Saddlecraft, a Knoxville firm, began operations in a recently vacated barn on the site of the old Cherokee boarding school. It had a five-year permit to manufacture moccasins and other tourist-related objects in return for training Cherokee workers. Within a year it was employing forty-three Indians, with a weekly payroll of $1,800.[7]

Some Cherokees believed the local agency was not doing enough to promote industrial growth, a contention hotly disputed by agent Richard D. Butts, who pointed out in 1957 that the reservation already had two industries, Saddlecraft and Whitetree Workshop, which also made souvenirs and employed ten Indians with a weekly payroll of $400. Butts's point seems well taken, for by decade's end the BIA and tribal council, along with nearby off-reservation towns, had collaborated in attracting the $300,000 Harn Manufacturing plant, the largest industry on the reservation to date. The company was to make plastic and cotton accessories for infants. Indian commissioner Emmons attended the plant's dedication in December 1959 and hailed it as a milestone: "This is the first structure of its kind to be built from top to bottom by an Indian tribal group specifically for leasing by an industrial concern." The president of Harn estimated the annual payroll at about $500,000. Arsene Thompson, a Cherokee elder, said this promising beginning offered bright prospects for future generations of his people.[8]

Despite Cherokee success in attracting small manufacturing plants, John Gulick and other anthropologists claimed in 1961 that many conservative Indians were finding it difficult to adapt to an industrial economy. They supposedly had a "don't care" attitude toward money, possessions, and job discipline. Stung by such charges, the BIA enlisted support from white businessmen for a counterattack. The president of Saddlecraft praised the Cherokees for their dedication to work and their low absenteeism; the latter was especially remarkable because of the Indians' lack of adequate transportation to work. According to him, "Their dependability on the job is above average. . . . Their capacity for learning is good. They have a native ability and what we in industry call 'good hands,' meaning the ability to do nice things with their hands. They are dedicated to their jobs and to the quality of their work."[9] In all likelihood both sides in this disagreement exaggerated a bit. Both resorted to stereotypical assessments of Cherokee behavior and abilities, when in fact the Indians varied widely. Part of the problem was that Gulick and his fellow anthropologists had conducted most of their research in the early stages of nontourist business development. If their fieldwork had continued another two or three years, they might well have been surprised by the economic growth and Cherokee adaptation. On the other hand, even today employers occasionally complain about the lack of job discipline among some Cherokees.

* * *

The anthropological fieldwork of the 1950s reflected both an outgrowth of earlier scholarly interest in the Band and a fresh interdisciplinary assessment of the tribe. The Tsali Institute, for example, was established in the early 1950s by several regional universities and concerned itself with various Cherokee-related projects. In 1952, moreover, the North Carolina State Board of Public Welfare conducted a report on the social status of the Band in cooperation with the Minneapolis area office of the BIA (no doubt as part of the current assessment of Cherokee readiness for termination). And Haverford College, a prestigious Quaker school in Pennsylvania, began sponsoring summer institutes in Big Cove so its students could learn more about Cherokee life.[10]

Most important of all were studies conducted in 1956–58 by the University of North Carolina's Cross-Cultural Laboratory of the Institute for Research in Social Sciences. Funded by the Ford Foundation, the laboratory's Cherokee research was directed by John Gulick and included a number of graduate students from various universities who produced a series of papers, masters' theses, and doctoral dissertations. Among those participating were Raymond D. Fogelson, Harriet Kupferer, Paul Kutsche, and Robert K. Thomas, all of whom became prominent in Cherokee studies. Like earlier anthropologists, they focused most of their research on Big Cove and, to a lesser extent, Paint Town. Those two communities were of special interest because they occupied opposite poles of Eastern Cherokee acculturation. The result was a wealth of information and insight on societal and cultural changes on Qualla Boundary during a critical period in tribal economic development.[11]

Big Cove continued to be the most conservative of the Qualla Boundary communities. Its population in the summer of 1957 was 472, divided among seventy-five households containing ninety families. Connected by a winding gravel road to the tourist attractions of Cherokee, the community was still relatively isolated. As late as January 1955 there were only eighteen privately owned automobiles in the Cove, but this had risen to thirty-four by late 1956. Still, most people preferred to hitch a ride to Cherokee with the mailman, take the community's single taxi, or walk. High-school students were transported to and from Cherokee by bus.[12]

In contrast to just a generation earlier, virtually all Big Cove adults could at least carry on a conversation in English, and a large majority could speak it fluently. And yet Cherokee continued to be a viable language, with more than half the residents speaking it at home and with other Indians. Even in most of the households where English was normally spoken, at least one family member could speak Cherokee. The continuation of Cherokee in the home explains why some very young children spoke it exclusively and would not pick up English until starting school.[13] As one might expect, the Cherokee language was less prevalent in Paint Town. In 75 percent of the households there it was never spoken, but in almost half of those where the head was a "fuller-blood" (three-quarters or more Cherokee) it was still used.[14]

Big Cove residents did a little logging and farming or sometimes hired out their labor. Despite federal efforts since World War II to improve Cherokee agriculture, farming in the Cove had generally declined, in part because many young men periodically left for unskilled jobs in large cities. Usually they would return to the reservation after a few months. In the winter many conservatives made weekly trips to Cherokee to sell handwoven baskets to souvenir shops and buy staples. Others earned a few dollars hunting ginseng or perhaps importing bootleg whiskey from East Tennessee.[15]

Amenities were notably lacking in Big Cove. Only forty houses (54 percent) had electricity, which was used mostly for illumination. Thirty-four households had radios, twenty-seven washing machines, and fourteen refrigerators. Among conservative families the woodburning stove was ubiquitous. The day school had the only telephone in the entire cove. Some homes had private privies, which were almost always in sorry condition, but many other houses had no sanitary facilities whatever.[16] Paint Town residents, in contrast, typically enjoyed more conveniences: 74 percent of their homes had electricity, 64 percent refrigerators, 36 percent television, 26 percent indoor plumbing, 24 percent electric ranges, 10 percent phones, and 5 percent gas ranges. About half the households had at least one automobile. Paint Town residences were mostly of frame construction, with a significant minority having brick or stone siding; only twelve log homes remained there by 1957. Other houses commonly found on the reservation were constructed of cinder blocks or rough-sawn lumber covered with asbestos shingles or tar paper.[17]

Conjuring was still common in Big Cove and elsewhere on Qualla Boundary and even included some members of the tribal council. Its practitioners, however, had generally reduced their activity and their claims about its efficacy. Many had easily reconciled conjuring with Christianity and modern medicine, demonstrating again the syncretic and eclectic nature of Cherokee society. Old-style conjuring seemed to be disappearing, and one of its last practitioners was Bird Partridge, who died in 1958 at age eighty-two. A longtime medicine man for the Bird Town stick-ball team, he was both loved and feared for his powers and "enjoyed a great reputation among the fast-dwindling circle of fullbloods."[18]

Like conjuring, the Cherokee ballplay continued on a diminished scale, but without the violence and political significance of earlier days. The only exception was a brief period after World War II when the game was again the "little brother of war" as veterans enthusiastically wreaked havoc on one another. By the mid-1950s it was different. Except for the obligatory contests staged for whites at the annual Cherokee fairs (later called fall festivals) and a series of games in the summers of 1958–59, there was little incentive for competing. Big Cove seldom even had rivals, though in later years Wolf Town would field dominant teams for the festivals. Snowbird apparently had not organized a team since the early years of the century. Even in Big Cove there had been no dances and other traditional pregame rituals since the late 1930s. Most Cherokees favored mainstream sports like softball, baseball, and basketball rather than the traditional ballplay.[19]

In Big Cove the old free labor companies—or gadugi—continued to operate, though not every conservative or full-blood belonged to one. To a certain extent the functions of the gadugi had been assumed by the community development clubs created in the late 1940s at the urging of the BIA and CHA. The same thing was happening in Paint Town and Snowbird.[20] After an initial period of enthusiasm, people in Big Cove were beginning to lose interest in the clubs, and anthropologists believed a kind of malaise existed there. Likewise interest among Paint Town residents was waning, in part because the clubs embodied white middle-class social values. One anthropologist concluded that kinship ties in Paint Town were stronger than any psychological identification with the community.[21]

Even in relatively acculturated Cherokee communities, there was a tendency for residents to remain close to their roots. In Paint Town 63 percent of the one hundred heads of households who were surveyed—or their spouses—had grown up there. Movement was either to white communities or to other tourist-oriented Cherokee communities along the highways. About 42 percent of all children listed by Paint Town households remained in that town, while 29 percent resided off reservation, 26 percent in Wolf Town, Cherokee, or Bird Town, and only 1 percent in Big Cove or Graham County. The last figure suggests that moving to more traditionalist communities held few attractions for Paint Town people. The number of adult children living off the reservation was even higher, 42 percent, and more than one-third of them were in military service. Indeed, serving in the armed forces was one of the foremost reasons Indians left the reservation.[22]

Cherokee, Paint Town, Wolf Town, and Bird Town reflected the influence of modern American society more dramatically than Big Cove and Snowbird. They all straddled major federal highways leading into the national park and were the scene of almost all tourist development. Most employees of such businesses lived there, as did, a bit later, those working in the new manufacturing plants. There were more Christian denominations in those communities, more automobiles, more paved roads, and more movement back and forth between the reservation and the outside world. These communities also had a smaller percentage of full-bloods and fuller-bloods than Big Cove and Snowbird.

Although Baptists and Methodists were still dominant, Qualla Boundary increasingly attracted other religious denominations, including Catholics, Episcopalians, and—much to the chagrin of certain preachers—Mormons. The Rev. Ewell Payne, representing the Southern Baptist Convention, viewed the appearance of Mormons in 1949 as a call to Armageddon and exhorted his faithful to repulse the outsiders. Through his influence the tribal council consistently denied the Mormons permission to build a church on the reservation—even on a convert's possessory tract. Along with the Catholics, Mormons were for a time forced to hold their services in the school auditorium, which was federal property. Eventually the Catholics built their own church in town and the Mormons built just outside the reservation boundary. As for the Reverend Mr. Payne, the tribal council declared him persona non grata in 1956 because of his alleged meddling in tribal politics.[23]

According to a 1959 report, most of the 596 families on the reservation had gardens or did a small amount of subsistence farming. The "farms" averaged about sixteen acres of open land, evenly divided between pasture and cropland. Since World War II many Cherokees had started growing burley tobacco to bring in a few dollars, but the average farm income was still only $600. Corn continued to be important both for human consumption and for livestock. Traditional colored Indian corn was still common because it was tasty and had ornamental value for tourist items. But there was no way farming could compete with tourism in the tribal economy or with wage labor on and off the reservation. Only 23 percent of the Paint Town heads of household, for example, even claimed to be farmers.[24]

Figures on Cherokee income during this period vary, depending on the criteria used. By 1950 reported average family income from all sources, including food grown at home, was $1,642. Even a decade later this was supposedly "higher than that of non-Indian families in the counties adjoining the reservation." But according to a 1952 report the estimated annual family income "from all sources in cash and in kind" was $1,264, or about $295 per capita. The compilers admitted, however, that these figures did not reflect the Cherokees' exemption from taxes on land and personal property and the fact they received many BIA services free of charge. Real Cherokee family income was therefore "somewhat higher" than $1,264. Estimated per capita income in 1950 for all of Swain, Jackson, and Graham counties was almost twice as high as for the reservation, $575, but whites of course did not receive BIA services. Other surveys, apparently limited to cash income, show Indian family and per capita incomes well below those of nearby whites throughout the 1950s.[25]

Whatever the correct statistics, a sharp division existed on the reservation between the haves and have-nots. A relatively few Cherokees were prospering while many others were impoverished. R. W. Quinn, the BIA supervisory program officer, said Cherokee society was primarily defined by economic status, and he saw three major divisions within the tribe: the first, representing more than half the population, comprised the "mountain folks" who were one or two generations behind other Cherokees in acculturation. In many respects the lives of these people mirrored those of poor mountain whites. The middle group of Cherokees consisted of more progressive farmers, small businessmen, and those with steady employment. These had "definitely charted their course towards American cultural behavior, morals and economic goals." The most progressive group, Quinn said, were so-called white Indians, but he cautioned that this was not exclusively a racial designation because it included many with at least one-half Cherokee blood.[26]

Quinn believed that nine families controlled most of the valuable business operations in Cherokee and the Soco Valley. "These business leaders," he said, "exert an expected strong influence on the tribal political situation. Their 'possessory holdings' provide returns in wealth and prestige so far out of proportion from that received by the other 'possessory right' holders as to make comparison [ridiculous].. . . . Neither are the successful tribesmen unaware of the nature of their advantage. Any action to motivate the conservatives to exerting their political potential would bring swift and certain [retaliatory] action." As he noted somewhat wryly, this is what the BIA meant by acculturation. "Our embarrassment lies in the fact that the beneficiaries who achieved goals did so at the expense and to the [detriment] of the rest of the beneficiaries."[27]

The "beneficiaries" of this economic growth made up what Robert K. Thomas calls the Cherokee middle class, the most acculturated of four tribal social divisions. The others, occupying a continuum from least to most acculturated, were the conservatives, generalized Indians, and rural white Indians. Unlike the other three, the middle class—or tribal bourgeoisie— had largely arisen since World War II in response to the tourist boom. Most of this class were white Indians, but there were a few notable full-bloods as well. In 1960–61 Harriet Kupferer modified Thomas's model by suggesting there were only two major cultural divisions, conservatives and modern Indians. A truly acculturative difference existed between the two, one group emphasizing the traditional harmony ethic and passivity (as well as other real or alleged aboriginal traits), the other subscribing to the capitalist—or "Protestant"—ethic. Kupferer suggested there were numerous gradations among modern Indians reflecting not so much degree of acculturation as socioeconomic differentiation.[28]

Cherokees in the lower socioeconomic strata often obtained assistance from one or more sources. In 1952 about 20 percent of tribal families received help from county departments of public welfare for old age, dependent children, and various disabilities. The tribal council also appropriated about $7,000 in welfare, mostly for food, while another $2,000 came from the BIA. Total public and tribal relief expenditures during the year amounted to almost $50,000, with church organizations providing additional help. Federal aid alone increased to $114,405 by 1960 (after other agencies besides the BIA began providing assistance), then dropped off to $55,303 in 1963 because of the economic boom. Predictably, public assistance was lowest during the tourist season and peaked in March and April.[29]

* * *

Not surprisingly, the economic changes on Qualla Boundary exacerbated political factionalism. As always, much of this conflict focused on the growing domination of mixed-bloods, especially white Indians. Osley Saunooke, ever responsive to the political situation, supported a number of conservatives who formed the "Qualla Association" and claimed they represented seven hundred Cherokees from all over the reservation. At congressional hearings in 1955 they complained about the lack of jobs, said the CHA should do more to help the tribe, and expressed fear over the lingering possibility of termination. Soon they also called for purging the tribal roll of members with less than one-sixteenth Cherokee blood. The revival of this old issue led Congress in 1957 to authorize revision of the Baker Roll for the first time since its compilation during the 1920s. The Eastern Band could set its own requirements for membership, and the roll would be continually revised as members died and new ones were born. The legislation also allowed the tribe to overturn the 1931 statute permitting individuals of any blood quantum to inherit membership from a bona fide member, incurring the wrath of Fred Bauer, who saw it as a denial of private property rights and the inheritance laws of North Carolina.[30]

After attempts to require a one-fourth blood quantum failed, the new roll, begun in 1959, specified a minimum of one-thirty-second Cherokee blood.[31] Four years later, however, opponents mustered enough strength to have it raised back to one-sixteenth. Councilwoman Myrtle Jenkins objected and claimed the new action resulted from a belief that the tribe was about to win damages from the Indian Claims Commission; many Cherokees, she said, did not want to share the money with white Indians. Her opposition had little effect, and tribal membership remained pegged at one-sixteenth. By 1968 enrolled Cherokees numbered about 6,700, with some 4,600 living on or near the reservation.[32]

Another source of political dispute during the 1960s was the question of replacing the Band's state charter with a new constitution. Principal Chief Jarrett Blythe, long a supporter of the BIA, readily cooperated with that agency in preparing a proposed constitution under the 1934 Indian Reorganization Act, which still applied to the Band. The ostensible purpose was to modernize tribal government.[33] After several drafts, the completed document was submitted to the Cherokees for comment. One of its more important provisions was to add two new delegates to the council, one each from "Big Y," a part of Wolf Town, and Tomotla, an enclave of white Indians in Cherokee County who were in the Snowbird electoral district. After "much opposition" to the new document, the tribal council voted in October 1966 to dismiss the constitution committee. The Band would continue to operate under its 1889 charter and subsequent amendments. Theodore C. Krenzke, the current Cherokee agent, hoped the Indians would reconsider, but Cherokee factionalism was too severe to permit such a change.[34] In 1973, however, Tomotla's disgruntled Indians ran their own candidates against those of Snowbird for control of the district's two council seats. They won, precipitating a political crisis that eventually brought about an informal system where Tomotla's white Indians share representation for the district with Snowbird's fuller-blood population.[35]

Tribal politics of the 1950s and 1960s were flavored by the contrasting personalities—and physiques—of its two leading figures. It was Osley Saunooke, more than 300 pounds of former wrestling champion, grappling with Jarrett Blythe, a wizened 120 pounds. The outcome seemed as fixed as a professional wrestling match, except that the script worked against Saunooke. He always lost. Periodically Jarrett Blythe would emerge from "retirement," confront his Goliath, slay him, and spend another four years leading his people. His fame among Native Americans earned him recognition by the National Indian Council as 1954's Outstanding Indian of the Year. It must have been an enormous frustration for Saunooke, who died in April

1965 from diabetic complications. Unfortunately, Blythe no longer had the vigor of earlier years and sometimes, in the midst of meetings, would simply put his head on the conference table and rest. He served his sixth and final term from 1963 to 1967 and then retired for good, the undisputed political champion of the Eastern Band. He died in April 1977 at age ninety.[36] Both he and Saunooke, though different in many ways, had worked diligently to attract business and jobs to the reservation.

Most Cherokees and BIA officials were enthusiastic participants in President Lyndon B. Johnson's "Great Society." Early in 1964 current Cherokee agent Don Y. Jensen stressed that breaking the "cycle of poverty" on the reservation required better economic and educational opportunities as well as changes in the "emotional and psychological climate."[37] During those heady days of Johnson's War on Poverty, the tribe benefited from a variety of services, and in 1966 it received a grant of nearly $484,000 from the Office of Economic Opportunity. The money was earmarked for Community Action Programs in Big Cove, Cherokee, Paint Town, Wolf Town, and Bird Town; Snowbird and the Cherokee County Indians became involved the following year. Among the projects were day-care centers, neighborhood information centers, beautification projects, family education programs, and other social services. The Community Action Programs were often in conjunction with other federal and state programs; efforts to construct low-cost housing, for example, dovetailed with efforts by the Department of Housing and Urban Development. A federally financed agency, Qualla Housing Authority, helped Cherokees construct or renovate four hundred homes by 1975.[38] Likewise the "temporary" management of the tribal hospital by the United States Public Health Service became permanent. Thus the Eastern Band eagerly embraced even more federal dependency, leading Jarrett Blythe to grumble that his people were getting "soft" from so many benefits.[39]

As in many tribes, Cherokee conservatives were not fully prepared to understand or participate in Great Society programs. In the spring of 1968 a delegation of full-bloods arrived in Washington to complain about being denied their share of benefits by tribal leaders and the BIA. Again they condemned the growing influence of white Indians, prompting one federal official to say the delegation "reflected problems which exist on many reservations today," notably the control of tribal assets by "progressive elements (mostly mixedbloods)."[40] Though accurate, the observation hardly helped resolve the differences between culturally conservative Cherokees and the more business-oriented mixed-bloods. In this case, Theodore Krenzke in-

6. Osley Bird Saunooke, world super heavyweight wrestling champion 1937–51.
Courtesy of Bertha and Pat Saunooke.

sisted the conservatives were actually well represented in the program benefits but still needed to become more involved in communitywide activities.[41]

Bolstered by federal programs and an ever-growing tourism, tribal economic development accelerated during the nationwide prosperity of the
1960s. Projected completion of a major new tourist attraction, Frontier-
land, was hailed in 1963 as another milestone for the Band. Even more ambitious was the council's decision to use $75,000 of tribal funds and a BIA

7. Osley Bird Saunooke, principal chief 1951–55, 1959–63. Courtesy of the
Cherokee Historical Association.

loan of $525,000 to build a plant in Cherokee for the Vassar Corporation,
a manufacturer of women's hair accessories.[42] These and similar developments helped fuel an unparalleled boom. Agent Jensen could be forgiven his
mild hyperbole when he claimed Qualla Boundary was the first fully indus-
trialized reservation, with "more jobs here than there are qualified Indians
to hold them."[43]

Jensen's optimism seemed well founded. By late 1965 three industrial plants provided year-round employment for about 340 Cherokees, with a total yearly payroll of some $650,000. Figures for that year show 691 Cherokees having permanent jobs. Besides the three factories, the biggest employers were Indian-owned private businesses with 87 workers and the BIA with 70. There were also 638 seasonal jobs—200 provided by the Cherokee Historical Association, which during 1950–66 paid Cherokees almost $1.8 million in salaries. The Neighborhood Youth Corps employed another 149 Cherokees seasonally, and 125 worked in tourist-related businesses. (These figures require caution because some Cherokees held more than one job.) Behind this growth was a swelling flood of tourists to Qualla Boundary, an estimated 5 million a year by 1968.[44]

The boom had many other consequences besides new jobs. During 1966 the 3 percent tribal sales levy brought in more than $148,000, and ninety-three members of the Eastern Band operated their own businesses. By then Qualla Boundary's road system had been modernized and included a paved highway to Big Cove. The growth of wage labor brought a noticeable decline in farming, and many families no longer even kept a garden, preferring to live from payday to payday.[45] The growing contact with tourists and a dynamic economy were also partly responsible for a rapid decline in spoken Cherokee throughout the reservation. By 1968, according to Theodore Krenzke, the average Cherokee family income had risen to about $5,100 a year, compared with family averages of about $8,000 for the nation, $7,000 for the state, $6,000 for rural western North Carolina, and $3,000 for all United States Indians. If correct, these figures reveal the remarkable economic strides the Eastern Band had made in the preceding decade. Although lagging behind most citizens (70 percent of Cherokee families were still below the national poverty level), they were better off than most other Indians. Their per capita income was higher, unemployment lower, and education better, and they had more amenities like automobiles, running water, and adequate sewerage.[46]

* * *

Paradoxically, existing side by side with a growing tribal dependency on federal funds was a new willingness by Cherokee individuals and communities to assume responsibility for running their own programs. The active participation in Community Action Programs provides a good example. Even more noteworthy was the Band's effort to assume more police power on the reservation. Here one can clearly discern the mixed system of government (or "concurrent jurisdiction") that had long prevailed, as well as a gradual shift toward more tribal self-determination. Ten "major crimes" were handled by federal authorities, while lesser offenses fell under state and county jurisdiction.[47]

Until 1951, the BIA employed a police officer on the reservation who worked closely with federal, state, and county law-enforcement agencies. But with the tremendous increase in visitors to Qualla Boundary, the need for a larger police force became apparent. In 1952 the Eastern Band, with the BIA's approval, used its new 3 percent sales levy to fund a Community Services Program that increasingly assumed responsibility for police protection and other services. This was the first time a tribe had paid for its own law enforcement. By 1959 the Band spent more than $15,000 a year to support five to seven policemen who were deputized by the BIA to enforce federal laws and by the sheriff of either Jackson or Swain county to uphold North Carolina laws. The latter arrangement, however, limited authority of tribal policemen to the county that had deputized them and prevented any effective reservationwide law enforcement.[48]

Another drawback was the way county politics intruded into the appointment of tribal police. Late in 1958 the Eastern Band established the first competitive examination for policemen and on this basis selected the top five candidates. The sheriff of Swain County, however, refused to issue their commissions because of political considerations.[49] It was a difficult situation for the Eastern Band. It was willing to relieve the counties of paying for law enforcement on the reservation but was denied an effective voice in appointing the policemen. Agent Butts protested this politicization to Governor Luther H. Hodges and advocated allowing tribal police to operate throughout the reservation. The governor responded that there was no law authorizing him to appoint such officers but suggested the representatives of Swain, Jackson, Graham, and Cherokee counties introduce suitable legislation.[50] This was done, and a subsequent act of the legislature gave the Cherokee deputies commissioned by Jackson and Swain counties authority to act in both counties, though still leaving them susceptible to local political whims.[51]

Gradually the Cherokees assumed more and more control over other services. The people of Snowbird, for example, constructed an improved sanitation system with the assistance of the United States Public Health Service, and thanks to the tribal levy the Eastern Band became the first tribe to establish its own sanitation and fire departments. In May 1965 the federal government transferred control of the reservation water system to the tribe, about the same time that North Carolina, after a long dispute over whether the tribe had to observe state fish and game laws, conveyed full authority to the Band to control its own fisheries.[52]

Perhaps the best example of growing Cherokee self-determination was the remarkable success of the Cherokee Boys Club, organized as an agricultural club in 1932 and incorporated in 1964 to offer training, employment, and recreation for Cherokee boys and young men. In the latter year it contracted with the federal government to provide transportation for Cherokee schoolchildren, becoming "the first non-governmental operator of school buses on an Indian reservation in the United States."[53] Little did anyone foresee that the club would assume such a prominent role in tribal life. Within four years it was furnishing a variety of agricultural, construction, and maintenance services and operating a fleet of sixteen school buses. As manager Raymond E. Kinsland remarked, "Our boys are really interested in doing things themselves. They want to get away from the welfare that many communities depend on today."[54] Later the club would contract to manage an array of social services for the tribe. For the Cherokees, self-determination within the comforting web of federal assistance was becoming a reality.

In education, too, the pattern was much the same. In 1962 the four elementary schools on Qualla Boundary were combined into one building near the BIA agency. The Eastern Band continued to rely on federal support but at the same time made significant strides toward cooperation with local white school districts. After the boarding facilities closed in 1954, Cherokees wanted either a new federal high school or a consolidated public school with Swain County.[55] Consolidation never occurred, but Cherokee children increasingly attended white schools. By the 1964–65 school year, 498 of the 1,503 Eastern Cherokee students were in public schools.[56] Gone were the days when white school districts steadfastly refused to admit students who were phenotypically Cherokees. Attracted by federal subsidies for educating Indians, the Graham County Board of Education invited the parents of Snowbird to send their children to the Robbinsville schools as soon as possible. Most were eager to do so because Indian children would be bused to a new twenty-room elementary school and given daily lunches. The local BIA school finally closed in July 1965. By that fall some seventy-seven Cherokee pupils were attending school in Robbinsville. Agent Jensen reported they were "well received and well thought of in the Robbinsville community. . . . We are very proud of our fine working relations with the public schools of North Carolina."[57]

In the meantime the campaign to construct a new BIA high school in Cherokee was becoming a crusade. Ever since education came to the forefront during the controversy over termination, critics had noted the school's inadequacies. Finally, in September 1970 it appeared that the budget for fiscal year 1972 would include appropriations for a new school on land purchased by the council for $80,000. Congressman Roy A. Taylor told secretary of the interior Walter J. Hickel that he was encouraged by this development because the existing facilities were a disgrace and "a most unfavorable reflection upon the Federal Government. They are all wooden structures built around the turn of the century and were condemned some twenty years ago."[58] When the new school was completed in the mid-1970s, it became a showcase for the BIA.

In other respects, however, Cherokee education lagged badly. According to a 1970 report, the generally low level of income on the reservation "made it difficult for many families to provide necessary books, magazines, newspapers, radios, television sets, and other contemporary modern day communication media found in the average American home today." Even with the success of a federal and tribal housing program, over 50 percent of reservation homes were classified as substandard, and poor sanitary conditions left many Cherokee pupils unhealthy. In 1966–67, for example, 92 percent were infected with roundworm. In addition, because of a continuing dietary imbalance 39 percent of the students were classified as obese. There was a high arrest rate among school-age Cherokees, and in 1969 92 percent of all arrestees between twelve and twenty-one years of age were under the influence of alcohol. Moreover, California Achievement Tests given that year showed "that 31% of all students were below age-grade level in communicative skills, and particularly in reading comprehension." Mostly because of this, Cherokee pupils also ranked very low on a battery of so-called intelligence tests. A survey showed that more than 45 percent of students in their senior year had no plans beyond graduation, while 46 percent of junior high pupils believed school was "a waste of time" and attended classes only because someone forced them to. Delinquency and unplanned pregnancies were other common problems for school-age Cherokees.[59]

In an earlier period Cherokee parents might well have been indifferent to these and other school-related matters, but there were signs of growing concern as they took increasingly active roles, serving on the community-elected Cherokee Advisory School Board and offering their help with innovative programs like Head Start and Follow Through. Discipline was another area of parental concern. Many blamed students' misbehavior on the

BIA's policy of prohibiting corporal punishment. In April 1970 the council authorized the local Advisory School Board to draw up comprehensive guidelines for administering corporal punishment and suspending or expelling troublesome students. As Theodore Krenzke noted, "Hopefully . . . the student's attitude of I can do what I want and nothing can be done will be eliminated."[60] The new policy was a radical departure from the traditional Cherokee inclination to indulge children and avoid physical punishment and no doubt represented the sentiments of more acculturated parents. That same year also witnessed a different kind of parental concern as instruction in the Cherokee language was offered for the first time in tribal schools—an odd counterpoint to recent developments.[61]

Within the local BIA administration, the same shift to more self-determination was gradually becoming apparent. Jeff Muskrat, Krenzke's successor as agent, was chosen in 1974 by the Eastern Cherokees themselves from a slate of candidates. His being a Western Cherokee, Muskrat admits, probably gave him a decisive edge over his competitors. While some councilmembers at first found him a bit condescending, they quickly asserted themselves and nudged the agreeable agent into more of an advisory role. When he retired in 1985, the council, as if making a point of its independence, deliberated a long time before formally approving Wilbur Paul (a Blackfeet) as his successor.[62]

* * *

With the increasing turmoil in American society over civil rights and the Vietnam War, the issue of past and present injustices to Indians also became a national issue. The Eastern Cherokees cooperated with moderate pan-Indian organizations like the National Congress of American Indians and the United South and Eastern Tribes but generally viewed the growing "Red Power" movement as a threat to their satisfactory working relationship with the BIA. Certainly a radical group like the American Indian Movement (AIM), headed by young urban Indians, held little appeal. In fact some Cherokees still evince considerable pride when discussing their forcible eviction of certain radical Indian organizers from the reservation in the late 1960s and early 1970s.[63]

Though hardly a radical, Laurence French, a sociologist at Western Carolina University, was treated like a pariah by many prominent Indians and whites because he publicly attacked the Cherokee Historical Association and its control of choice tourist attractions. Among other things, he claimed the organization had failed to live up to its original objectives, had violated tribal law, and had benefited the tribe's haves at the expense of the have-nots. French also leveled a barrage at his employer, saying that Western Carolina was in effect a coconspirator with the CHA in exploiting the Eastern Band. For a brief time in 1976–77 an underground newspaper supposedly edited by some of French's Cherokee students attacked the "ruling class" on the reservation with charges of greed, corruption, and nepotism. French left Western Carolina in 1977, but his campaign perhaps influenced the CHA to turn over administration of its newly completed Museum of the Cherokee Indian to the tribal council.[64]

Tribal members were sometimes willing to take a stand on timely issues relating specifically to themselves and not requiring the kind of self-criticism demanded by French and his supporters. In the mid-1960s a number of Cherokees joined conservationists and other opponents of TVA's plans to build Tellico Dam on the Little Tennessee River in eastern Tennessee. Cherokees were angry because the new reservoir would flood the sites of historic Indian villages, including Chota, the tribe's former principal town. In April 1965 opponents of Tellico Dam carefully orchestrated a visit by Supreme Court Justice William O. Douglas, an ardent conservationist. Meeting with him were various citizens' action groups and a delegation of the Eastern Band, which presented Douglas with both a petition opposing destruction of the archaeological sites and a gaudy Sioux warbonnet (more of an attention getter than a Cherokee souvenir).[65]

TVA director Aubrey "Red" Wagner attempted to mollify the Indians by working with certain factions to promote development of the reservation's resources. TVA also sponsored archaeological digs under the auspices of the University of Tennessee in an effort to retrieve precious artifacts and data before Chota and other sites were inundated. Beginning in 1968, TVA would spend more than $4 million on the Tellico excavations. When the Cherokee Nation in Oklahoma protested construction of the dam, TVA paid for a trip by a delegation of that tribe so they could see the archaeological work. This wining and dining paid off, for the Nation quickly withdrew its protest and even complimented TVA for its sensitivity to the Cherokee heritage. TVA also encouraged the University of Tennessee to hire Indian youths to help on the digs.[66]

However, some Eastern Cherokees joined with the small United Keetowah Band of Cherokees from Oklahoma to continue protesting both the "desecration" of the archaeological sites and the impending completion of the dam. Reacting to this pressure, the tribal council voted in August 1972 to oppose both projects, and Chief Noah Powell requested that Tennessee's Governor Winfield Dunn and President Richard Nixon intervene. Especially vehement in his denunciation of the dam and the ongoing disruption of Indian burial grounds was councilman Jonathan L. Taylor, vice president of the United South and Eastern Tribes, a consortium of Indian groups with some 19,000 members. Though neither Dunn nor Nixon was inclined to offer more than sympathy, the National Congress of American Indians soon passed a resolution against the dam. Before long popular writers and the national media were featuring the Tellico controversy.[67]

Noah Powell was fundamentally a conservative compromiser who wished to resolve any differences with Aubrey Wagner and TVA. As he told a friend (who relayed the information to Wagner), the chief "just did not have the strength to fight many battles anymore."[68] Most of the tribal council likewise seemed to backtrack from an open confrontation with TVA; it was as if they had made an obligatory bow to the more radical tribal faction and were reluctant to do more. Such vacillation simply invited trouble. Given the context of the time, it was perhaps inevitable that firebrands would appear on the scene and vehemently denounce TVA, Tellico Dam, the BIA, conservative tribal officials, and American injustice in general. Without a doubt the most flamboyant of such characters was Hawk Littlejohn, who rather mysteriously appeared on Qualla Boundary and claimed to be a Western Cherokee. For a while he was a darling of the media with his denunciations. Completely without support among tribal leaders, Littlejohn had his season of glory and then in 1974 disappeared from view almost as quickly as he had appeared.[69]

After their protests of the early 1970s, the Eastern Band generally remained aloof over the controversy surrounding Tellico Dam, evidently believing a well-organized coalition of environmentalists would be sufficient to prevent its completion. Certainly it was in the tribe's best interests to remain on good terms with TVA, especially since the agency was making every effort to placate tribal leaders, even to the point of offering to develop Cherokee-related tourist facilities near the new reservoir.[70] Both sides wanted the Cherokees as allies. In 1977 opponents of Tellico Dam met with a number of Indians and again enlisted their somewhat wavering support, but the tribe was never a significant force in the crusade. The end was not long in coming. TVA's defenders in Congress finally managed to get the dam approved, and the reservoir began to fill in November 1979, despite a last minute lawsuit filed by the Eastern Band and the Keetowah Cherokees.[71]

Although the Cherokees lost part of their tribal heritage to Tellico Dam, they reclaimed another part in a settlement with the federal government. In May 1972, twenty-one years after the tribe brought suit in the Indian

Claims Court, the United States offered a settlement of $1,855,254.50 for loss of lands and other injustices. The following month, at a "grand council" at Mountainside Theater, some 500 Cherokees voted decisively to accept the offer. After considerable debate, the tribe later decided to distribute the money per capita among some 7,200 members, amounting to about $250 each. Hardly a bonanza, the individual payments were nonetheless welcome income and an acknowledgment of ancient wrongs.[72]

Tellico Dam and the Band's victory in court were minor skirmishes among the many battles fought by Indians during the 1960s and early 1970s. With more self-assurance, more education, and the emergence of radical organizations like the American Indian Movement, Native Americans insisted on charting their own destiny. At the same time, however, many still feared possible termination of federal responsibility. Termination threatened their tribal existence, their identity. This ambivalence over independence and dependency was reflected in federal policy. Throughout the administrations of John F. Kennedy and Lyndon Johnson the government disavowed termination without tribal consent. Johnson also emphasized maximum tribal participation in the variety of social service programs constituting the Great Society.[73]

After Richard M. Nixon was inaugurated in 1969, he carried this process a step further. In a major message on Indian Affairs in July 1970, he summed up the trend of the previous decade by forthrightly calling for self-determination without termination. As he put it:

> It is long past time that the Indian policies of the Federal government began to build upon the capacities and insights of the Indian people. Both as a matter of justice and as a matter of enlightened social policy, we must begin to act on the basis of what the Indians themselves have long been telling us. The time has come to break decisively with the past and to create the conditions for a new era in which the Indian future is determined by Indian acts and Indian decisions.[74]

The Native American could remain an Indian—could even define that Indianness—and still receive federal assistance.

For longtime advocates of Americanism and acculturation, Nixon's speech seemed a step backward. In a letter to Congressman Roy Taylor, Fred Bauer said that the 1953 congressional resolution providing for termination (HCR 108) offered Indians their only hope of becoming respected and full-fledged citizens. Repeal of termination, he believed, "would give the [BIA] the Brass ring for another ride on the merry-go-round." More specifically, he again claimed that the Eastern Cherokees owned their lands indivdually and that Nixon's support of tribalism threatened those property rights. As an accent note, that very year Bauer published *Land of the North Carolina Cherokees*, a diatribe against the BIA and tribalism. Filled with vim and vitriol, it articulated the author's interpretation of the Band's history and legal status as well as the baneful effects of federal policy. It was Bauer's last, most defiant stand. He died in May 1971.[75]

Nixon's ideas regarding Indian policy finally took shape with passage of the Indian Self-Determination and Education Assistance Act of January 4, 1975. According to the act's preamble, the United States had an obligation to respect Indians' desires for self-determination by allowing them to participate to the maximum in directing federal programs affecting them. At the same time, the government was committed to maintaining its "unique and continuing relationship with and responsibility to the Indian people."[76] Thus the new act merely reflected what had already occurred among some tribes, including the Eastern Band. During the previous twenty years the Band had successfully forestalled termination and, building upon its tourist base, undertaken significant economic development. It had also assumed increasing responsibility in administering its internal affairs and many federal programs. And yet . . . and yet "self-determination" within a continuing federal context left unresolved the old puzzle of how the Cherokees—or any tribe—could be both modern Americans and Indians.

9

Cherokee Americans

OUTWARDLY Cherokee life has changed little since the 1970s. Tribal members, numbering 9,590 as of January 1990, still argue about who qualifies as a "real" Indian and who does not. The core of their homeland, a reservation of 56,621 acres held in trust by the federal government, remains intact and inviolate.[1] Despite numerous new businesses, the town of Cherokee looks much the same, still a creature of the seasonal rhythm of tourism. After the October colors signal a gaudy farewell to visitors, the reservation begins a six-month hibernation interrupted only by weekend bingo games.

Although tourism is part of a familiar pattern, it has made today's Cherokees even more subject to the vagaries of national and international economic developments as periodic oil shortages and recessions bring sharp drops in the number of visitors. In July 1979, for example, agent Jeff Muskrat said the reservation had "suffered a tremendous decline" in tourism, with downtown businesses, especially craft shops, showing drops of from 30 to 65 percent. Attendance at "Unto These Hills" was also down sharply.[2] Surprisingly, the 1982 Knoxville World's Fair brought a decline in tourist visits to the reservation as vacationers apparently decided they had time and money for the fair but not the Indians. As the acting agent put it in August of that year, "The Cherokee community is experiencing one of the poorest tourist seasons in recent years. Everyone had anticipated an excellent year due to the fact that the World's Fair is in Knoxville. However, the Fair has apparently been detrimental rather than helpful and many people who found jobs earlier in the season have been laid off."[3] In contrast, approximately 10.2 million visitors came to the Great Smoky Mountains National Park during the prosperous 1987 season, with many also stopping in Cherokee.[4]

Competition for tourist dollars is fierce, as rival communities like Gatlinburg and Pigeon Forge, Tennessee, siphon off most of the park visitors. After a recent excursion to those towns, current chief Jonathan L. Taylor said, "If Cherokee could draw people like this, we would not have to worry about the government cut-backs."[5] A marketing survey by Keith T. Stephens, a Western Carolina University professor, verifies the competitive strength of Gatlinburg and Pigeon Forge. Stephens sent questionnaires to 1,000 people who had made inquiries during 1987 to Cherokee Travel and Promotion Services, and about 40 percent of the 468 respondents said Cherokee was not their primary destination; most of those 40 percent listed the two Tennessee cities.[6] These figures are particularly ominous because the group surveyed was obviously skewed in favor of Cherokee.

In two respects, however, the Eastern Band has a decisive edge over its rivals. First, the Western Carolina marketing survey shows that many tourists want to see Cherokees and learn more about their history and culture. Second, as a federally recognized reservation, Qualla Boundary is exempt from restrictive state gaming laws, and since 1982 the Cherokees have sponsored what they tout as the world's largest ongoing bingo extravaganza. Well-advertised games with cash prizes sometimes amounting to hundreds of thousands of dollars attract busloads of eager players from all over the eastern United States. In Soco Valley a cavernous building once occupied by the now defunct Vassar Corporation accommodates more than 4,000 players. Shrouded by a pall of cigarette smoke, row after row of contestants, ranging from blue-haired old ladies to young couples with coolers of food and drink, test their luck. Originally Cherokee Bingo operated under a tribal license held by rather shadowy white outsiders who employed a management firm headed by two local Indians. Although the tribe expected to reap about $2 million a year from the games, it reportedly received only about $1 million from an estimated gross of $33 million during the first three years.[7]

Later revelations of wrongdoing led to the conviction of several whites and one Indian for skimming and fraud and a lawsuit filed by Chief Robert Youngdeer to force an accounting from the enterprise. The council repudiated Youngdeer for this and in February 1987, over the chief's strenuous objections, bought out Cherokee Bingo and began operating it on a tribal basis, usually hosting games two weekends a month. During the first year under tribal auspices the games reportedly drew nearly 50,000 players, employed some 200 Cherokees, and brought in $954,000, more than a third of the Band's operating budget that year. In addition, Cherokee Bingo generates considerable off-season income for motels, restaurants, souvenir shops, and other businesses. As Chief Taylor notes, bingo revenue helps make up for cutbacks in Indian services since Ronald Reagan's inauguration in 1981.[8]

An example of bingo's scope and economic clout is the "Super Bingo" game of May 14, 1988, which drew a crowd of 3,915 to compete for over $450,000 in cash and other prizes. Receipts from this one date enabled Cherokee Bingo to reduce its line of credit by $140,000 and also pumped more than $63,000 into the tribal treasury through the Band's 6 percent sales levy. Despite continuing allegations of corruption and mismanagement, most Cherokees have learned to accept the games as an economic necessity and a fact of life. Efforts by North Carolina and other states to limit high-stakes bingo on reservations have been defeated in federal courts, but the BIA and FBI are subjecting tribal management contracts to closer scrutiny.[9]

Except for bingo and talk of building golf courses, ski slopes, and dog-racing tracks, tourism on Qualla Boundary conforms to the same patterns as a decade or two ago. Exhibits in the Museum of the Cherokee Indian remain basically unaltered, souvenir shops sell the same stock items, and many Cherokee artists produce predictable works for a predictable market. Major attractions like "Unto These Hills" and Oconaluftee Indian Village are much as they were a generation ago. Why argue with success? By 1987 the outdoor drama had attracted about 4.6 million paying customers since its 1950 debut, and Oconaluftee Village was almost as successful.[10] An additional tribal attraction, the Sequoyah Birthplace Museum near Vonore, Tennessee, opened in 1986 on land donated by TVA as penance for building the Tellico Dam.[11]

During the tourist season the rhythm of life hardens into daily routine. Every morning, like exotic sentries, Cherokee "chiefs" dressed in the warbonnets of Plains Indians begin their vigils along U.S. 441 and U.S. 19. Standing beside little tepees in front of gift shops, they pose for photographs with squealing children and sheepish housewives and assure curious visitors that, yes, they *are* "real" Indians. For added drama, one may pose with a ferocious-looking stuffed bear conveniently mounted on wheels so it can be shifted for suitable lighting. Then it's back into the car for a lurching, bumper-to-bumper crawl through Cherokee's strip of shops and fast-food franchises.

For those who "look" Indian with copper skins, raven-black hair, hawk

8. Carl Standingdeer "chiefing" in downtown Cherokee, late 1940s. Courtesy of the Museum of the Cherokee Indian.

noses, and appropriate costuming, "chiefing" can be very profitable. Henry Lambert has been at it for years, as well as Joseph George and other regulars along the federal highways. They make money from photographs and tips and also lure customers to the particular souvenir shop they represent. That their Plains regalia and tepees are quite un-Cherokee bothers them not at all. Lambert admitted that once, when much younger, he tried an experiment

9. Cherokee baskets. Courtesy of the Museum of the Cherokee Indian.

where he worked one day wearing a warbonnet, the second dressed in modest Cherokee clothing and beadwork, and the third with flashy Plains attire again. The warbonnet and tepee of the Plains tribes brought him $80 the first day and $82 the third; Cherokee attire on the second netted him only $3. On his all-time best day with a warbonnet, he made $803 and could have cleared $1,000 had he not quit early. "Hey," Lambert said a few years ago, "I'm not stupid. I stuck with the warbonnet." He has even market tested his costume by asking women to evaluate swatches of fabric. "Women can make or break my business," he admitted. During the season he wears ten different costumes, all in variations of red, orange, and black. "This won't clash with what my customer has on. These look well with anything." [12]

Liquor for thirsty tourists is an ongoing problem as the town of Cherokee tries to compete against the well-watered attractions of Gatlinburg and Pigeon Forge. Federal reservations may pass their own liquor legislation, but the Cherokees have always chosen to remain officially dry, partly because of the Baptist influence and partly from an understanding of alcohol's deleterious effects. As recently as 1980 the Cherokees defeated a proposal for liquor sales by a two-to-one margin. The light turnout perhaps indicated

10. Robert Bushyhead as Elias Boudinot in "Unto These Hills." Courtesy of the
Museum of the Cherokee Indian.

either apathy or a conviction that the measure would fail.[13] In 1986 the tribal
council, under considerable pressure, narrowly voted to kill a proposal for
liquor sales. But a recent poll suggests that changes may not be far off; it
shows a significant number of Cherokees favoring some kind of controlled
sale of liquor on the reservation.[14] Tribal politicians and businessmen are
ever wary in discussing alcohol sales, yet many will privately admit that the

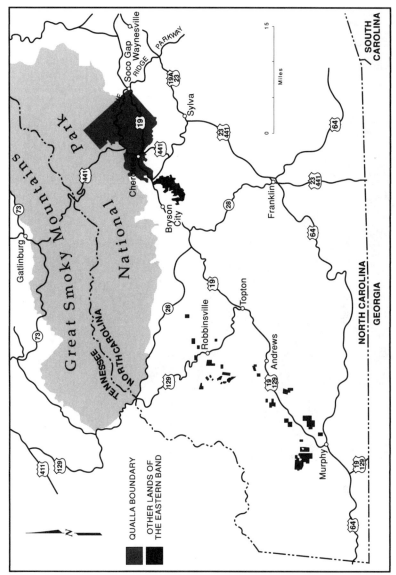

Western North Carolina, 1990

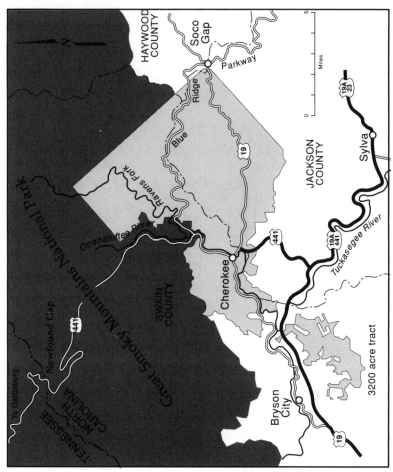

Qualla Boundary and environs, 1990

only effect of the reservation's dry status is to encourage tourists to go else-where. Indians can readily obtain their own liquor in Bryson City and Sylva, and like many reservations Qualla Boundary has a problem with substance abuse. Jeff Muskrat complained in the late 1970s about the ready availability of liquor and hard drugs, even for minors, and by the early 1980s about 140 DUI cases were processed annually in the tribal court.[15]

An investigation of police reports shows that of 220 automobile crashes on the reservation from October 1985 through September 1987, a relatively low thirty-eight were alcohol related (17.3 percent). However, all six fatalities in these accidents resulted from alcohol abuse. The Community Injury

Control Program concluded that alcohol-related automobile crashes and injuries were probably underreported and that they "are a significant problem on the Cherokee Indian reservation."[16] A recent tribal report estimated that three out of four families on the reservation were affected in one way or another by alcohol, and articles on its dangers appear in almost every issue of the *Cherokee One Feather*, the tribal newspaper. Duane King, an anthropologist with extensive experience among the North Carolina and Oklahoma Cherokees and other tribes, believes alcohol abuse is more prevalent among the Eastern Cherokees than those in Oklahoma, but he adds that neither group has as much of a problem as many tribes in the West.[17]

Despite repeated efforts to attract light industry and other sources of permanent employment, success has been limited since the 1960s, and the town of Cherokee remains a sleepy mountain village during the off-season. Unemployment often soars to 30 or 40 percent, with a commensurate increase in general assistance. Jeff Muskrat noted some of the problems:

> In an area that is blessed or cursed (depending on one's point of view) with a seasonal tourism business that booms in the summer months and literally dies in the winter and therefore greatly relies upon Federally funded work programs such as CETA, unemployment insurance, and welfare payments to stabilize the community's economic base, it is extremely difficult to promote and encourage career training motivation that will result in full time employment. The fact of the matter is that "Training" in and of itself has become a major activity on this reservation.[18]

Local politics have also affected employment opportunities. Muskrat said it was an "undeniable fact that tribal politics and preferential treatment and even pettiness with regard to job selection and personnel policies [occur], and the most qualified applicant does not get the job regardless of an individual's education or training."[19] One major problem in attracting industries and other businesses is the peculiar system of landholding that combines individual possessory rights with reservation status. Even with so-called leasehold mortgages backed by the tribal government, lending institutions are skeptical about using Cherokee properties as collateral. Whatever the reasons, the Eastern Band has not been as successful as the Mississippi Choctaws in attracting light industry to the reservation. On the other hand, the Choctaws do not have a solid tourist base like the Cherokees.[20]

One alternative to on-reservation economic development is to invest tribal funds in enterprises elsewhere. In the autumn of 1986 the Eastern

Band decided to pay $28.8 million for the Carolina Mirror Company, one of the world's largest manufacturers of mirrors. Nothing could better illustrate how today's Native Americans have become participants in the modern world of finance. An outside investment banking company assisted the tribe in effecting a leveraged buyout employing "junk" bonds. The tribe used $1.5 million from a bank loan and its own assets, while a New York securities firm sold $32 million in bonds to a group of private investors. Company assets serve as collateral, and the loan will be repaid from future profits.[21]

Located in North Wilkesboro, North Carolina, and Houston, Texas, the mirror company was seen as a money-making venture that would bring benefits to all Eastern Cherokees. An enthusiastic Chief Youngdeer interpreted it as a release from the reservation's constraints: "We've been in jail here for 150 years." After vocal opposition from some tribal members, most Cherokees adopted a wait-and-see attitude toward Carolina Mirror. By late 1989, however, Chief Taylor viewed the company as at best a long-term investment the tribe could not afford and was forcefully advocating its sale.[22]

Meanwhile many Qualla Boundary Cherokees continue to find work in nearby towns like Waynesville and Sylva, while Snowbird Indians work for the National Forest Service, TVA, or the Stanley Furniture Company in Robbinsville. For adventurous individuals interested in more distant opportunities, military service and the construction industry are viable options. But the attractions of home are always strong. Like white southern mountain people, Cherokees have an abiding sense of place and kinship. Examples of successful Indians who have returned to the reservation include former chief Youngdeer, a retired military man and BIA law enforcement officer, and Richard Welch, a navy veteran and former Orlando resident who is chairman of the tribal council and editor of the *Cherokee One Feather*.

Most Cherokees consider education a tribal priority, but results in this area are mixed at best. Virtually all Cherokee children attend school, either on the reservation or in the public systems of Bryson City, Sylva, or Robbinsville. The BIA compensates those systems for each Cherokee student. BIA-operated facilities include an elementary school and the Cherokee Central School, a beautiful modern building accommodating grades seven through twelve. Usually called Cherokee High School, it had 450 students in 1985.[23] Both institutions have up-to-date equipment and dedicated teachers and administrators. Yet some Cherokee parents believe their children will receive a better education in the public schools because of a more competitive academic atmosphere or because of an alleged lack of discipline at

Cherokee schools. Richard Welch, who graduated from Cherokee Central School a generation ago, said he did not realize how poorly educated he was until he joined the navy. And even today too many students do not finish their education. One recent high-school graduate says, "In ninth grade you'll have ninety people in your class and by the time you are a senior, half of them have dropped out." On the other hand, the BIA is clearly proud of Cherokee Central School and nominated it for special recognition by the United States Department of Education. After a visit by a panel of judges, it was selected in 1989 as one of 218 outstanding schools throughout the nation.[24]

Whatever their feelings about BIA institutions versus public schools, Cherokee parents fiercely defend their rights to federally subsidized education. During the mid-1980s a BIA proposal to limit educational benefits to tribal members with an Indian blood quantum of at least one-fourth created a storm of opposition because it would have affected a sizable percentage of the Band.[25] Frederick Bradley, a teacher and former school board member, complained to the BIA that such a change would destroy the local school system and expose Indians with even a low blood quantum to racism in the public schools. In closing he wrote, "FUND THE SCHOOLS AT CHEROKEE FOR CHILDREN AND NOT DEGREE OF BLOOD." Tribal leaders, along with those of other tribes, lobbied successfully in Washington to squelch a one-fourth requirement both for education and for receiving Indian Health Service benefits at the modern Cherokee Hospital, which opened in 1981.[26]

Only a minority of Cherokee high-school graduates continue their education, despite the availability of both federal and tribal funds to assist them. A common attitude is that college is basically irrelevant for someone who intends to remain on the reservation. Most of those going on for education stay nearby, some enrolling at Southwestern Community College in Sylva and others at that school's Cherokee branch. Nearby Western Carolina University probably has more Cherokee students than any other four-year institution (about twenty in 1979), but Eastern Cherokees have also attended many other state universities as well as private institutions like Emory, Harvard, and Brigham Young. Sixty-nine Eastern Cherokees were in college in 1985.[27] That same year William Carson, a New Jersey businessman, established a fund at North Carolina's Guilford College to provide full scholarships for qualified Eastern Cherokees. So far twelve have attended Guilford, but some had difficulty adjusting and dropped out.[28] A few tribal members have earned their Ph.D.s, and recently Frances Owl-Smith became the first female Cherokee—and only the second tribal member—to earn an M.D. (at the University of North Carolina).[29] Persuading such successful students to return to the reservation's limited opportunities is understandably difficult.

Relations with whites in Swain, Jackson, Graham, and Cherokee counties appear to be good, though in recent years Cherokees have charged Swain and Jackson County law-enforcement officers with abusing tribal members. Even when relations are calm there is a certain tension or wariness. For example, some whites resented Chief John A. Crowe's assertion in 1976 that there was no reason for Indians to celebrate the nation's bicentennial.[30] This resentment flared even more because the Band and the Cherokee Historical Association had opened their new $2 million Museum of the Cherokee Indian earlier that year and then received a federal grant of $962,500 to improve the fall festival grounds and other tribal facilities. An application by Swain County for federal assistance for its own community facilities was rejected.[31]

Reacting to this rebuff, Swain County commissioners complained in February 1977 to their congressional delegation that this was evidence of discrimination against the white majority and asked that the grant be revoked. They also said the Band's claim in its grant application of a 44 percent unemployment rate was an "outright myth." Then, in a return to the rhetoric of the termination era, they said, "It is about time the Indians be released from the custody of the Bureau of Indian Affairs and allowed to become full-fledged taxpaying citizens and become a part of the community in which they live."[32] Fortunately this was just a momentary spat, and most white residents recognize the benefits of a Cherokee tribal presence.

It is much more common to find Cherokee pitted against Cherokee, and factionalism remains a fact of life on the reservation. Chief Youngdeer won election in 1983 with only a small plurality in a field of several candidates and defeated his chief rival, councilman Dan McCoy, by a mere seven votes. The two men remained at odds for Youngdeer's entire term, mostly because of McCoy's connection with the bingo games. Youngdeer also alienated some constituents—and councilmembers—by campaigning for a new tribal constitution and by his military, no-nonsense approach to government. His term ended with the council decisively repudiating him for his attacks on Cherokee Bingo. In 1987 he lost his bid for reelection, but in the runoff campaign the two finalists, Jonathan Taylor and Dan McCoy, bitterly attacked one another. Taylor finally won. Even though he has attempted to reconcile competing factions, letters in the *Cherokee One Feather* regularly attack various individuals for favoritism and dirty politics.[33] Such factionalism is not

11. John A. Crowe, principal chief 1975–83. Courtesy of the Museum of the Cherokee Indian.

uncommon in American politics, but it can be particularly virulent on the Cherokee reservation.

Tensions between fuller-bloods and white Indians were especially high in the early 1980s over a proposed tribal constitution. James Cooper, a prominent businessman in Cherokee and a trustee of Western Carolina University, attended a grand council to discuss the matter and expected the

12. Robert S. Youngdeer, principal chief 1983–87. Courtesy of the Museum of the
Cherokee Indian.

new constitution would enable the tribal government to become more busi-
nesslike and progressive. But he was stunned to learn that people he had
known all his life wanted to include a restrictive membership requirement
that would exclude his heirs from the roll.[34] Many Cherokees had the same
fears as Cooper (by 1986 an estimated 62 percent of the tribe had less than
one-half Cherokee blood) or were simply afraid to abandon the 1889 state
charter that governs the Band. In a surprisingly light turnout in October
1984, voters decisively rejected the constitution. Both Chief Youngdeer and

13. Jonathan L. Taylor, principal chief 1987–. Courtesy of the Museum of the Cherokee Indian.

Wilbur Sequoyah, a fuller-blood councilman from Big Cove, favored the constitution but ruefully admitted that white Indians saw it as a threat.[35]

Two years later the power of mixed-bloods was again evident when voters revised the charter in several fundamental ways: first, they over-turned the old requirement that the chief and vice chief have at least one-half Cherokee blood. Now any enrolled member is eligible to run for those offices, a development that permitted the energetic Jonathan Taylor to be elected chief in 1987 after many years on the council. Another change re-

14. The tribal council in session. Courtesy of the Cherokee Historical Association.

flecting the strength of mixed-bloods and white Indians is one allowing the first-generation, nonenrolled descendants of a tribal member to inherit that individual's possessory rights. Thus a person with an insufficient degree of Cherokee blood for enrollment can still enjoy the benefits of his enrolled parent's estate. Feelings over this issue were so strong at one grand council that some participants, reflecting a traditional Cherokee avoidance of unpleasantness, left rather than confront the hostility. Voters finally approved the measure 639 to 397.[36]

Still another indication of the mixed-blood impact in tribal politics is the way Cherokee County (or Tomotla), consisting almost entirely of white Indians, has worked out an informal arrangement with Snowbird whereby each community has one of the two representatives elected from the combined district. This has enabled Tomotla to lobby successfully for increased funding from the tribal government. On the other hand, electoral changes in 1981 should mean progressively less influence for both Snowbird and Tomotla. Because of federal insistence on "one man one vote" representation in state and local elections, the Eastern Band restructured its council representation. The most attractive—and imaginative—approach was to retain its system of two council members from each of six districts, but to give

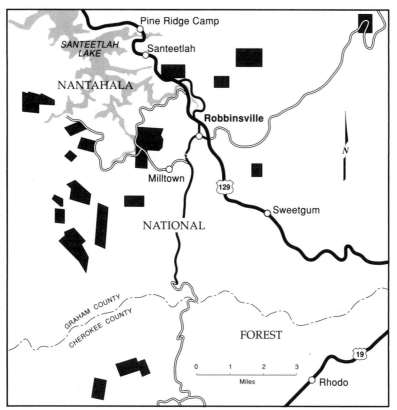

Snowbird community, 1990

representatives from more populous towns more "points." Every ten years a tribal census will determine how a total of one hundred points will be divided among the twelve council members. That spells increasing political clout for the larger towns of Cherokee, Bird Town, and Wolf Town.[37]

Chief Taylor's style as a tribal leader is quite different from that of his predecessor, Robert Youngdeer. With almost continuous service in tribal government dating back to the early 1970s, Taylor is more adept in the art of political compromise than Youngdeer, a former military man. Taylor is quite familiar with the workings of the Washington bureaucracy and of the BIA in particular, making many trips to the capital and appearing to enjoy the give and take of lobbying. In almost every issue of the *Cherokee One Feather* he describes and justifies his recent activities, often including a verbatim transcript of his testimony before a congressional committee. His main objective in office, as he puts it, is "jobs, jobs and jobs."[38] He is clearly

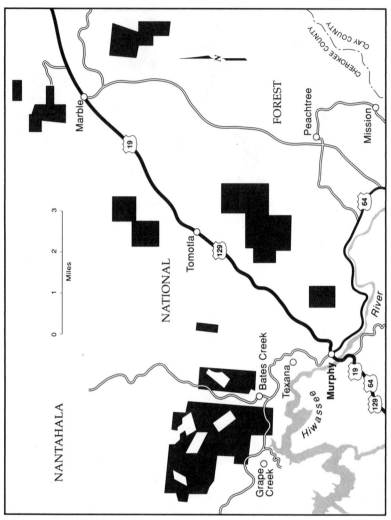

Cherokee (Tomotla) community, 1990

the dominant figure in tribal government, while current agent Wilbur Paul assumes a supporting role as the BIA's representative.

Chief Taylor seeks more federal funding and economic development for the Band and has strongly resisted proposed legislation to designate most of the Great Smoky Mountains National Park a wilderness. Despite reassurances from wilderness advocates, Taylor believes such a designation would impede Cherokee economic development and eventually lead to closing of

U.S. 441, the only highway across the park.[39] His approach to politics, then, is just as canny and issue oriented as that of a veteran member of Congress. This kind of expertise has been especially important with cutbacks in federal funding for Indians during President Reagan's two administrations. On the eve of his retirement as agent in 1985, Jeff Muskrat estimated that his budget had been reduced by about 25 percent since his appointment in 1974. Of particular concern has been the lack of adequate funding for Indian Health Services.[40] This austerity in appropriations for Native Americans seems likely to continue during the presidency of George Bush.

Women also have prominent roles in Eastern Cherokee politics, though there has been no counterpart to Wilma Mankiller, who was elected chief of the Cherokee Nation in Oklahoma. Mollie Blankenship, daughter of the redoubtable Lula Gloyne, was the first woman elected to the council (in 1947), and for many years she was an indispensable employee of the BIA. She remains active in a variety of tribal and regional projects and is frequently honored. Bertha Saunooke, the widow of former chief Osley Saunooke, has been a council member since 1969, the longest uninterrupted service of any Eastern Cherokee. Likewise, Glenda Sanders has often represented her Tomotla constituents in the council (and incurred the enmity of some traditionalists). This is hardly tokenism, for in September 1989 female candidates won six of the twelve council seats.[41]

Probably the most famous Eastern Cherokee woman is Maggie Wachacha, a traditionalist from Snowbird who for many years was council scribe and translated proceedings into the Cherokee syllabary. In 1984 the joint councils of the Eastern Band and Cherokee Nation designated her a "Beloved Woman" of the Cherokees, and in 1985, along with ninety-six-year-old Lula Gloyne, she was one of forty-one nominees for the Distinguished Women of North Carolina award. Nominated again the following year, the ninety-two-year-old Wachacha was one of five women to receive the award from Governor James G. Martin.[42]

* * *

By the late 1970s the old questions surrounding the Band's legal status had largely been answered. Several court decisions had systematically repudiated the contentions of the late Fred Bauer and generations of state officials by holding that the Eastern Band is indeed a tribe, that it occupies a reservation that, whatever its origins, is similar to other Indian reservations, and that federal authority is preeminent and virtually identical to that exercised over other federally recognized tribes. North Carolina's attempts to require

15. Lula Owl Gloyne, 1955. Courtesy of the Cherokee Historical Association.

Indians to pay taxes on reservation properties and income have been defeated, and it appears the state will even have to reimburse the tribe for state gasoline taxes. The United States has sole jurisdiction over the ten major crimes, and since 1980 the tribe has operated its own Court of Indian Offenses to handle misdemeanors and minor civil actions involving Cherokees. With North Carolina's recent conferral of state police authority on Chero-

16. Maggie Wachacha. Courtesy of *Cherokee One Feather*.

kee deputies, the tribal police now have the right to arrest whites and other non-Indians suspected of committing crimes on the reservation.[43]

In recent years North Carolina has become more solicitous about the welfare of its Indian citizens. With six tribes and more than 65,000 self-proclaimed Indians, it has the largest Native American population of any state east of the Mississippi. In 1971 it established the North Carolina Commission of Indian Affairs to promote Indian history, culture, and welfare, and in 1981, after considerable goading by the Cherokees, it created a task force specifically to review state relations with the Band. North Carolina also designated 1986 the Year of the Native American.[44]

During the past decade or so the Eastern Cherokees' awareness of other Indians has sharpened, especially regarding their fellow Cherokees in Oklahoma. On the weekend of April 6–7, 1984, representatives of the Eastern Band met with those of the Cherokee Nation at the Red Clay council grounds near Cleveland, Tennessee, the site of the last full-scale Cherokee council before most of the tribe embarked on the Trail of Tears. Relays of runners celebrated the event by carrying the tribe's eternal flame over the mountains to Red Clay from Cherokee. An estimated 1,000 Eastern Cherokees and 500 Western Cherokees attended, as well as many more whites, and total attendance for the two days was about 35,000. National newspapers and television networks covered the events, and President Reagan even sent a personal message (which unfortunately offended some Indians by calling the gathering a "powwow"). It marked the first time since removal that Western and Eastern Cherokees had officially met to affirm their brotherhood. A joint council of the two tribes passed a series of resolutions, including a demand for the return of skeletal remains exhumed from archaeological sites.[45] Although the symbolism of the Red Clay meeting was foremost, business was not forgotten. Sid Grant, an Eastern Cherokee "chief," set up shop selling traditional Indian fry bread. "What's this mean to me?" he responded when asked about the occasion. "Money. A chance to make some money."[46]

The Oklahoma Cherokees (consisting of the Nation and smaller groups) still have no formal relationship with the Eastern Band, but the Band and the Nation alternate special council sessions once a year at Cherokee and Tahlequah, Oklahoma, the Nation's capital. This sense of shared heritage was enhanced during 1988–89 as Cherokees all over America observed the sesquicentennial of the Trail of Tears in a variety of official and unofficial ways. This brotherhood continues more informally with the annual Trail of Tears sings hosted by the Snowbird Indians, events that draw Oklahoma Cherokees as well as hundreds of whites from western North Carolina. As a result of these gatherings and countless individual contacts in recent years, many Western and Eastern Cherokees have formed close friendships and in some cases reestablished family ties. Western Cherokee traditionalists like Crosslin Smith have visited Qualla Boundary and discussed tribal lore and possible revival of traditionalist societies.[47]

Both former chief Youngdeer and current chief Taylor have been involved in national pan-Indian organizations. Taylor, especially, has been active for years in such groups as the National Congress of American Indians, the National Tribal Chairman's Council, and the United South and Eastern Tribes, and he has frequently served as an officer.[48] He is less enthusiastic, however, about socializing with the numerous Lumbees of eastern North Carolina. In the eyes of many Cherokees the Lumbees are not "real" Indians at all and, worse, even dared at one time to call themselves Cherokees. The state has recognized the Lumbees as a tribe, but Congress, while acknowledging them as Indians, has noted their confused historical and genealogical past and specifically denied them valuable services available to federally recognized tribes. Despite Lumbee pressures, Taylor and other Cherokees are not about to help them obtain these services, reasoning that the available federal pie is not going to get any larger and that recognition of the Lumbees would simply diminish the slice the Cherokees and other "true" Indians receive. They usually phrase their opposition more diplomatically, saying they believe the Lumbees have not followed federal guidelines for obtaining recognition. It can be a bit awkward, because some whites in North Carolina fail to understand the legitimate basis of Cherokee concern and view them as obstructionists or even as traitors to their own race.[49]

* * *

The issue of Lumbee recognition raises the obvious question of how today's Eastern Cherokees view themselves. What is their identity? What are their aspirations? There are no ready answers except to restate what should be apparent: the Cherokees vary widely in these respects. They are certainly distinct from their white neighbors in having a well-defined reservation and a language that, though fading, is still used by older Indians. They have traditions and attachments to the mountains that predate those of whites and a history that emphasizes their distinctiveness. Likewise, they also differ from the Oklahoma Cherokees. According to Jeff Muskrat, a Western Cherokee and former agent, the reservation is critical in explaining why, in his eyes, the Eastern Cherokees are "more Indian" than their western counterparts. Reservation life forces the Eastern Cherokees to confront their Indianness every day, whereas the Nation's reservation in Oklahoma was long ago allotted.[50] The many off-reservation Eastern Cherokees typically retain family connections there and often return for visits.

Unlike Muskrat, anthropologist Duane King sees more similarities than differences between Eastern and Western Cherokees, especially among conservatives who retain certain traits like generosity, being good neighbors, and passivity in the presence of whites. He concedes, however, that the Eastern Cherokees retain more of their myths, legends, and traditional dances (albeit in modified form), and their version of the ballplay is probably closer to the original Cherokee game. According to King the Western Cherokees, now numbering some 100,000, have many more Cherokee speakers, but he estimates there are at least 1,000 among the Band who still speak the language.[51] And yet, despite the eagerness of many adults to take instruction in Cherokee and a brief, compulsory introduction to it in Cherokee schools, the language is rapidly disappearing on the reservation as anything more than a curiosity. A Big Cove woman who grew up with Cherokee as her first language laments its decline in the past generation. Despite her own fluency and dedication to the language's preservation, her son is not interested in learning it. Equally pessimistic is Snowbird's Lois Calonehuskie, a translator for elderly Cherokee speakers interviewed in an oral history project appropriately called "Fading Voices." She is fatalistic about the lack of Cherokee speakers younger than thirty, conceding that Indian children need to concentrate on English in order to advance.[52] Ironically, many of the most eager students in Cherokee language classes on and off the reservation are non-Indians.

Among the large majority of Eastern Cherokees who do not speak the language, there are great differences in how they perceive themselves and their objectives. Some wish to pick up the standard of the late Fred Bauer and swear allegiance to Americanism, individualism, and complete assimilation. Former chief Youngdeer on occasion has argued that viewpoint quite forthrightly. In a 1985 commencement address at Southwestern Technical College, he said: "The Cherokees in western North Carolina have been reservation Indians for at least 115 years. Isn't that a long time to be someone different? At one time we weren't accepted, but now through education and schools like Southwestern Tech and dedicated educators, we, like you, have accepted the challenge to excel and blend into the whole of American society."[53] More recently he remarked, "We hate to lose them, but the old ways don't put bread on the table."[54] Others on the reservation—especially those with extensive experience in the outside world—agree with such sentiments.

Others, however, are simply confused, uncertain about their identity. This seems especially true of the children. All are aware of their Indian status (even if uninformed about their history and culture), yet all are daily confronted with the reality of a larger world outside the reservation, a world both alluring and intimidating.[55] For many it seems safer to remain on the reservation than to face possible failure in the outside world.

Whatever their uncertainties, most Cherokees apparently believe it is possible to be both modern Americans and Indians. They wish to retain the tribal identity and land base while developing more and more self-sufficiency. At present they contract most of their services with the BIA and have taken a strong—even forceful—role in the operation of their school system. Indeed, in 1987 the school board characterized a BIA financial plan as "inadequate, not in the best interests of the students or community, and [the board] exercises its statutory authority by rejecting the Plan."[56] And yet it would be naive to suggest the Indians do not value the comforting safety net of federal assistance available to recognized tribes. After all, why should Cherokees eschew something the Lumbees and other nonrecognized groups prize so highly? What has emerged on the reservation is a blend of self-reliance and dependency not unlike that found on other reservations. The Cherokees, because of their tourist industry, may be wealthier and further along the road to self-sufficiency than most tribes, but they still have a long way to go.[57] In the meantime Cherokee leaders will fight every step of the way to retain federal benefits. Nothing attests to this more conclusively than their use of a lobbyist in Washington and the many trips there by Chief Taylor, the tribal attorney, and members of the council.

What this suggests is that an important part of Cherokee self-identity is legal and contractual in nature. Eastern Cherokees see themselves as a distinct group entitled to certain privileges and funds from the federal government. They have a legal standing different from that of most other Americans and occupy a well-defined reservation protected by the United States. Such an attitude is common to federally recognized tribes and has always distinguished Indians from other minorities in the United States, explaining why they have been careful to separate their cause from that of American blacks. This even extends to one tribe's relations with another. The Eastern Cherokees, for example, while recognizing a common heritage with Oklahoma Cherokees, nevertheless emphasize their own identity as a unique tribe with distinct interests and rights shaped by law and historical experience.

This legalistic concept of Cherokee identity is heightened among the Eastern Band by the related issues of enrollment and Indian blood quantum. Unlike their ancestors who favored an inclusive membership extending in some cases to outsiders, today's Eastern Cherokees carefully guard their prerogatives by adhering to a membership defined by a specified degree of

Indian blood. Many who are enrolled are attacked by others as white Indians whose ancestors bought their tribal affiliation. Amid such hostility, lesser-bloods are seeking to preserve the fruits of their economic investments for their children. The recent charter amendment allowing certain privileges to first-generation nonenrolled heirs resembles the adoption of the Half-way Covenant among seventeenth-century Puritans, a desperate attempt to secure the benefits—if not the status—of membership for those otherwise unqualified. With such adjustments, lesser-bloods may well maintain at least a quasi-Indian identity for another generation or so.

Also powerfully influencing today's Cherokee identity is the tourist industry and its curious attendant dichotomy: on the one hand, it has made the Eastern Cherokees a people who appreciate the increased opportunities of modern America; on the other hand, it has also made them aware of their Cherokee identity and the necessity of maintaining it—at least to the extent of keeping tourism alive. Not surprisingly, tourism on Qualla Boundary promotes an ersatz Indian image in order to appeal to the gullibility of visitors whose only exposure to "Indians" is in novels or Hollywood westerns. Thus the gift shops feature toy tomahawks made in Taiwan, craft items of dubious authenticity, and "chiefs" wearing gaudy regalia resembling that of the Plains tribes. Clearly, the entrepreneurial ethic is firmly enough entrenched among many Cherokees to give customers what they want.

This identification of the tourist business with a nonspecific, generic "Indian" conforming to white stereotypes is common on the reservation, and most Cherokees seem to accept it as a necessary cost of doing business. Anthropologists and historians might wince at the spectacle, and celebrated German film director Werner Herzog might use Cherokee as a metaphor for American vacuity and pretense by having his protagonist in *Stroszek* kill himself there. Yet one should remember that tourism also sustains worthwhile attractions like the Museum of the Cherokee Indian, Oconaluftee Indian Village, and the Qualla Arts and Crafts Cooperative. Thus it entails certain trade-offs; the tacky merchandise exists in symbiotic embrace with more worthy attractions offering visitors—and the Cherokees themselves—an informed insight into the tribe. More important, tourism puts food on the table. Fortunately most Cherokees seem to understand the difference between the stereotypical image they project and the Cherokee identity they claim.

Inevitably, the economic impact of tourism has also sown seeds of discord among the Eastern Band. The unique system of landholding has resulted in gross disparities in property holdings and wealth as more sophisticated, educated, and acculturated individuals acquire the choicest tourist properties. If downtown commercial property in Cherokee could ever be sold on the open market, it would likely bring $25,000 an acre.[58] These inequities have led some fuller-bloods to proclaim themselves the only "true" Cherokees and to attack lesser-bloods vehemently, as if a higher proportion of Cherokee ancestry will somehow offset their opponents' wealth. It is a curious form of discrimination, reflecting economic disparities more than cultural or genetic differences.

In short, the Eastern Band's identity varies considerably, depending on the groups or individuals involved. The benefits derived from the federal attachment and especially tourism will probably sustain at least a generalized Cherokee identity for the immediate future. But the larger reality is that virtually all tribal members—from the entrepreneurs along U.S. 441 and 19, to the conservatives of Big Cove and Snowbird, to the white Indians of Tomotla, to those living out of state—understand that their Indian identity is subsumed within a national context. The twentieth century has brought a sometimes painful rapprochement between them and the American government. They value their citizenship and the opportunities of modern America. Like their white neighbors, they shamelessly lobby their congressmen and senators, vote according to self-interest, and accept the many federal benefits. In return they offer allegiance and present themselves as modern-day warriors ready to defend—and perhaps die for—America's institutions. They have endured the changing currents of Indian policy, adjusted as necessary, argued among themselves, survived, and in the end called themselves both Cherokees and Americans.

ABBREVIATIONS

BIA   Bureau of Indian Affairs

CA   Cherokee Agency, Correspondence, Record Group 75, Federal Records Center, East Point, Ga.

CACF   Cherokee Agency, Chronological File, Cherokee, N.C.

CIA   Commissioner of Indian Affairs

FRCS   Federal Records Center, Suitland, Md. Record Group 75, Cherokee Agency

M-685   Microcopy M-685, Records Relating to Enrollment of Eastern Cherokees by Guion Miller, 1908–10, National Archives

M-1059   Microcopy 1059, Selected Letters Received by the Office of Indian Affairs Relating to the Cherokees of North Carolina, 1851–1905, National Archives

NA   National Archives, Washington, D.C.

NCDAH   North Carolina Division of Archives and History, Raleigh, N.C.

OIA   Office of Indian Affairs

RG   Record Group

SHC   Southern Historical Collection, University of North Carolina, Chapel Hill, N.C.

SI   Secretary of the Interior

T-623   Microfilm T-623, Population Schedules of the Twelfth United States Census, 1900, National Archives

WCU   Western Carolina University, Cullowhee, N.C.

Notes

PREFACE

1. Frank W. Porter III, ed., *Strategies for Survival: American Indians in the Eastern United States* (Westport, Conn.: Greenwood Press, 1986). In 1956 Congress extended a limited recognition to the Lumbees but specifically denied them services available to federally recognized tribes. Cherokee opposition to Lumbee efforts to receive these services is discussed in chapter 9 of this work.

2. Mooney, *Myths of the Cherokee*, Nineteenth Annual Report of the Bureau of American Ethnology, part 1 (Washington, D.C.: Government Printing Office, 1900).

3. Helen C. Rountree, "The Indians of Virginia: A Third Race in a Biracial State," in *Southeastern Indians since the Removal Era*, ed. Walter L. Williams (Athens: University of Georgia Press, 1979), 27–48. Harry A. Kersey, Jr., "Those Left Behind: The Seminole Indians of Florida," in ibid., 174–90; Kersey, "Florida Seminoles in the Depression and the New Deal, 1933–1942: An Indian Perspective," *Florida Historical Quarterly* 65 (Oct. 1986): 175–95; Kersey, *The Florida Seminoles and the New Deal, 1933–1942* (Boca Raton: Florida Atlantic University Press, 1989); W. McKee Evans, "The North Carolina Lumbees: From Assimilation to Revitalization," in Williams, *Southeastern Indians since the Removal Era*, 49–71; Adolph Dial and David K. Eliades, *The Only Land I Know: A History of the Lumbee Indians* (San Francisco: Indian Historian Press, 1975); Karen I. Blu, *The Lumbee Problem: The Making of an American Indian People* (New York: Cambridge University Press, 1980); Ronald N. Satz, "The Mississippi Choctaw: From the Removal Treaty to the Federal Agency," in *After Removal: The Choctaw in Mississippi*, ed. Samuel J. Wells and Roseanna Tubby (Jackson: University of Mississippi Press, 1986), 3–32; Kendall Blanchard, *The Mississippi Choctaws*

at Play: The Serious Side of Leisure (Urbana: University of Illinois Press, 1981); John H. Peterson, Jr., "Three Efforts at Development among the Choctaws of Mississippi," in Williams, *Southeastern Indians since the Removal Era*, 142–53; J. Anthony Paredes, "Back from Disappearance: The Alabama Creek Indian Community," in ibid., 123–41; Ernest C. Downs, "The Struggle of the Louisiana Tunica Indians for Recognition," in ibid., 72–89; Max E. Stanton, "Southern Louisiana Survivors: The Houma Indians," in ibid., 90–109; Fred B. Kniffen, Hiram F. Gregory, and George A. Stokes, *The Historic Indian Tribes of Louisiana: From 1542 to the Present* (Baton Rouge: Louisiana State University Press, 1987); Charles M. Hudson, "The Catawba Indians of South Carolina: A Question of Ethnic Survival," in Williams, *Southeastern Indians since the Removal Era*, 110–20; Charles M. Hudson, *The Catawba Nation* (Athens: University of Georgia Press, 1970); Charles M. Hudson, *The Southeastern Indians* (Knoxville: University of Tennessee Press, 1976).

CHAPTER 1

1. Twelfth U.S. Census, 1900, Population, vol. 1, part 1 (Washington, D.C.: Government Printing Office, 1900), 466.

2. The early history of the Eastern Band is discussed in John R. Finger, *The Eastern Band of Cherokees, 1819–1900* (Knoxville: University of Tennessee Press, 1984). Population figures for Indians (Cherokees) in Swain, Jackson, Cherokee, and Graham counties are in Twelfth U.S. Census, 550.

3. Twelfth U.S. Census, 466; North Carolina Corporation Commission, Railroad Map prepared by H. C. Brown (Raleigh: Rand, McNally, 1900).

4. Henry Spray to CIA, March 28, April 21, 1900, CA.

5. Twelfth U.S. Census, 466; North Carolina Corporation Commission, railroad map; Twelfth U.S. Census, 1900, Population, Microfilm T-623, Roll 1196; James Mooney and Frans M. Olbrechts, *The Swimmer Manuscript: Cherokee Sacred Formulas and Medicinal Prescriptions*, Bureau of American Ethnology Bulletin 99 (Washington, D.C.: Government Printing Office, 1932), 10.

6. Twelfth U.S. Census, 466; North Carolina Corporation Commission, railroad map; the prevalence of these mixed-bloods is apparent in M-685, "Records Relating to Enrollment of Eastern Cherokees by Guion Miller, 1908–1910."

7. Information on Cherokee households is in T-623, Rolls 1188, 1196, 1201, and 1218. Fuller discussion of community life is in chapter 4. As late as the 1930s, there was apparently a significant clan identification among the Eastern Cherokees. William H. Gilbert, Jr., *The Eastern Cherokees* (Washington, D.C.: Government Printing Office, 1943), 201, 203–7.

8. Excellent accounts of these changes include Grace Steele Woodward, *The Cherokees* (Norman: University of Oklahoma Press, 1963); Henry Thompson Malone, *Cherokees of the Old South: A People in Transition* (Athens: University of Georgia Press, 1956); Charles Hudson, *The Southeastern Indians* (Knoxville: University of Tennessee Press, 1976); Theda Perdue, *Slavery and the Evolution of Cherokee*

Society, 1540–1866 (Knoxville: University of Tennessee Press, 1979); and two books by William G. McLoughlin: *Cherokees and Missionaries, 1789–1839* (New Haven: Yale University Press, 1984), and *Cherokee Renascence in the New Republic* (Princeton: Princeton University Press, 1986). See also Ronald D. Eller, *Miners, Millhands, and Mountaineers: Industrialization of the Appalachian South, 1880–1930* (Knoxville: University of Tennessee Press, 1982).

9. The most comprehensive compilation of these myths and legends is James Mooney, *Myths of the Cherokee*, Nineteenth Annual Report of the Bureau of American Ethnology, part 1 (Washington, D.C.: Government Printing Office, 1900).

10. Twelfth U.S. Census, 32, 514–15, 550–51.

11. M-685, "Records Relating to Enrollment of Eastern Cherokees by Guion Miller, 1908–1910."

12. CIA *Annual Report*, 1900, 56 Cong., 2 sess., *House Doc.* 5, Serial 4101 (Washington, D.C.: Government Printing Office, 1900), 666; CIA *Annual Report*, 1901, 57 Cong., 1 sess., *House Doc.* 5, Serial 4290 (Washington, D.C.: Government Printing Office, 1902), 716; Henry Spray to CIA, Dec. 9, 1901, CA; report by Lincoln Crowell, Deputy Supervisor of Forests, April 1916, in report of William Heritage, Regional Forester, April 1946, RG 75, 61A-182, Box 123B, File 24316, NA. The 1835 figures are in William G. McLoughlin and Walter H. Conser, Jr., "The Cherokees in Transition: A Statistical Analysis of the Federal Cherokee Census of 1835," *Journal of American History* 64(Dec. 1977): 678–703.

13. CIA *Annual Report*, 1898, 55 Cong., 3 sess., *House Doc.* 5, Serial 3557 (Washington, D.C.: Government Printing Office, n.d.), 218–19; CIA *Annual Report*, 1900, *House Doc.* 5, Serial 4101, 306–7; CIA *Annual Report*, 1901, *House Doc.* 5, Serial 4290, 716–17; CIA *Annual Report*, 1902, 57 Cong., 2 sess., *House Doc.* 5, Serial 4458 (Washington, D.C.: Government Printing Office, 1903), 260–61.

14. See sources in note 13.

15. Henry Spray to CIA, March 28, April 21, May 31, Sept. 1, 1900; Jan. 31, 1901, CA; T-623, Roll 1218 (for list of pupils and school staff).

16. Finger, *Eastern Band of Cherokees*, 138–39, 149–52, 156–62, 174.

17. *Private Laws of the State of North Carolina*, session of 1897 (Winston, N.C.: M. I. and J. C. Stewart, 1897), chap. 207, secs. 1–2. Smith's career is discussed in Finger, *Eastern Band of Cherokees*, chaps. 7–8.

18. Finger, *Eastern Band of Cherokees*, chaps. 6–8; George E. Frizzell, "The Politics of Cherokee Citizenship, 1898–1930," *North Carolina Historical Review* 61(April 1984): 205–30; George E. Frizzell, "The Legal Status of the Eastern Band of Cherokee Indians" (M.A. thesis, Western Carolina University, 1981), 84–123. Major cases relating to the Band's status are discussed in Ben Oshel Bridgers, "An Historical Analysis of the Legal Status of the North Carolina Cherokees," *North Carolina Law Review* 58(Aug. 1980): 1075–1131.

19. Finger, *Eastern Band of Cherokees*, chap. 8.

20. There was frequent commentary on the Eastern Cherokees' unusual land tenure. See, for example, CIA *Annual Report*, 1902, *House Doc.* 5, Serial 4458, 261.

21. Francis Paul Prucha, *The Great Father: The United States Government and the American Indian*, 2 vols. (Lincoln: University of Nebraska Press, 1984), vol. 2, chap. 26, for discussion of the Dawes Act. The allotment controversy as it applied to the Eastern Band is discussed in chapter 3 of the present work.

22. Finger, *Eastern Band of Cherokees*, chaps. 7–8; Eller, *Miners, Millhands, and Mountaineers*, 86–112; Report of Lincoln Crowell, April 1916, in report of William Heritage, Regional Forester, April 1946, RG 75, 61A-182, Box 123B, File 24316, NA; CIA *Annual Report*, 1901, *House Doc.* 5, Serial 4290, 294.

23. Finger, *Eastern Band of Cherokees*, chap. 8.

24. These tensions and changes are discussed more fully in chapter 2.

25. Locations and information on acculturation are in T-623, Rolls 1188, 1196, 1201, 1218; and M-635, "Records Relating to Enrollment of Eastern Cherokees by Guion Miller, 1908–1910." Cherokee travel on the reservation and its environs is described in Joan Greene, ed., "The Story of My Life as Far Back as I Can Remember," *Journal of Cherokee Studies* 9(Fall 1984): 89–99; G. M. Edwards to Hiram Wilburn, Oct. 8, 1935, Wilburn Papers, WCU, and "Maggie Wachacha: The Cherokees Venerate Their Beloved Women," *Winston-Salem Journal*, Aug. 24, 1986.

26. T-623, Roll 1196, Graham County.

27. T-623, Roll 1188, Cherokee County.

28. T-623, Roll 1201, Jackson County; Finger, *Eastern Band of Cherokees*, 153, 156–62. Blythe's and Bauer's political careers are discussed in chapters 5–7.

29. T-623, Roll 1218, Swain County.

30. Ibid. My division of Oconalufty Township into distinct communities is based on known locations of certain individuals and institutions. Information on the Bradleys and Swayneys is given in Robert K. Thomas, "Eastern Cherokee Acculturation," May 1958, unpublished paper for the Cross-Cultural Laboratory of the Institute for Research in Social Sciences, University of North Carolina, Chapel Hill, 15–17.

31. T-623, Rolls 1188, 1196, 1201, 1218; CIA *Annual Report*, 1901, *House Doc.* 5, Serial 4290, 696; Henry Spray to CIA, Nov. 23, 1901, CA. See also information on English literacy in chapters 2 and 4.

32. T-623, Rolls 1188, 1196, 1201, 1218.

33. Finger, *Eastern Band of Cherokees*, chaps. 7–8. For a survey of education on the Cherokee reservation see Joan Greene, "Federal Policies in the Schools of the Eastern Cherokees, 1892–1932" (M.A. thesis, Western Carolina University, 1986).

34. CIA *Annual Report*, 1900, *House Doc.* 5, Serial 4101, 307; CIA *Annual Report*, 1902, *House Doc.* 5, Serial 4458, 261; Henry Spray to CIA, May 8, 1901; Spray to Estelle Reel, July 29, 1902, CA. The persistence of the ballplay throughout the

nineteenth century suggests that the competition was part of a large and well-integrated culture pattern for the Eastern Cherokees. See Raymond D. Fogelson, "The Cherokee Ball Game: A Study in Southeastern Ethnology" (Ph.D. diss., University of Pennsylvania, 1962), 49. See also James Mooney, "The Cherokee Ball Play," *American Anthropologist,* old series, 3(1890): 105–32. Cultural continuity and change are discussed in chapter 4.

35. Catherine L. Albanese, "Exploring Regional Religion: A Case Study of the Eastern Cherokee," *History of Religions* 23(May 1984): 358. See also Raymond D. Fogelson, "A Study of the Conjuror in Eastern Cherokee Society" (M.A. thesis, University of Pennsylvania, 1958), 65–66, 68, 112, and Mooney and Olbrechts, *Swimmer Manuscript,* 135.

36. A good example is Horace Kephart, *Our Southern Highlanders* (New York: Outing, 1913; reprinted Knoxville: University of Tennessee Press, 1976); also John C. Campbell, *The Southern Highlander and His Homeland* (New York: Russell Sage Foundation, 1921). A more sophisticated—and revealing—analysis of one community of these people is Durwood Dunn, *Cades Cove: The Life and Death of a Southern Appalachian Community, 1818–1937* (Knoxville: University of Tennessee Press, 1988). See also Rodger Cunningham, *Apples on the Flood: The Southern Mountain Experience* (Knoxville: University of Tennessee Press, 1987).

37. Examples are CIA *Annual Report,* 1904, 58 Cong., 3 sess., *House Doc.* 5, Serial 4798 (Washington, D.C.: Government Printing Office, 1905), 266, and James E. Henderson to Roger Mumblehead, Dec. 22, 1915, Box 16, CA.

38. Hans Kohn stresses similar components in the evolution of nationalism. See *The Idea of Nationalism: A Study in Its Origins and Backgrounds* (New York: Macmillan, 1944), introduction. Likewise, Fredrik Barth emphasizes self-definition and other ascriptive values in defining ethnic groups. See Fredrik Barth, ed., *Ethnic Groups and Boundaries: The Social Organization of Culture Difference* (Boston: Little, Brown, 1969), introduction.

39. The work of Mooney's successors among the Cherokees is discussed in chapter 4.

40. Mooney, *Myths of the Cherokee,* 236–37 (quotation on 237).

41. *Ethnic Groups and Boundaries,* introduction. Karen I. Blu makes the same point in regard to the Lumbee Indians of eastern North Carolina. See *The Lumbee Problem: The Making of an American Indian People* (New York: Cambridge University Press, 1980), 4–5.

CHAPTER 2

1. The best analysis of these regional changes is Ronald D. Eller, *Miners, Millhands, and Mountaineers: Industrialization of the Appalachian South, 1880–1930* (Knoxville: University of Tennessee Press, 1982).

2. C. F. Nesler to SI, Aug. 3, 1904, M-1059, 7:793. An overview of lumbering in the area is Robert S. Lambert, "Logging the Great Smokies, 1880–1930," *Tennessee Historical Quarterly* 21(Dec. 1961): 350–63.

3. *Private Laws of the State of North Carolina,* session of 1895 (Winston, N.C.:

M. I. and J. C. Stewart, 1895), chap. 166, secs. 23–24; *Private Laws of the State of North Carolina*, session of 1897 (Winston, N.C.: M. I. and J. C. Stewart, 1897), chap. 207, secs. 22–23, 25; John R. Finger, *The Eastern Band of Cherokees, 1819–1900* (Knoxville: University of Tennessee Press, 1984), chap. 8.

4. J. S. Holmes to CIA, Sept. 11, 1900, M-1059, 7:218–19. For Indian disappointment with the tribal council, see Climbing Bear to CIA, Aug. 7, 1900, M-1059, 7:171–74.

5. E. A. Hitchcock to CIA, Oct. 4, 1900, M-1059, 7:190–92.

6. DeWitt Harris to CIA, Oct. 4, 1906; Harris to Gryson and Black, Nov. 20, 1906, CA. The purchasers were Wirt C. Ward and Elihu Hutton of Huttonsville, West Virginia.

7. Examples include Henry Spray to W. T. Mason Lumber Co., July 26, 1901; Spray to CIA, April 27, 1903; DeWitt Harris to CIA, May 28, 1907, Oct. 16, 1908, CA. Many aspects of the lumber business, including the matter of compliance, are in C. F. Nesler to CIA, Aug. 3, 1904, M-1059, 7:793–803.

8. CIA *Annual Report*, 1901, 57 Cong., 1 sess., *House Doc.* 5, Serial 4290 (Washington, D.C.: Government Printing Office, 1902), 294 (quotation). Examples include Henry Spray to Mrs. C. Y. Dunlap, May 1, 1902, CA; David Murphy and Mary Dunlap to CIA, May 5, 1902, M-1059, 7:File 571; DeWitt Harris to CIA, April 3, 1908; Frank Kyselka to CIA, Oct. 10, 1911, CA.

9. Examples of desire to sell outlying tracts are Henry Spray to CIA, April 5, 1900; DeWitt Harris to CIA, Feb. 27, Oct. 7, 1905, CA; Finger, *Eastern Band of Cherokees*, 147–49.

10. Sharlotte Neely Williams, "The Role of Formal Education among the Eastern Cherokee Indians, 1880–1971" (M.A. thesis, University of North Carolina, Chapel Hill, 1971), 28–30; George E. Frizzell, "The Legal Status of the Eastern Band of Cherokee Indians" (M.A. thesis, Western Carolina University, 1981), 65; CIA *Annual Report*, 1904, 58 Cong., 3 sess., *House Doc.* 5, Serial 4798 (Washington, D.C.: Government Printing Office, 1905), 265. Harris transferred to Cherokee from Pipestone reservation in Minnesota.

11. CIA *Annual Report*, 1904, *House Doc.* 5, Serial 4798, 265–66; DeWitt Harris to CIA, Jan. 25 (quotation), Feb. 4, 1905; Dec. 24, 1907, CA.

12. CIA *Annual Report*, 1901, *House Doc.* 5, Serial 4290, 716; Spray to CIA, Dec. 9, 1901, CA.

13. CIA *Annual Report*, 1904, *House Doc.* 5, Serial 4798, 625; Henry Spray to CIA, July 16, 1900; Spray to N. Downs, Sept. 24, 1902; Spray to Henry Hodges, Feb. 20, 1903; DeWitt Harris to CIA, Feb. 13, May 15, 1907; Frank Kyselka to CIA, July 24, 1912; James Henderson to CIA, Dec. 1, 1913, CA.

14. Horace Kephart, *Our Southern Highlanders* (New York: Macmillan, 1929), 38–39; CIA *Annual Report*, 1901, *House Doc.* 5, Serial 4290, 294; CIA *Annual Report*, 1902, 57 Cong., 2 sess., *House Doc.* 5, Serial 4458 (Washington, D.C.: Govern-

ment Printing Office, 1903), 260; James Henderson to CIA, July 2, 1915, Box 14; O. H. Lipps to CIA, Dec. 16, 1915, Box 8, CA.

15. CIA *Annual Report*, 1904, *House Doc.* 5, Serial 4798, 266; Board of Survey to CIA, Dec. 27, 1901; [?] to CIA, Nov. 20, 1906; Frank Kyselka to CIA, May 11, 1909, CA; John Parris interview of Arsene Thompson, "The Scars Have Healed," *Asheville Citizen*, Dec. 3, 1959.

16. Henry Spray to CIA, March 28, April 21, 1900; Spray to G. R. Loyal, May 31, 1900, CA. John Parris interview of Arsene Thompson, "The Scars Have Healed," *Asheville Citizen*, Dec. 3, 1959.

17. Kyselka to CIA, Jan. 23, May 11, 1909; Jan. 17, April 23, Dec. 6 (quotation), Dec. 19, 1910, CA.

18. James Henderson to CIA, Feb. 8, 1917, Box 8, CA.

19. R. L. Spalsbury to CIA, Oct. 24, 1933, Box 8; Harold W. Foght to CIA, Nov. 2, 1934, Box 9, CA.

20. Author's interview with Lois Farthing, April 24, 1985; Kephart, *Our Southern Highlanders*, 138, 231–33; James Henderson to CIA, Aug. 8, 1922, Box 8, CA; Fred B. Bauer, *Land of the North Carolina Cherokees* (Brevard, N.C.: George E. Buchanan, 1970), 27.

21. *Cherokee Nation et al. v. U.S.*, 40 *Court of Claims Reports* (1905), 252–365; M-685, "Records Relating to Enrollment of Eastern Cherokees by Guion Miller, 1908–1910"; DeWitt Harris to CIA, Nov. 20, 1906, CA.

22. M-685, "Records Relating to Enrollment of Eastern Cherokees by Guion Miller, 1908–1910"; Harris to CIA, Dec. 3, 1906; March 9, June 24, Sept. 27, Nov. 18, 1907, CA; CIA *Annual Report*, 1908, 60 Cong., 2 sess., *House Doc.* 1046, Serial 5453 (Washington, D.C.: Government Printing Office, 1908), 99–100. Frank Kyselka and some Indians believed Guion Miller included Negroes on his roll. Kyselka to CIA, Oct. 10, 1911, CA. In addition to the 3,436 "Cherokees" living east of the Mississippi, 27,384 residing west of that river were included on Miller's final, approved roll.

23. CIA *Annual Report*, 1909, 61 Cong., 2 sess., *House Doc.* 107, Serial 5747 (Washington, D.C.: Government Printing Office, 1910), 36; Frank Kyselka to CIA, Jan. 31, Feb. 3, June 3, 1910, CA; *Senate Report* 1479, 71 Cong., 3 sess., Serial 9323 (Washington, D.C.: Government Printing Office, 1931), 2 (quotation).

24. Spray to Merrill E. Gates, Dec. 16, 1902; Kyselka to CIA, Dec. 6, 1910, CA; CIA *Annual Report*, 1909, *House Doc.* 107, Serial 5747, 36–37.

25. For the Band's legal status in the nineteenth century, see Finger, *Eastern Band of Cherokees*, especially 172–74 regarding the Boyd decision. CIA *Annual Report*, 1904, *House Doc.* 5, Serial 4798, 266; James Henderson to W. Swayney, Feb. 17, 1914, CA. In classic understatement, Kyselka said in 1910, "The political status of the Eastern Cherokee is peculiar and has never been definitely settled." By 1912, however, he emphasized their citizenship while noting certain peculiari-

ties in their status. Kyselka to CIA, Dec. 6, 1910; April 1, 1912, CA. Annual CIA reports usually listed the Indians as citizens.

26. Harris to CIA, Aug. 4, 1908, CA.

27. Smith to CIA, May 20, 1901, M-1059, 7:469–75. In 1911 the acting superintendent at Cherokee noted the educational qualifications for voting but said "quite a number of the younger men who have attended school vote at state and national elections." See B. H. Dooley to CIA, Aug. 11, 1911; see also Frank Kyselka to CIA, April 1, 1912, CA. George E. Frizzell is probably closer to the truth when he concludes that, for whatever reasons, few Cherokees were able to vote after 1900. See Frizzell, "The Politics of Cherokee Citizenship, 1898–1930," *North Carolina Historical Review* 61(April 1984): 217.

28. J. E. Jenkins to CIA, Jan. 30, 1900, M-1059, 7:223; Frizzell, "Legal Status of the Eastern Band of Cherokee Indians," 89–90.

29. *Private Laws of North Carolina*, 1897, chap. 207, sec. 1; Harris to CIA, Jan. 25, Feb. 4, April 19, 1905, CA.

30. Harris to CIA, April 19, 1905 (quotation), CA. For more on the allotment policy and its effects, see Francis Paul Prucha, *The Great Father: The United States Government and the American Indian*, 2 vols. (Lincoln: University of Nebraska Press, 1984), vol. 2, chaps. 26, 29, 34.

31. Harris to CIA, Aug. 15, 1908, CA.

32. Kyselka to CIA, July 21, 22, 1909, CA; *S. Rept.* 1479, Serial 9323, 1–2. See also Kyselka's letter of Nov. 23, 1911, to CIA. Special agent Charles L. Davis had also proposed a plan for giving members of the Band individual titles. Bauer, *Land of the North Carolina Cherokees*, 26–27.

33. Long to SI, April 28, 1905, M-1059, 7:901–4. For comments on alleged Indian attitudes regarding allotment, see John Will to CIA, March 3, 1902, M-1059, 7:610; Spray to CIA, April 30, 1902; DeWitt Harris to CIA, July 29, 1908, CA.

34. Second Assistant CIA to John Talala, n.d., 1910, Special Agent's Letterbook, Charles L. Davis, Box 4, CA.

35. Finger, *Eastern Band of Cherokees*, chaps. 7–8; Williams, "Role of Formal Education among the Eastern Cherokee Indians," 19–38; Joan Greene, "Federal Policies in the Schools of the Eastern Cherokees, 1892–1932" (M.A. thesis, Western Carolina University, 1986), 43–49, 55–60.

36. Greene, "Federal Policies in the Schools of the Eastern Cherokees," 45–46, 61, 67–68; Joan Greene, "Goingback Chiltoskey, Master Carver," *Now and Then* (Johnson City, Tenn., Center for Appalachian Studies and Services/Institute for Appalachian Affairs) 3(Autumn 1986): 8 (quotation); author's interview with Goingback and Mary Chiltoskey, April 18, 1985.

37. One of many letters relating to nonattendance is Henry Spray to CIA, Oct. 24, 1902, CA.

38. Harris to CIA, Jan. 2, June 13, 1905, CA. Greene, "Federal Policies in the Schools

of the Eastern Cherokees," 75–76. During much of this time the Cherokee boarding school could not have accommodated all eligible children. On Jan. 7, 1905, Harris wrote Major W. W. Stringfield that without a compulsory attendance law Cherokee children "will soon become as worthless as the young Negros growing up among us without any education" (CA).

39. DeWitt Harris to CIA, Jan. 2, 1905; Harris to Major W. W. Stringfield, Jan. 7, 1905; Harris to Hon. A. S. Patterson, Feb. 4, 1905; Harris to W. S. Campbell, Feb. 20, 1905, CA; *Public Laws and Resolutions of the State of North Carolina . . . Session of 1905* (Raleigh: E. M. Uzzell, 1905), chap. 213; Greene, "Federal Policies in the Schools of the Eastern Cherokees," 76–77.

40. 145 *North Carolina Reports* 440; *Public Laws and Resolutions of the State of North Carolina . . . Session of 1909* (Raleigh: E. M. Uzzell, 1909), chap. 848; DeWitt Harris to J. U. Gibbs, Jan. 22, 1908; Harris to CIA, July 29, 1908; Frank Kyselka to CIA, Feb. 1, 1909; Aug. 11, 1911; Wadsworth to Norwood Lumber Co., April 13, 1913, CA; Greene, "Federal Policies in the Schools of the Eastern Cherokees," 77–81.

41. Finger, *Eastern Band of Cherokees*, chap. 7. As late as 1898 public funds of Swain and Jackson counties were used to operate small schools at Bird Town and in Soco. In that year Henry Spray said there was no justification for continuing either one. CIA *Annual Report*, 1898, 55 Cong., 3 sess., *House Doc.* 5, Serial 3757 (Washington, D.C.: Government Printing Office, n.d.), 219. See also Kyselka to CIA, March 1, Aug. 31, Sept. 10 (quotation), 1909, CA; Greene, "Federal Policies in the Schools of the Eastern Cherokees," 37–42.

42. Kyselka to CIA, Aug. 31, 1909; Jan. 26, Aug. 23, 1910; Jan. 11, 1911; Jan. 18, 22, 1912, CA; Greene, "Federal Policies in the Schools of the Eastern Cherokees," 42. The federal government earlier had paid Graham County a small amount when the latter was providing separate educational facilities for Indians. The practice of counties' returning a portion of Cherokee taxes to support the tribal school had been common in earlier years. See Henry Spray to W. R. Sherrill, Aug. 12, 1901; Spray to J. N. Wilson, Aug. 12, 1901, CA. Sometimes the money in question was simply diverted to pay part of the Cherokees' other taxes.

43. John A. Hyde to James Henderson, Oct. 9, 1914, Box 4, CA.

44. James Henderson to Mrs. Awee Tooni, April 22, 1914, Miscellaneous, 121, CA; Greene, "Federal Policies in the Schools of the Eastern Cherokees," 33–37; Robert A. Trennert, "From Carlisle to Phoenix: The Rise and Fall of the Indian Outing System, 1878–1930," *Pacific Historical Review* 52(Aug. 1983): 267–91.

45. Finger, *Eastern Band of Cherokees*, 162, 169; Elizabeth C. Duran, "David Owl, Eastern Cherokee among New York Iroquois," *Journal of Cherokee Studies* 6(Spring 1981): 4–13; Frank Kyselka to Caroline W. Andrus, July 20, 1911, CA. Kyselka believed that Hampton graduates made better reservation employees than those of any other school he was acquainted with.

46. Luzena Swayney to Mother, Aug. 11, 1914, Box 16, CA; James Henderson to [O. H.] Lipps, Feb. 25, 1916, Box 16, CA. Other examples include Henry Spray to R. H. Pratt, July 16, 30, Aug. 12, 1901, CA.

47. Henry W. Spray to CIA, Sept. 24, 1902, CA. Two Chilocco students had a similar experience. P. R. Wadsworth to CIA, March 20, 1913, CA.

48. James Henderson to O. H. Lipps, Oct. 3, 1914, Box 1 (1915–19), CA.

49. Harvey K. Meyer to James Henderson, July 7, 1916; J. R. Wise to Henderson, July 22, 1916; Edgar A. Alley to Henderson, July 24, 1916; William H. Scoville to Henderson, Aug. 18, 1916, Box 16, CA.

50. "Returned Student Survey," Jan. 30, 1917, Box 8; Henderson to Roger Mumblehead, Dec. 22, 1915, Box 16, CA.

51. Henry Spray to CIA, Sept. 1, 1900, CA.

52. William Munn Colby, "Routes to Rainey Mountain: A Biography of James Mooney, Ethnologist" (Ph.D. diss., University of Wisconsin–Madison, 1977), 90–91; Leo L. Elliott to James Henderson, April 28, 1914, Box 8, CA.

53. Leo L. Elliott to James Henderson, April 28, 1914, Box 8; Spray to Joseph G. Bulloch, Jan. 4, 1901; Spray to CIA, Jan. 12, 1901, CA. Raymond D. Fogelson contends that though conjuring was still a potent force during this period it had lost much of its earlier flexibility. Fogelson, "A Study of the Conjuror in Cherokee Society" (M.A. thesis, University of Pennsylvania, 1958), 59.

54. Henry Spray to CIA, July 31, 1900; Joseph G. Bulloch to CIA, Jan. 26, 1902; DeWitt Harris to CIA, July 5, 1906; Oct. 4, 1907; June 5, 1908; Mary E. Wolfe to James Henderson, Nov. 9, 1914, Box 3, CA; Greene, "Federal Policies in the Schools of the Eastern Cherokees," 51–53.

55. Henry Spray to CIA, Dec. 2, 1902; Frank Kyselka to CIA, Feb. 9, 1910; various materials in Box 2, esp. Assistant CIA E. B. Meritt to James Henderson, June 4, 1914; Meritt to Henderson, Oct. 26, 1914; Henderson to CIA, Aug. 10, 1917, CA.

56. For a sampling, see agents' letters of Sept. 21, 1901; Oct. 24, 1905; May 25, July 29, 1908; Feb. 9, March 1, April 27, Oct. 14, 1909; Sept. 5, Dec. 6, 1910, CA.

57. James Henderson to CIA, April 5, 1915; OIA Circular 1002, July 15, 1915; J. J. Wolfe to Henderson, Sept. 15, 1915, Box 8, CA.

58. CIA Annual Report, 1902, House Doc. 5, Serial 4458, 261; Spray to Reel, July 29, 1902, CA; Greene, "Federal Policies in the Schools of the Eastern Cherokees," 56. Early official interest in Indian crafts is discussed in Robert Fay Schrader, The Indian Arts and Crafts Board: An Aspect of New Deal Indian Policy (Albuquerque: University of New Mexico Press, 1983), chap. 1.

59. Joan Greene, ed., "The Story of My Life as Far Back as I Can Remember," Journal of Cherokee Studies 9 (Fall 1984): 90; Harris to CIA, March 8, 1907, CA.

60. CIA Annual Report, 1911, 62 Cong., 2 sess., House Doc. 120, Serial 6223 (Washington, D.C.: Government Printing Office, 1912), 137; P. C. Wadsworth to Mrs. J. M. Skinner, July 3, 1913; James Henderson to J. S. Robinson, March 30,

1915, Box 14; Henderson to Mrs. C. J. Thompson, Sept. 13, 1916, Box 1 (1915–17), CA; John Preston Arthur, *Western North Carolina: A History (from 1730 to 1913)* (Raleigh: Edwards and Broughton, 1914), 510.

61. Frank Kyselka to CIA, July 18, 1912; P. C. Wadsworth to CIA, May 19, 1913; Henderson to CIA, March 30, 1914, CA. Kyselka to Gudger, Sept. 21, 1914; Henderson to CIA, April 15, 1915 (quotation), Box 1 (1914–15), CA; Mary Ulmer Chiltoskie, *Cherokee Fair and Festival: A History thru 1978* (Asheville, N.C.: Gilbert Printing, 1979), 5–8.

62. Chiltoskie, *Cherokee Fair and Festival*, passim; Henderson to CIA, April 5, 1915 (quotation), Box 1 (1914–15), CA.

63. James Henderson to E. S. Millsaps, Nov. 3, 1916 (quotation); J. H. Harwood to Henderson, Sept. 27, 1916, Box 1, CA; Eastern Band of Cherokee Indians, Council Records, Nov. 17, 1916, Microfilm, NCDAH.

CHAPTER 3

1. Accounts of American involvement in the war include Allen Churchill, *Over Here! An Informal Re-creation of the Home Front in World War I* (New York: Dodd, Mead, 1968), and Harvey DeWeerd, *President Wilson Fights His War: World War I and the American Intervention* (New York: Macmillan, 1968). Statistics on Indians immediately preceding the war are in CIA *Annual Report*, 1916, 64 Cong., 2 sess., *House Doc.* 1899, Serial 7160 (Washington, D.C.: Government Printing Office, 1917), 74, 88. For the status of the Eastern Band see John R. Finger, *The Eastern Band of Cherokees, 1819–1900* (Knoxville: University of Tennessee Press, 1984); George E. Frizzell, "The Politics of Cherokee Citizenship, 1898–1930," *North Carolina Historical Review* 61(April 1984): 205–30; and Ben Oshel Bridgers, "An Historical Analysis of the Legal Status of the North Carolina Cherokees," *North Carolina Law Review* 58(August 1980): 1075–1131.

2. The following account of Cherokee participation in World War I is a revised condensation of John R. Finger, "Conscription, Citizenship, and 'Civilization': World War I and the Eastern Band of Cherokee," *North Carolina Historical Review* 63(July 1986): 283–308 (copyright 1986 by the North Carolina Division of Archives and History). A good overview of Indian participation in the war is Michael L. Tate, "From Scout to Doughboy: The National Debate over Integrating American Indians into the Military, 1891–1918," *Western Historical Quarterly* 17(Oct. 1986): 417–37.

3. Jackson to James E. Henderson, Aug. 10, 1915, Box 14, CA.

4. 40 Stat. 76–83.

5. William Preston, Jr., *Aliens and Dissenters: Federal Suppression of Radicals, 1903–1933* (Cambridge: Harvard University Press, 1963), chaps. 4–5; H. C. Peterson and Gilbert C. Fite, *Opponents of War, 1917–1918* (Madison: University of Wisconsin Press, 1957). Recent studies of conscription are John Whiteclay Chambers II, *To Raise an Army: The Draft Comes to Modern America* (New York:

Free Press, 1987), and J. Garry Clifford, *The First Peacetime Draft* (Lawrence: University of Kansas Press, 1986).

6. Henderson to John A. Hyde and Sheriffs of Graham and Cherokee counties, May 22, 1917; Henderson to Stone Chekelelee, May 25, 1917; Henderson to John Francis, Jr., May 29, 1917; and Henderson to the principal, Hampton Institute, May 29, 1917, Box 17, CA.

7. [Walter] David Owl to Henderson, June 1, 1917, Box 17, CA. David Owl's career is discussed in Elizabeth C. Duran, "David Owl, Eastern Cherokee among New York Iroquois," *Journal of Cherokee Studies* 6(Spring 1981): 4–13.

8. J. Fowler Hyde to James Henderson, June 6, 1917; Henderson to Deputy Marshal C. T. Roane, June 11, 1917, Box 17, CA.

9. Henderson to CIA, June 8, 1917; Edgar B. Meritt to Henderson, June 21, 1917, Box 17, CA. By September 1918, 170 Cherokees had registered: 94 in Swain County, 59 in Jackson County, and 17 in Graham County. Census of draft-age Indians, large packet, Box 18, CA.

10. James Henderson to David Owl, July 25, 1917; Henderson to George Owl, July 31, 1917, Box 17, CA; Joe Jennings to Donald Q. Palmer, Nov. 26, 1946, folder marked "Inspection Report—Donald Q. Palmer," Correspondence, 1926–52, Box 46, CA; *Jackson County Journal*, July 27, 1917, Oct. 11, 1918.

11. David Owl to Henderson, Sept. 14, 1917, Box 13, CA; article on Owl family, *Asheville Citizen-Times*, May 6, 1973.

12. Henderson to David Owl, Sept. 19, 1917, Box 13, CA. The 1916 report of the commissioner of Indian affairs, in almost total disregard of the complex history and status of the Eastern Band, listed them as citizens and voters. See *House Doc.* 1899, Serial 7160, 88.

13. Churchill, *Over Here!* 74; Richard N. Ellis, "'Indians at Ibapah in Revolt': Goshutes, the Draft, and the Indian Bureau, 1917–1919," *Nevada Historical Society Quarterly* 19(Fall 1976): 163–70; Laurence M. Hauptman, *The Iroquois and the New Deal* (Syracuse: Syracuse University Press, 1981), 9; Hazel W. Hertzberg, *The Search for an Indian Identity: Modern Pan-Indian Movements* (Syracuse: Syracuse University Press, 1971), 175; Tate, "From Scout to Doughboy," 428–29; Alison R. Bernstein, "Walking in Two Worlds: American Indians and World War Two" (Ph.D. diss., Columbia University, 1986), 46–47.

14. Coleman C. Cowan to W. S. Wilson, Oct. 1, 1917, Military Collection, World War I, part 2, Box 49, NCDAH, hereafter cited as World War I Papers; Cowan to Charles A. Webb, March 30, 1918; Governor Thomas W. Bickett to E. H. Crowder, June 27, 1918; Bickett to Newton D. Baker, July 10, 1918; Cowan to Bickett, July 27, 1918; and Bickett call for leniency, July 29, 1918, Governor Bickett Papers, NCDAH.

15. Sells to Jack, Charley, and Posey Wachacha, Jan. 22, 1918, Box 17, CA.

16. James Henderson to Helen H. Hennett, Jan. 30, 1918, Box 9; Henderson to Miss Bell Reichal, May 23, 1921; service record of Sylvester Long, Box 18, CA.

17. Meritt to Provost Marshal General, Feb. 26, 1918, Box 18, CA. The Boyd decision is 83 F. 547 (4th Cir., 1897).

18. Henderson to CIA, Oct. 25, 1917, Box 17, CA.

19. See Henderson's statement of March [n.d.] 1919, War–Red Cross Drive folder, Box 18, CA.

20. Henderson to CIA, Oct. 25, 1917, Box 17, CA.

21. Phillips to Adjutant General, Jan. 30, 1918; and Phillips to James Henderson, Sept. 11, 1917, Box 17, CA.

22. Duran, "David Owl," 7–8.

23. John H. Dillard to Cato Sells, July 4, 1918, Box 17, CA.

24. Meritt to John H. Dillard, Aug. 21, 1918; J. Fowler Hyde to James Henderson, Sept. 7, 1918, Box 17, CA.

25. Service Records, Box 18, CA.

26. Ellis, "'Indians at Ibapah in Revolt,'" 169. At various times reformers had espoused Indian military service as a means of acculturation but could not agree whether it was best to have segregated units. By World War I those favoring integration of Indians into white units had prevailed. See Tate, "From Scout to Doughboy," passim.

27. Varying estimates of the number of Indians serving in the war are in Francis Paul Prucha, *The Great Father: The United States Government and the American Indian*, 2 vols. (Lincoln: University of Nebraska Press, 1984), 2:771; Nancy Ann Haynie, ed., *Native Americans and the Military: Today and Yesterday* (Fort McPherson, Ga.: U.S. Army Forces Command, Public Affairs Command Information Branch, 1984), 7; Arrell M. Gibson, *The American Indian: Prehistory to the Present* (Norman: University of Oklahoma Press, 1980), 534. Figures for Eastern Cherokee servicemen also vary slightly, but most evidence indicates there were sixty-eight. See also Service Records; James Henderson to Chiltoskie Nick, Nov. 20, 1918; letter of Sergeant George S. Case, July 24, 1918, Box 18, CA; *Asheville Citizen-Times*, Dec. 28, 1941; and "Report of Inducted Men from Local Board Swain County, Bryson City, N.C.," 5, and typescript list of Indians drafted in Graham County, part 5, Box 8, World War I Papers. In Jackson County no distinction was made in listing white and Indian draftees, whereas Negroes were listed separately.

28. Service Records, Box 18, CA; Clarence Walton Johnson, *The 321st Infantry "Wildcats," 81st Division* (Columbia, S.C.: R. L. Bryan, 1919), 3, 83, 187–90; George W. McIver, "Service with the 81st Division at Camp Jackson, August, 1917, to May, 1918," typescript, chap. 15, pp. 9–10, part 6, Box 34, World War I Papers. McIver greatly overestimated the number of Cherokees serving in the 321st. See also George Owl to Edgar B. Meritt, Oct. 14, 1917; Owl to Nancy [?], Feb. 18, 1918; Owl to James Henderson, May 29, 1918, Box 17, CA.

29. McIver, "Service with the 81st Division," chap. 15, pp. 9–10.

30. Littlejohn to James Henderson, Feb. 16, 1918, Box 17, CA.

31. McIver, "Service with the 81st Division," chap. 15, p. 10. At that time Lumbee Indians were usually referred to as "Croatan" or even "Cherokee," though they had no relation to the Eastern Band. See T. L. Johnson to Captain T. B. McCargo, Sept. 15, 1918; and Johnson to Governor T. W. Bickett, Sept. 5, 1918, Governor Bickett Papers.

32. James Henderson to Miss Hayes, April 23, 1918, Box 18; J. W. Fuller to Henderson, Sept. 18, 1918, Box 1, CA.

33. Eastern Band of Cherokee Indians, Council Records, June 27, 1918, Microfilm, NCDAH;. James Henderson to CIA, May 11, 1918, Box 18, CA; *Asheville Times* as quoted in the *Jackson County Journal*, March 22, 1918.

34. *Jackson County Journal*, July 5, 1918. See also front-page editorial in issue of July 26, 1918. Jackson County did considerably better in a later drive.

35. Council Records, Oct. 7, 1918. Despite their general impoverishment, American Indians contributed about $75 per person to the Liberty Loan drives, a remarkable show of support. See Ellis, "'Indians at Ibapah in Revolt,'" 168–69.

36. Service Records, including Stephen Youngdeer, Box 18, CA; *Asheville Citizen-Times*, Dec. 28, 1941; *Jackson County Journal*, Oct. 11, 1918. Additional information on Youngdeer is in Joe Jennings to Donald Q. Palmer, Nov. 26, 1946, folder marked "Inspection Report—Donald Q. Palmer," correspondence, 1926–52, Box 46, CA. A detailed account of Youngdeer's outfit, the 115th Machine Gun Battalion, is in [?] to Mrs. A. A. McLean, Dec. 15, 1918, part 3, Box 4, World War I Papers; and *Operations, Thirtieth Division, Old Hickory* (n.p., n.d.), part 3, Box 3, World War I Papers. It is possible Youngdeer was also a victim of the 1918 Spanish influenza pandemic, which ravaged American troops and often resulted in pneumonic complications.

37. *Asheville Citizen-Times*, Dec. 28, 1941.

38. McIver, "Service with the 81st Division"; *The Jacksonian: Home-coming, Souvenir Edition* (Columbia, S.C.: [1920?]), part 3, Box 56, World War I Papers; "Operations, a Speech, a Memorandum," part 3, Box 56, World War I Papers; Geddings Crawford, "With the Three Twenty First," *State* (Columbia, S.C.), Sept. 19, 1920, 35; Johnson, *321st Infantry*, 37–38; "Operations Report Covering Operations of the Regiment, November 9th–11th, 1918," Nov. 17, 1918, folder marked "321st Infantry," part 4, Box 34, World War I Papers.

39. "Operations Report Covering Operations of the Regiment."

40. Ibid.; Operations, 81st Division, Jan. 16, 1919, folder marked "Operations, a Speech, a Memorandum," 6, part 3, Box 56, World War I Papers; Service Records, Box 18, CA.

41. *State*, Sept. 19, 1920; *Jacksonian Home-coming*.

42. Author's interview with Jefferson Thompson, June 14, 1984; Henderson to John A. Welch, Dec. 27, 1918, Box 18, CA.

43. Author's interview with Youngdeer, Cherokee, N.C., Feb. 21, 1985. See also Joan Greene, "Federal Policies in the Schools of the Eastern Cherokees, 1892–1932" (M.A. thesis, Western Carolina University, 1986), 45.

44. CIA *Annual Report*, 1919, 66 Cong., 2 sess., *House Doc.* 409, Serial 7706 (Washington, D.C.: Government Printing Office, 1920), 8–9.

45. *The American Indian in the World War*, Office of Indian Affairs Bulletin 15 (Washington, D.C.: Government Printing Office, 1922).

46. Eastern Band of Cherokee Indians, Council Records, Nov. 6, 1919, 97–101, microfilm, NCDAH. The final disposition of tribal assets was to proceed according to a plan discussed on September 27, 1917, by assistant Indian commissioner Edgar B. Meritt. See 76 Cong., U.S. Senate, *Survey of Conditions of the Indians in the United States*, part 37 (Washington, D.C.: Government Printing Office, 1940), 20815–21. See also Fred B. Bauer, *Land of the North Carolina Cherokees* (Brevard, N.C.: George E. Buchanan, 1970), 28–29.

47. James Henderson to W. David Owl, Feb. 1, 1921, Box 13; James Henderson to Earl Y. Henderson, Sept. 25, 1923, Box 15, CA.

48. "An Act Granting Citizenship to Certain Indians," Nov. 6, 1919, 41 Stat. 350.

49. James Henderson to CIA, Feb. 20, 1924, Box 15, CA. Tate, "From Scout to Doughboy," 435, says that nationally "the numbers who requested the status were relatively few."

50. Frizzell, "Politics of Cherokee Citizenship," 218–19, 222–23; Henderson to Owl, Feb. 1, 1921, Box 13, CA. Henderson further said the unscrupulous whites "went about it in such a high handed way as to cause it to act as a boomerang upon the deserving as well as the undeserving Indians." See also his letter to CIA of Feb. 20, 1924, Box 15, CA. Frederick E. Hoxie, *A Final Promise: The Campaign to Assimilate the Indians, 1880–1920* (Lincoln: University of Nebraska Press, 1984), chap. 7, notes that by 1920 the Indian Office embraced only a limited concept of Indian citizenship, one not necessarily including the vote.

51. Frizzell, "Politics of Cherokee Citizenship," 218–22.

52. Ibid., 223–24.

53. 43 Stat. 253. Gary C. Stein argues that the citizenship act was part of the progressive crusade, an attempt to limit the powers of the Bureau of Indian Affairs. See "The Indian Citizenship Act of 1924," *New Mexico Historical Review* 47 (July 1972): 257–74; Prucha, *Great Father*, 2:793–94.

54. Frizzell, "Politics of Cherokee Citizenship," 224–25; James Henderson to Earl Y. Henderson, Sept. 25, 1923; W. David Owl to James Henderson, Feb. 12, March 17, 1924; James Henderson to Owl, Feb. 15, 1924, Box 15, CA; Sibbald Smith to Zebulon Weaver, Oct. 16, 1928, Weaver Papers.

55. Owl to James Henderson, March 17, 1924 (quotations), Box 15, CA; 43 Stat. 376–82; Frizzell, "Politics of Cherokee Citizenship," 224–25.

56. 43 Stat., sec. 21, p. 381; Frizzell, "Politics of Cherokee Citizenship," 226; si Ray Lyman Wilbur to Lynn J. Frazier, Dec. 4, 1930, *Senate Report* 1479, 71 Cong., 3 sess., Serial 9323 (Washington, D.C.: Government Printing Office, 1931), 1.

57. Frizzell, "Politics of Cherokee Citizenship," 226; Sibbald Smith to Smith Coffy, Oct. 15, 1926, blamed Swain County's opposition to Indian voters on James Henderson. See Box 22, Personal Correspondence, Superintendent, CA. For

continuing efforts to tax Swain County Indian lands, see James Henderson to CIA, June 8, July 28, 1927, Box 7, CA. The Circuit Court case was *U.S. v. Wright*, 53 F. 2d 300 (4th cir. 1931).

58. 43 Stat. 376 (sec. 3); *House Report* 1475, 67 Cong., 4 sess., Serial 8157 (Washington, D.C.: Government Printing Office, 1923), 5–8; James Henderson to CIA, June 24, 1926, Box 7, CA.

59. James Henderson to CIA, June 24, Nov. 10, 26, 1926, Box 7, CA; SI Ray Lyman Wilbur to Lynn J. Frazier, Dec. 4, 1930, *Senate Report* 1479, Serial 9323, 2; 43 Stat., secs. 8–9, p. 378; 76 Cong., *Survey of the Condition of the Indians in the United States*, 20794–97; Bauer, *Land of the North Carolina Cherokees*, 30–31. The secretary of the interior also had the discretion of awarding monetary equivalents for allotments to any member of the Band with less than one-sixteenth Indian blood.

60. SI Ray Lyman Wilbur to Lynn J. Frazier, Dec. 4, 1930, *Senate Report* 1479, Serial 9323, 2; L. W. Page to CIA, Sept. 10, 1929; March 20, 1930; Cherokee Council Petition to SI and CIA, Nov. 7, 1929, Box 7, CA.

61. See various materials in 1928 inspection report of H. W. Gilman, folder, Box 45, CA.

62. Frizzell, "Politics of Cherokee Citizenship," 226–28. Stanion's comments about political "sleight of hand" in 1924 confusing Cherokee citizenship brought an angry response from Zebulon Weaver, who believed Stanion had impugned his motives and actions. Weaver to Stanion, Oct. 5, 1928, Weaver Papers. See also E. L. McKee to Weaver, Oct. 9, 1928, and Sibbald Smith to Weaver, Oct. 16, 1928, Weaver Papers.

63. Frizzell, "Politics of Cherokee Citizenship," 228; 45 Stat. 1094; *House Doc.* 1762, 71 Cong., 2 sess., Serial 9193 (Washington, D.C.: Government Printing Office, 1930), 3–4.

64. 46 Stat. 787; Frizzell, "Politics of Cherokee Citizenship," 229–30 (quotation on 229). See also *House Doc.* 1762, Serial 9193. When possible county registrars continued to refuse Cherokees registration on grounds of illiteracy—although the real reason, as Harold W. Foght said, was a belief in "'no taxes, no vote.'" See Foght to CIA, Nov. 12, 1936, Box 9, CA.

65. Prucha, *Great Father*, vol. 2, chaps. 31, 34; Lewis Meriam et al. for Brookings Institution, Institute for Government Research, *The Problem of Indian Administration* (Baltimore: Johns Hopkins University Press, 1928).

66. Cherokee Council petition to SI and CIA, Nov. 7, 1929, Box 7; see also R. L. Spalsbury to CIA, April 23, 1932, Box 8, CA.

67. Council Records, March 19, 1930; L. W. Page to CIA, March 20, 1930, Box 7, CA; Wilbur to Lynn J. Frazier, Dec. 4, 1930, *Senate Report* 1479, Serial 9323, 1–3. See also J. A. Tahquette and John Wolfe to Wilbur, Feb. 15, 1930, 76 Cong., *Survey of the Conditions of the Indians in the United States*, 20828–30.

68. Wilbur to Lynn J. Frazier, Dec. 4, 1930, *Senate Report* 1479, Serial 9323, 2–3.

69. 46 Stat. 518.

70. Council Records, Feb. 11–12, 1931.

71. Ibid., Jan. 11, 1932.

72. This phrase is borrowed from Michael Kammen, *People of Paradox: An Inquiry concerning the Origins of American Civilization* (New York: Alfred A. Knopf, 1972).

CHAPTER 4

1. Henderson to S. W. Black, May 31, 1921, Box 13, CA.

2. James Henderson to CIA, Aug. 8, 1922, Box 8, CA; Robert S. Lambert, "Logging the Great Smokies, 1880–1930," *Tennessee Historical Quarterly* 21 (Dec. 1961): 361–62; Michael Frome, *Strangers in High Places: The Story of the Great Smoky Mountains*, rev. ed. (Knoxville: University of Tennessee Press, 1980), chap. 13.

3. James Henderson to CIA, June 2, 1926, Box 7; Henderson to Arthur Dixon, Sept. 9, 1925, Box 4; Henderson to W. Gentry Hall, Jan. 31, 1921, Box 11, CA. Throughout the late nineteenth and early twentieth centuries, Cherokee agency files are filled with complaints about timber trespass.

4. Lambert, "Logging the Great Smokies," 362; Ralph P. Stanion to CIA, Feb. 21, 1929, Box 7, CA; Ellen Englemann Black, "A Study of the Diffusion of Culture in a Relatively Isolated Mountain County" (M.A. thesis, University of Chicago, 1928), 16, 43–44. A list of annual cuts on the reservation in 1917–45 is in report of William Heritage, Regional Forester, April 1946, NA, no. 61A-182, Box 123B, File 24316.

5. Stanion to CIA, Feb. 21, 1929; L. W. Page to CIA, Nov. 11, 1929; Page to CIA, Dec. 9, 1930, Box 7, CA; 71 Cong., 3 sess., U.S. Senate, *Survey of the Conditions of the Indians in the United States*, part 16 (Washington, D.C.: Government Printing Office, 1931), 7495, 7510; William H. Gilbert, Jr., *The Eastern Cherokees* (Washington, D.C.: Government Printing Office, 1943), 213–14; Raymond D. Fogelson, "A Study of the Conjuror in Cherokee Society" (M.A. thesis, University of Pennsylvania, 1958), 49; Raymond D. Fogelson and Paul Kutsche, "Cherokee Economic Cooperatives: The Gadugi," in *Symposium on Cherokee and Iroquois Culture*, ed. William N. Fenton and John Gulick, Bureau of American Ethnology Bulletin 180 (Washington, D.C.: Government Printing Office, 1961), 106.

6. O. H. Lipp to Henderson, Feb. 12, 1916, Box 16; Henderson to David Bird, May 28, 1917, Box 17; Henderson to Mrs. Charles L. Schaefer, March 27, 1919, Box 9; Henderson to J. E. Coburn, Aug. 4, 1919, Box 14; Stanion to CIA, Feb. 23, 1929, Box 7, CA; Black, "Study of the Diffusion of Culture," 14, 28.

7. For perceptive contemporary commentary on the automobile, see Frederick Lewis Allen, *Only Yesterday: An Informal History of the Nineteen-Twenties* (New York: Harper and Brothers, 1931); a more recent assessment is James J. Flink, *The Car Culture* (Cambridge: MIT Press, 1975).

8. Allen, *Only Yesterday*; Flink, *Car Culture*.

9. Black, "Study of the Diffusion of Culture," 1, 31–32.

10. Ibid., 32–33; Earl Y. Henderson, "Report on the Cherokee Indian Reservation, North Carolina," June 25, 1924, Box 15, CA, 14–15.

11. James Henderson to Frank L. O'Rurk, Dec. 4, 1917, Box 3; L. W. Page to CIA, Nov. 11, 1929, Box 7; R. L. Spalsbury to CIA, May 18, 1928, Box 7, CA; Earl Y. Henderson Report, June 25, 1924, Box 15, CA, p. 15; R. L. Spalsbury to CIA, Sept. 5, 1932, Box 8, CA; 71 Cong., 3 sess., *Survey of the Conditions of the Indians in the United States*, 7507.

12. Good general accounts of the park are Carlos C. Campbell, *Birth of a National Park in the Great Smoky Mountains* (Knoxville: University of Tennessee Press, 1960), and Frome, *Strangers in High Places*, chaps. 14–16.

13. Henderson to CIA, Aug. 2, 1927, Box 7, CA.

14. Kephart, *Cherokees of the Smoky Mountains* (Ithaca, N.Y.: Atkinson Press, 1936; reprinted Gatlinburg, Tenn.: Great Smoky Mountains Natural History Association, 1983); examples of such interest include *Raleigh News and Observer*, Oct. 16, 1927, Sept. 20, 1931; B. T. Groome to James Henderson, Nov. 1, 1921, Box 1 (1914–15); Mrs. F. M. Weaver to Henderson, April 28, 1924, Box 15, CA; *Charlotte Observer*, July 5, 1931; *Bryson City Times*, Oct. 14, 1932.

15. James Mooney and Frans M. Olbrechts, *The Swimmer Manuscript: Cherokee Sacred Formulas and Medicinal Prescriptions*, Bureau of American Ethnology Bulletin 99 (Washington, D.C.: Government Printing Office, 1932), xvii; Gilbert, *Eastern Cherokees*, 193–94; John Witthoft, "Will West Long, Cherokee Informant," *American Anthropologist* 50(April–June 1948): 355–59. Mooney's career is discussed in L. G. Moses, *The Indian Man: A Biography of James Mooney* (Urbana: University of Illinois Press, 1984).

16. John Witthoft, *Green Corn Ceremonialism in the Eastern Woodlands*, Occasional Contributions from the Museum of Anthropology of the University of Michigan 13 (Ann Arbor: University of Michigan Press, 1949), 31–50; Frank G. Speck and Leonard Broom, in collaboration with Will West Long, *Cherokee Dance and Drama*, rev. ed. (Norman: University of Oklahoma Press, 1983), preface to the first edition, introduction; Robert K. Thomas, "Culture History of the Eastern Cherokee," May 1959, unpublished paper for the Cross-Cultural Laboratory of the Institute for Research in Social Sciences, University of North Carolina, Chapel Hill, 17, 19–20. See also relevant comments in John Gulick, *Cherokees at the Crossroads* (Chapel Hill: University of North Carolina Press, 1960), xi–xii, 200–201.

17. Mooney and Olbrechts, *Swimmer Manuscript*, 8; Gilbert, *Eastern Cherokees*, 201; Earl Y. Henderson report, June 25, 1924, p. 10, Box 8, CA. Photographs of many Cherokee homes are in "Industrial Survey," 1922–23, Box 8, CA.

18. Gilbert, *Eastern Cherokees*, 201–2, 212; Thomas, "Culture History of the Eastern Cherokee," 18–19; Fogelson and Kutsche, "Cherokee Economic Cooperatives: The Gadugi," 100–110; John Witthoft, "Observations on Social Change among the Eastern Cherokees," in *The Cherokee Nation: A Troubled History*, ed. Duane H.

King (Knoxville: University of Tennessee Press, 1979), 204–5; Mooney and Olbrechts, *Swimmer Manuscript*, 80, 135–36.

19. Henderson to Daniel Ranenel, Aug. 20, 1919 (quotation), Box 1, CA; B. T. Groome to Henderson, Nov. 1, 1921, and Henderson to Groome, Nov. 7, 1921, Box 1 (1914–15); telegram of Daniel B. Henderson to James Henderson, May 7, 1923; James Henderson to CIA, May 17, 1923; James Henderson to Daniel Henderson, May 6, 1923; W. L. Reynolds to James Henderson, May 10, 1923, Box 15, CA.

20. Kyselka to CIA, Oct. 14, 1909; Dec. 6, 1910 (quotation), CA; Horace Kephart article on Cherokee fair in *Raleigh News and Observer*, Oct. 16, 1927; *Bryson City Times*, Oct. 14, 1932; Thomas, "Culture History of the Eastern Cherokee," 22–23; Fogelson, "Study of the Conjuror in Eastern Cherokee Society," 107–9; Raymond D. Fogelson, "The Conjuror in Eastern Cherokee Society," *Journal of Cherokee Studies* 5(Fall 1980): 81–82; Annual Statistical Report, Narrative Section, March 15, 1932, p. 7, Box 8, CA. The most detailed discussion of the Cherokee ballplay is Raymond D. Fogelson, "The Cherokee Ball Game: A Study in Southeastern Ethnology" (Ph.D. diss., University of Pennsylvania, 1962); see especially chap. 6.

21. Joe Jennings to Donald Q. Palmer, Nov. 26, 1946, Inspection Report, Correspondence, 1926–52, Box 46; Kyselka to CIA, Jan. 6, 1910; May 15, 1912, CA; Fogelson, "Cherokee Ball Game," 307; Benjamin G. Rader, *American Sports: From the Age of Folk Games to the Age of Spectators* (Englewood Cliffs, N.J.: Prentice-Hall, 1983), 93, 140–44. One example of progressive attitudes toward sports is Cary Goodman, *Choosing Sides: Playground and Street Life on the Lower East Side* (New York: Schocken Books, 1979).

22. Lawrence S. Ritter, *The Glory of Their Times: The Story of the Early Days of Baseball Told by the Men Who Played It* (New York: Macmillan, 1966), chap. 11; Robert W. Wheeler, *Jim Thorpe, World's Greatest Athlete*, rev. ed. (Norman: University of Oklahoma Press, 1979); Elizabeth C. Duran, "David Owl, Eastern Cherokee among New York Iroquois," *Journal of Cherokee Studies* 6(Spring 1981): 4–13; John R. Finger, "Conscription, Citizenship, and 'Civilization': World War I and the Eastern Band of Cherokee," *North Carolina Historical Review* 63(July 1986): 294–95, 297–98; 1925 correspondence regarding Thomas Owl, Box 15, 31a-630, CA; 71 Cong., 3 sess., *Survey of the Conditions of the Indians in the United States*, 7520; article on Ben Powell, *Asheville Citizen*, April 6, 1973.

23. L. W. Page to CIA, March 4, 1930, Box 7, CA.

24. Ralph P. Stanion to CIA, Feb. 13, 1929, Box 7, CA.

25. Gilbert, *Eastern Cherokees*, 188–89; Secretary [?] to George Junkin, March 28, 1933, Box 29, CA; author's interview with Duane H. King, May 9, 1988; Dorothy Andora Arnold, "Some Recent Contributions of the Cherokee Indians of North Carolina to the Crafts of the Southern Highlands" (M.S. thesis, University of Tennessee, 1952).

26. Charles H. Burke "to All Indians," Feb. 24, 1923 (quotation), Box 15, CA; Speck

and Broom, *Cherokee Dance and Drama*, 12 (quotation); Raymond D. Fogelson and Amelia B. Walker, "Self and Other in Cherokee Booger Masks," *Journal of Cherokee Studies* 5 (Fall 1980): 88–102; *Raleigh News and Observer*, Oct. 16, 1927; Annual Statistical Report, Narrative Section, March 15, 1932, p. 7, Box 8, CA.

27. Mooney and Olbrechts, *Swimmer Manuscript*, 10; Gilbert, *Eastern Cherokees*, 199.

28. Peyton Carter report, April 6, 1922; E. B. Meritt to James Henderson, May 5, 1922; Henderson to CIA, May 15, 1922 (two letters), Box 8, CA.

29. Menu for May 16–22, 1922, Box 8, CA. A decade earlier school diets depended largely on the amount and kind of food raised on the school farm; by the 1920s, however, there was less emphasis on farming among boarding-school students. Joan Greene, "Federal Policies in the Schools of the Eastern Cherokees, 1892–1932" (M.A. thesis, Western Carolina University, 1986), 50–51. See also comments of John C. Campbell, *The Southern Highlander and His Homeland* (New York: Russell Sage Foundation, 1921), 199.

30. Carter report, April 6, 1922, Box 8, CA. Bushyhead is quoted in Greene, "Federal Policies in the Schools of the Eastern Cherokees," 42–43.

31. Carter report, April 6, 1922, Box 8, CA.

32. Ibid.; for enrollment requirements see E. B. Meritt to James Henderson, March 20, 1920, Box 4, CA.

33. Carter report, April 6, 1922, Box 8, CA.

34. Henderson to CIA, May 15, 1922; Jan. 12, Feb. 23 (quotation), 1925, Box 8, CA. He was even more negative in comments about the Big Cove people. Henderson to CIA, Dec. 13, 1927, Box 7, CA.

35. James Henderson to J. H. Moody, Jan. 6, 1925, Box 8; L. W. Page to CIA, Oct. 3, 1929; Dec. 8, 1930, Box 7, CA; Francis Paul Prucha, *The Great Father: The United States Government and the American Indian*, 2 vols. (Lincoln: University of Nebraska Press, 1984), 2:836–40. A few years later officials were sharply critical of Snowbird school and replaced it with a new federally operated facility.

36. Greene, "Federal Policies in the Schools of the Eastern Cherokees," 46–53, 100–101; Robert K. Thomas, "Eastern Cherokee Acculturation," May 1958, unpublished paper for the Cross-Cultural Laboratory of the Institute for Research in Social Sciences, University of North Carolina, Chapel Hill, 18–19; Thomas, "Culture History of the Eastern Cherokee," 22.

37. James Henderson to Commissioner of Pensions, March 26, 1926, Box 18, CA; Mooney and Olbrechts, *Swimmer Manuscript*, 34–35; Fogelson, "Conjuror in Eastern Cherokee Society," 70; Fogelson, "Study of the Conjuror in Eastern Cherokee Society," 80–81.

38. Mooney and Olbrechts, *Swimmer Manuscript*, 15, 17, 35–39.

39. Harris to CIA, May 1, 1908, CA; CIA *Annual Report*, 1906, 59 Cong., 2 sess., *House Doc.* 5, Serial 5118 (Washington, D.C.: Government Printing Office, 1907), 292; Leo L. Elliott to James Henderson, April 28, 1914, Box 8, CA; Mooney and Olbrechts, *Swimmer Manuscript*, 39–50, 83–109. See also Ray-

mond D. Fogelson, "Change, Persistence, and Accommodation in Cherokee Medico-magical Beliefs," in *Symposium on Cherokee and Iroquois Culture*, ed. William N. Fenton and John Gulick, Bureau of American Ethnology Bulletin 180 (Washington, D.C.: Government Printing Office, 1961), 215–25.

40. Examples are found in James Axtell, *The Invasion Within: The Contest of Cultures in Colonial North America* (New York: Oxford University Press, 1985), chaps. 5–6, and Neal Salisbury, *Manitou and Providence: Indians, Europeans, and the Making of New England, 1500–1643* (New York: Oxford University Press, 1982), 74–75, 136–38.

41. *Asheville Citizen*, Jan. 21, 1934 (quotation); Fogelson, "Conjuror in Eastern Cherokee Society," 84; Fogelson, "Study of the Conjuror in Eastern Cherokee Society," 112; Mooney and Olbrechts, *Swimmer Manuscript*, 108–10.

42. Alfred H. Crosby, *Epidemic and Peace, 1918* (Westport, Conn.: Greenwood Press, 1976), says the commonly cited figure of 21 million deaths resulting from Spanish influenza is probably "a gross underestimation" (p. 207). The influenza was often accompanied by pneumonic complications and was especially deadly among young adults. Health-related materials for the Cherokee reservation include correspondence of Dec. 28, 1918; Feb. 27, 1919; Feb. 20, 1920; June 23, 1921, all in Box 4, CA; [?] Hooper to Henderson, Jan. 15, 1923, Box 4; Henderson to CIA, Oct. 31, 1927, Box 7, CA.

43. Stevens report, 1923, Box 8, CA.

44. Ibid.

45. Gilbert, *Eastern Cherokees*, 196; Walter S. Stevens, "Medical and Sanitary Report," Sept. 18–20, 1930, Box 45, CA.

46. Report of Walter S. Stevens, 1923, Box 8; Henderson to CIA, July 9, 1926; Aug. 2, 1927; R. L. Spalsbury to CIA, May 7, 1928; L. W. Page to CIA, Oct. 10, 1929, Box 7; Stanion[?] to CIA, Jan. 14, 1931, Box 8, CA; article on Gloyne in *Cherokee One Feather*, June 21, 1989.

47. [?] to CIA, Oct. 23, 1922, Box 8; James Henderson to CIA, July 18, 1927, Box 7, CA.

48. Forrest Carter, *The Education of Little Tree* (New York: Delacorte Press, 1976; reprinted Albuquerque: University of New Mexico Press, 1986). A few of the many letters pertaining to alcohol include correspondence of Aug. 8, 1922; 1925 materials regarding Smith, 14c–34, Box 8; L. W. Page to CIA, Sept. 22, 1930, Box 7, CA.

49. Henderson to CIA, Dec. 13, 1927, Box 7, CA.

50. Russell Thornton, "Tribal History, Tribal Population, and Tribal Membership Requirements: The Cases of the Eastern Band of Cherokee Indians, the Cherokee Nation of Oklahoma, and the United Keetowah Band of Cherokee Indians in Oklahoma," in *Toward a Quantitative Approach to American Indian History*, Occasional Papers Series 8 (Chicago: Newberry Library, 1987).

51. Information on the Catt family comes from Betty Duggan, doctoral candidate

in anthropology, University of Tennessee, Knoxville; Thomas, "Eastern Chero-kee Acculturation," 12–18; Thomas "Culture History of the Eastern Chero-kee," 20–21; G. M. Edwards to Hiram Wilburn, Oct. 8, 1935, Hiram Wilburn Papers, WCU.

52. Thomas, "Eastern Cherokee Acculturation," 12–27 (quotation on 23). Thomas also considers a fourth group, "a new middle class," that emerged after 1930 and will be discussed later. A synopsis of and elaboration upon Thomas's cultural continuum is in Gulick, *Cherokees at the Crossroads*, 127–46. See also Harriet J. Kupferer, *The 'Principal People,' 1960: A Study of Cultural and Social Groups of the Eastern Cherokee*, Bureau of American Ethnology Bulletin 196 (Washington, D.C.: Government Printing Office, 1966), 311–17; Witthoft, "Observations on Social Change among the Eastern Cherokees," 205–7; and Annual Statistical Report, Narrative Section, Oct. 19, 1935, p. 1, Box 9, CA.

53. Kyselka to CIA, Aug. 12, 1912; Kyselka to R. F. Jarrett, July 7, 1911, CA; Gilbert, *Eastern Cherokees*, 201.

54. Gilbert, *Eastern Cherokees*, 201, 203–7; Leonard Bloom, "The Cherokee Clans: A Study in Acculturation," *American Anthropologist* 41 (April–June 1939): 266–68. See also Thomas, "Culture History of the Eastern Cherokee," 17–18, and Gulick, *Cherokees at the Crossroads*, 65–69.

55. Blythe's earlier career is discussed in John R. Finger, *The Eastern Band of Chero-kees, 1819–1900* (Knoxville: University of Tennessee Press, 1984), chap. 8.

56. Henderson to Fred H. Olds, March 16, 1920, Box 13, CA.

57. Henderson to Rev. W. R. L. Smith, Dec. 31, 1920, CA; Duran, "David Owl," 4–13; articles on the Owl family, *Asheville Citizen*, Aug. 26, 1962; *Asheville Citizen-Times*, May 6, 1973. Many years later Asheville columnist John Parris referred to Moses Owl, rather than David, as the Cherokee Uncle Remus. *Asheville Citizen*, Nov. 13, 1966.

58. John Witthoft, "Will West Long, Cherokee Informant," 355–59.

59. Ibid.

60. Mooney and Olbrechts, *Swimmer Manuscript*, 9; Speck and Broom, *Cherokee Dance and Drama*, passim; Gulick, *Cherokees at the Crossroads*, 67.

61. Mooney and Olbrechts, *Swimmer Manuscript*, 9, 109–11, 114. See also his com-ments on other medicine men, 111–16.

62. Witthoft, "Will West Long, Cherokee Informant," 358–59; Speck and Broom, *Cherokee Dance and Drama*, xix–xx. A recent appraisal of Long is in Carma-leta Littlejohn Montieth, "The Role of the Scribe in Eastern Cherokee Society, 1821–1985" (Ph.D. diss., Emory University, 1985), 128–54.

63. "Industrial Survey," 1922–23, Box 8, CA. For example, see Harold W. Foght to Dr. B. Youngblood, Dec. 31, 1934, Box 9, CA.

64. Thomas, "Eastern Cherokee Acculturation," 20; Thomas, "Culture History of the Eastern Cherokee," 19 (quotation); Fogelson, "Study of the Conjuror in Eastern Cherokee Society," 111–12.

65. Eastern Band of Cherokee Indians, Council Records, Nov. 8, 1919; July 1921, microfilm, NCDAH; *Private Laws of the State of North Carolina*, session of 1897 (Winston, N.C.: M. I. and J. C. Stewart, 1897), chap. 207, sec. 18; Annual Statistical Report, Narrative Section, March 15, 1932, p. 7, Box 8, CA; Fogelson, "Study of the Conjuror in Eastern Cherokee Society," 65–66.

CHAPTER 5

1. L. W. Page to CIA, Sept. 29, 1930, Box 7; Narrative Section, Annual Statistical Report, March 15, 1932, pp. 3–4, Box 8, CA.

2. L. W. Page to CIA, Nov. 11, 1929, Box 7; Narrative Section, Annual Statistical Report, March 15, 1932, pp. 3–4 (quotation); R. L. Spalsbury to CIA, July 11, 1933, Box 8, CA. Discussion of reimbursable agricultural plans is in Francis Paul Prucha, *The Great Father: The United States Government and the American Indian*, 2 vols. (Lincoln: University of Nebraska Press, 1984), 2:892–93.

3. Examples of assistance include Eastern Band of Cherokee Indians, Council Records, Nov. 5, 1919; Nov. 22, 1923; June 25, 1924; June 13, 1925; and Nov. 9, 1927, microfilm, NCDAH. See also R. L. Spalsbury to CIA, Feb. 20, April 27, May 29, 1933, Box 8, CA; R. L. Spalsbury to CIA, May 18, 1934, Box 9, CA; William H. Gilbert, Jr., *The Eastern Cherokees* (Washington, D.C.: Government Printing Office, 1943), 202, 212.

4. William Heritage, "Report Forestry Activities Cherokee Indian Reservation," April 1946, RG 75, Accession no. 61A-182, Box 123B, File 24316, NA; Narrative Section, Annual Statistical Report, March 15, 1932, pp. 8–9; R. L. Spalsbury to CIA, Dec. 8, 1932, Box 8; Clyde M. Blair to Lee Muck, Jan. 24, 1938, Box 10, CA.

5. Narrative Section, Annual Statistical Report, March 15, 1932, p. 10 (quotation); R. L. Spalsbury to CIA, Jan. 15, 1934, Box 8; Harold W. Foght to CIA, Jan. 10, 1935, Box 9; Foght to CIA, April 28, 1937, Box 10, CA.

6. Narrative Section, Annual Statistical Report, March 15, 1932, pp. 8–9, Box 8; Harold W. Foght to CIA, June 4, 1935, Box 9, CA; John Gulick, *Cherokees at the Crossroads* (Chapel Hill: University of North Carolina Press, 1960), 20–21; Raymond D. Fogelson, "A Study of the Conjuror in Eastern Cherokee Society" (M.A. thesis, University of Pennsylvania, 1958), 48–49.

7. Spalsbury to CIA, Oct. 17, 1932; April 27, 1933, Box 8. Spalsbury later favored reimbursable assistance. See his letter to CIA, May 17, 1933, Box 8, CA.

8. Michael Frome, *Strangers in High Places: The Story of the Great Smoky Mountains*, rev. ed. (Knoxville: University of Tennessee Press, 1980), chap. 14; Carlos C. Campbell, *Birth of a National Park in the Great Smoky Mountains* (Knoxville: University of Tennessee Press, 1960), passim. The park was formally established on June 15, 1934, and was dedicated by President Roosevelt on September 2, 1940.

9. Page to CIA, Jan. 14, 1931, Box 8, CA. This was state highway 107, later to become part of U.S. 19 and 441.

10. Spalsbury to CIA, Sept. 27, 1932, Box 8, CA.

11. Kenneth R. Philp, *John Collier's Crusade for Indian Reform, 1920–1954* (Tucson: University of Arizona Press, 1977); Prucha, *Great Father*, vol. 2, part 8; Lawrence C. Kelly, *The Assault on Assimilation: John Collier and the Origins of Indian Policy Reform* (Albuquerque: University of New Mexico Press, 1983); John Collier, *From Every Zenith: A Memoir and Some Essays on Life and Thought* (Denver: Sage Books, 1963).

12. Prucha, *Great Father*, vol. 2, chap. 37; Philp, *John Collier's Crusade for Indian Reform*, chaps. 7–8.

13. Spalsbury to CIA, May 15, 1934, Box 9, CA; Philp, *John Collier's Crusade for Indian Reform*, 139.

14. Quoted in Charles J. Weeks, "The Eastern Cherokee and the New Deal," *North Carolina Historical Review* 53 (July 1976): 313; Foght to CIA, Jan. 21, 1935, Box 9, CA. Foght had lobbied extensively for Cherokee acceptance of the IRA. *Asheville Citizen*, Dec. 19, 1934.

15. R. L. Spalsbury to CIA, April 27, 1933, Box 8, CA.

16. Harold W. Foght to CIA, June 29, Oct. 16, 1936, Box 9, CA; Weeks, "Eastern Cherokee and the New Deal," 310–11; Prucha, *Great Father*, 2:946–47. *Asheville Citizen*, June 17, 1939, 12th Annual Rhododendron Number. Foght discussed the variety of New Deal programs among the Cherokees in the Narrative Section of his Annual Statistical Report, Oct. 19, 1935, Box 9, CA.

17. 48 Stat. 596; Narrative Section, Annual Statistical Report, Oct. 19, 1935, Box 9; inspection report of Walter S. Stevens to CIA, April 12, 1938, Box 46, CA; *Asheville Citizen*, June 17, 1939, 12th Annual Rhododendron Number.

18. Narrative Section, Annual Statistical Report, Oct. 19, 1935, p. 2 (quotation), Box 9, CA. Examples of such land-related matters include R. L. Spalsbury to CIA, June 3, 1932; Jan. 15, 17, 1934, Box 8; Harold W. Foght to CIA, Feb. 17, 1936, Box 9; March 17, April 28, 1937, Box 10; Clyde M. Blair to CIA, Feb. 14, July 11, 1940, Box 11; Blair to William Zimmerman, Sept. 2, 1941; Dec. 29, 1942; Nov. 9, 1943, Box 12, CA.

19. Prucha, *Great Father*, 2:951 (quotations); Charles H. Burke "to All Indians," Feb. 24, 1923 (quotation), Box 15, CA.

20. Foght to CIA, Aug. 28, 1934, Box 9, CA.

21. Ibid., March 16, 1935.

22. Spalsbury to CIA, April 28, 1932; June 8, 1933, Box 8, CA; Minutes of Council Records, Dec. 7, 1932; *Asheville Citizen-Times*, May 7, 1933. Spalsbury apparently referred to the Southern Highland Handicrafts Guild, organized in 1928 in Penland, North Carolina, which included craftsmen and craftswomen from Penland, Gatlinburg, and other areas of the southern Appalachians. Frome, *Strangers in High Places*, p. 234, chap. 17. For more on the Indian New Deal's support of crafts, see Robert Fay Schrader, *The Indian Arts and Crafts Board: An Aspect of New Deal Indian Policy* (Albuquerque: University of New Mexico Press, 1983).

23. An example is Foght to CIA, April 24, 1936, Box 9, CA.

24. Author's interview with Goingback and Mary U. Chiltoskey, April 18, 1985; Joan Greene, "Goingback Chiltoskey, Master Carver," *Now and Then* (Johnson City, Tenn., Center for Appalachian Studies and Services/Institute for Appalachian Affairs) 3(Autumn 1986): 8–9; *Asheville Citizen*, June 17, 1939, 12th Annual Rhododendron Number; Spalsbury to CIA, Jan. 12, 1934, Box 8, CA.

25. Foght to CIA, Aug. 22, 1934 (quotation), Box 9; Foght to Ruth Cass, Sept. 26, 1934, Box 29. And yet less than a year later an estimated two hundred Indians worked at least part time on crafts. Secretary [?] to George Junkin, March 28, 1935, Box 29, CA.

26. Spalsbury to CIA, Sept. 27, 1932, Box 8, CA.

27. R. L. Spalsbury to CIA, May 10, 1933, Box 8; Spalsbury to John E. Freeman et al., Jan. 18, 1934, Letters to Others, CA.

28. Harold W. Foght to CIA, May 5, 1936, Box 9. Materials on the tribe's legal disputes with the railroad include R. L. Spalsbury to CIA, Oct. 24, 1933, Box 8; Foght to CIA, Aug. 21, Nov. 2, Dec. 7, 1934, Box 9, CA.

29. Foght to Dr. B. Youngblood, Dec. 31, 1934; Foght to CIA, Oct. 16, Nov. 15, 1934; Oct. 23, 1935; Narrative Section, Annual Statistical Report, Oct. 19, 1935, pp. 18–19, Box 9, CA.

30. Philp, *John Collier's Crusade for Indian Reform*, chaps. 8–9; Graham D. Taylor, "The Divided Heart: The Indian New Deal," in *The American Indian Experience, a Profile: 1524 to the Present*, ed. Philip Weeks (Arlington Heights, Ill.: Forum Press, 1988), 240–59.

31. The romantic story of Bauer's parents is told in Carmine Andrew Prioli, "The Indian 'Princess' and the Architect: Origin of a North Carolina Legend," *North Carolina Historical Review* 60(July 1983): 283–303; see also William B. Bushong, "A. G. Bauer, North Carolina's New South Architect," *North Carolina Historical Review* 60(July 1983): 304–32. Fred Bauer and the Blythes are listed in the 1900 census for Jackson County (T-623, Roll 1201).

32. Spalsbury to CIA, July 31, 1934; Harold W. Foght to CIA, Aug. 22, 1934, Box 9, CA. Bauer's forceful views were best expressed in his *Land of the North Carolina Cherokees* (Brevard, N.C.: George E. Buchanan, 1970).

33. Spalsbury to CIA, Sept. 5, 1932; March 20, 1933, Box 8, CA.

34. Spalsbury to CIA, May 18, 1934, Box 9, CA.

35. Ibid.

36. Foght to CIA, March 18, 1935, Box 9, CA.

37. Foght to CIA, July 31, 1934, Box 9, CA.

38. Foght to CIA, April 13, 1935; Foght to Catherine A. Bauer, April 30, 1935; Foght to A. G. Monahan, May 1, 1935, Box 9, CA.

39. Alice Lee Jemison, "Report on Hearings before the Senate Committee on Indian Affairs," Feb. 24, 1937, Josiah Bailey Papers, Senatorial Series, Insular Affairs, Duke University; Foght to CIA, April 13, 1935, Box 9, CA.

40. Quoted in Weeks, "Eastern Cherokee and the New Deal," 314.

41. Ibid., 314–15.

42. Foght to A. G. Monahan, May 1, 1935 (quotation); R. L. Spalsbury to CIA, June 27, 1934; Foght to CIA, Jan. 22, 1935, Box 9, CA.

43. Foght to CIA, Aug. 8, 1935, Box 9, CA.

44. A good analysis of the AIF is Laurence M. Hauptman, "The American Indian Federation and the Indian New Deal: A Reinterpretation," *Pacific Historical Review* 52(Nov. 1983): 378–402. See also Weeks, "Eastern Cherokee and the New Deal," 316–18; Philp, *John Collier's Crusade for Indian Reform*, 170–74, 200–205; and Laurence M. Hauptman, "Alice Jemison: Seneca Political Activist, 1901–1964," *Indian Historian* 12(Summer 1979): 16.

45. Hauptman, "American Indian Federation and the Indian New Deal," 395; Weeks, "Eastern Cherokee and the New Deal," 317.

46. Joseph Bruner to Senate Committee on Indian Affairs, May 9, 1936, Bailey Papers; Jemison, "Report on Hearings," Feb. 24, 1937, Bailey Papers.

47. Jemison to Bailey, Jan. 18, 1937; Bailey to Jemison, Jan. 16, 1937, Bailey Papers.

48. Collier to Bailey, Jan. 28, 1937, Bailey Papers. Harold Foght later admitted he had briefly threatened opponents with loss of jobs. Foght to John Collier, March 15, 1937, Box 10, CA. See also Cherokee testimony in 76 Cong., 3 sess., House of Representatives, Committee on Indian Affairs, *Hearings . . . on S. 2103* (Washington, D.C.: Government Printing Office, 1940).

49. Jemison, "Report on Hearings," Feb. 24, 1937, Bailey Papers; Weeks, "Eastern Cherokee and the New Deal," 317.

50. Foght to CIA, Aug. 29, 1935, Box 9, CA.

51. Ibid. More than a year and a half later Foght claimed opponents of the constitution had held "many weird night meetings," had attempted to usurp legal tribal authority, and in Bird Town had even drawn knives and threatened his life. Foght to CIA, March 15, 1937, Box 10, CA. Tom Underwood, a teenager at the time, recalls that opponents threatened to "hang" Foght. Author's interview with Underwood, April 24, 1985.

52. Foght to CIA, Nov. 15, 1935; March 30, 1936, Box 9, CA. Foght said Bauer and McCoy "should, if at all possible, be removed from the tribal council." See also Prioli, "Indian 'Princess' and the Architect," 287, 300–301, and n. 75. The 1900 census for Jackson County lists Bauer as one-quarter Cherokee and his maternal uncle James Blythe as one-half, whereas tribal records list them as three-eighths and six-eighths, respectively.

53. Foght to CIA, Oct. 23, 1935, Box 9, CA. The diminished scope of the program is apparent in Foght to CIA, Oct. 26, 1936, Box 9, CA.

54. Herbert D. Miles to Harold L. Ickes, Sept. 5, 1934, George Stephens Papers, SHC; Ickes to Governor Ehringhaus, Nov. 10, 1934, *Addresses, Letters and Papers of John Christoph Blucher Ehringhaus, Governor of North Carolina, 1933–1937* (Raleigh: Council of State, State of North Carolina, 1950), 382–88. The standard

account of the parkway is Harley E. Jolley, *The Blue Ridge Parkway* (Knoxville: University of Tennessee Press, 1969).

55. The best background on the Cherokees' relationship with the parkway is in 76 Cong., 1 sess., House of Representatives, Committee on Public Lands, *Hearings on House Resolution 6668, a Bill to Grant the State of North Carolina a Right of Way across the Cherokee Reservation in North Carolina* (Washington, D.C.: Government Printing Office, 1939); see also Jolley, *Blue Ridge Parkway*, chap. 8; R. L. Spalsbury to CIA, Jan. 11, 1934, Box 8; Spalsbury to CIA, June 27, 1934; Harold W. Foght to CIA, June 25, 1935, Box 9, CA.

56. Foght to CIA, June 25 (quotation), July 13, 1935, Box 9, CA; Jolley, *Blue Ridge Parkway*, 96–97; testimony of Fred Bauer, 76 Cong., 1 sess., *Hearings on House Resolution 6668*.

57. *Asheville Citizen*, July 9, 1935; Foght to CIA, July 13, 1935, Box 9, CA.

58. Foght to William Zimmerman, Jr., March 17, 1937, Box 10, CA; *House Report 931*, 75 Cong., 1 sess., Serial 10084 (Washington, D.C.: Government Printing Office, 1937).

59. Blythe to CIA, Sept. 14, 1937, Box 10, CA; SI Harold L. Ickes to Rene L. DeRouen, June 23, 1939, in *Senate Report 1491*, 76 Cong., 3 sess., Serial 10429 (Washington, D.C.: Government Printing Office, 1940); act of Aug. 19, 1937, 50 Stat. 699.

60. Blair to CIA, June 2, 1938, Box 10, CA; *Bryson City Times*, June 2, 1938.

61. Stephens to Curtis B. Johnson, Aug. 19, 24, 1938, Stephens Papers, SHC.

62. 76 Cong., 1 sess., *Hearings on House Resolution 6668*, 7, 13–15, 20–28, 49, 70; *Senate Report 1491*, Serial 10429. Bauer had earlier sent a statement protesting HR 6668 to every member of Congress. A somewhat garbled account of the deliberations is in the *New York Times*, Aug. 26, 1939.

63. Clyde M. Blair to CIA, Oct. 28, 1938, Box 11, CA.

64. Hauptman, "American Indian Federation and the Indian New Deal," 398; Blair to William Zimmerman, Aug. 4, 1939, Box 11, CA.

65. Author's interview with Underwood, April 24, 1985; *Bryson City Times*, Sept. 14, 1939; see also Clyde M. Blair to William Zimmerman, Aug. 4, 1939, Box 11, CA.

66. *Asheville Citizen*, June 17, 1939, 12th Annual Rhododendron Number; Statement of Zebulon Weaver, 76 Cong., 1 sess., *Hearings on House Resolution 6668*, 16.

67. Blair to CIA, Oct. 28, 1939; Feb. 17, 1940, Box 11, CA; Council Records, Feb. 12, 1940; Weeks, "Eastern Cherokee and the New Deal," 317–19; Jolley, *Blue Ridge Parkway*, 100–101.

CHAPTER 6

1. Spalsbury to CIA, Jan. 15, 1934, Box 8, CA.

2. Foght to CIA, June 18, 1935 (quotation), Box 9, CA; author's interview with Goingback and Mary U. Chiltoskey, April 18, 1985 (quotation).

3. Harold W. Foght to CIA, May 21, June 18, July 17, 1935, Box 9, CA; Eastern

Band of Cherokee Indians, Council Records, May 6, 1933, microfilm, NCDAH.

4. Foght to CIA, Aug. 22, 1934, Box 9, CA; author's interview with Underwood, April 24, 1985.

5. Spalsbury to CIA, Jan. 15, 1934, Box 8, CA.

6. Foght to CIA, May 21, 1935, Box 9, CA. Foght said they would "present again" a pageant, suggesting that one had been staged in 1934.

7. "Cherokee Indian Phoenix," typescript, May 1936, Box 9; Foght to CIA, May 3, 1937 (quotations), Box 10, CA; 76 Cong., U.S. Senate, *Survey of Conditions of the Indians in the United States*, part 37 (Washington, D.C.: Government Printing Office, 1940), 20476–78.

8. *Asheville Citizen-Times*, June 27, Aug. 15, 1937; *Bryson City Times*, July 1, 1937; Foght to J. L. Walters, Aug. 17, 1937, Box 10, CA; Fred B. Bauer, *Land of the North Carolina Cherokees* (Brevard, N.C.: George E. Buchanan, 1970), 54; testimony in 76 Cong., 3 sess., House of Representatives, Committee on Indian Affairs, *Hearings . . . on S. 2103* (Washington, D.C.: Government Printing Office, 1940), 240. Original plans called for eight performances, but factionalism was likely responsible for reducing the number to six.

9. Foght to CIA, Aug. 22, 1934, Box 9, CA.

10. See chapter 5.

11. C. M. Blair to CIA, Aug. 15, 1939, Box 11, CA; article on Lois Farthing, *Blueridge Parkway Gazette*, no. 7 (Pinehurst, N.C.: Gazette Newspapers, 1984).

12. Foght to CIA, Nov. 13, 1936, Box 9; Foght to William Zimmerman, Oct. 28, 1937, Box 10, CA.

13. Foght to William Zimmerman, June 18, 1936, Box 10, CA; McCoy to Senator Clyde R. Hoey, Jan. 26, 1947, Clyde R. Hoey Papers, Box 150, Duke University.

14. Foght to William Zimmerman, April 1, 1937, Box 10; article on Lois Farthing, *Blueridge Parkway Gazette*, no. 7, 1984.

15. *Blueridge Parkway Gazette*, no. 7, 1984 (quotation); author's interview with Lois Farthing, April 24, 1985.

16. McCoy article in *Bryson City Times*, June 1, 1939; see also *Bryson City Times*, Sept. 7, 1939.

17. *Asheville Citizen*, 12th Annual Rhododendron Number, June 17, 1939; Blair to CIA, Dec. 23, 1940, Box 11, CA.

18. Foght to Dr. B. Youngblood, Dec. 31, 1934, Box 9, CA.

19. McCoy article, *Bryson City Times*, June 1, 1939; McCoy to Senator Clyde R. Hoey, Jan. 26, 1947, Hoey Papers, Duke University.

20. The businessman was R. L. McLean; see chapter 5.

21. Clyde M. Blair to CIA, Feb. 14, July 20, 26, 1940, Box 11; Blair to William Zimmerman, Sept. 2, 1941; Blair to CIA, Nov. 5, Dec. 29, 1942, Box 12, CA.

22. Blair to CIA, Dec. 16, 1940, Box 11, CA.

23. Blair to CIA, July 7, 1945, Box 12, CA.

24. Clyde M. Blair to CIA, Feb. 23, 1941, Box 11; Nov. 5, 1942, Box 12, CA.

25. Blair to CIA, Aug. 15, 1939, Box 11, CA.

26. Ibid.; McCoy to Senator Clyde R. Hoey, Jan. 26, 1947, Hoey Papers, Box 150, Duke University. See also chapter 7.

27. Blair to CIA, Aug. 14, 1940, Box 11; July 15, 1941, Box 12; Jack Easton to Jarrett Blythe, April 17, 1941, Box 31, CA.

28. Clyde M. Blair to CIA, Dec. 31, 1941; Aug. 17, 1942 (quotation); Dec. 16, 1943, Box 12, CA.

29. Blair to CIA, July 7, 1942, Box 12, CA.

30. Blair to CIA, Sept. 4, 1942, Box 12, CA.

31. Blair to Charles Collier, June 20, 1942, Box 23, CA.

32. Early Bullard to SI Harold Ickes, Oct. 7, 1940; John H. Libby to Clyde M. Blair, Oct. 19, 1940; William Zimmerman to Blair, Dec. 14, 1940, RG 75, no. 54A-367, Box 475, NA.

33. Blair to Chairman of Election Board, Swain County, Oct. 28, Nov. 4, 1940; Blair to Chairman of Election Board, Jackson County, Oct. 28, 1940, RG 75, no. 53A-367, Box 475, NA; Council Records, Nov. 5, 1940, microfilm, NCDAH.

34. Council Records, Nov. 5, 1940.

35. Blair to CIA, Nov. 25, 1940, Box 11, CA.

36. Zimmerman to Blair, Dec. 14, 1940, RG 75, no. 53A-367, Box 475, NA.

37. Monthly service reports, RG 75, no. 53A-367, Box 475, NA.

38. "'Best Damn Soldiers in the Army'—Opinion of Indian Troopers," *Asheville Citizen-Times*, Nov. 29, 1942; monthly service reports, RG 75, no. 53A-367, Box 475, NA.

39. Monthly service reports, RG 75, no. 53A-367, Box 475, NA; William W. Wood, Jr., "War and the Eastern Cherokee," *Southern Indian Studies* 2(1950): 50; Tom Holm, "Fighting a White Man's War: The Extent and Legacy of American Indian Policy in World War II," *Journal of Ethnic Studies* 9(Summer 1981): 70; Donald L. Fixico, *Termination and Relocation: Federal Indian Policy, 1945–1960* (Albuquerque: University of New Mexico Press, 1986), 4. See also Alison R. Bernstein, "Walking in Two Worlds: American Indians and World War II" (Ph.D. diss., Columbia University, 1986).

40. Quoted in Holm, "Fighting a White Man's War," 71; see also Bernstein, "Walking in Two Worlds," 76–79. Similar remarks appear in "'Best Damn Soldiers in the Army'—Opinion of Indian Troopers," *Asheville Citizen-Times*, Nov. 29, 1942. A recent example of such stereotyping by an Indian scholar is Fixico, *Termination and Relocation*, 6–8.

41. Holm, "Fighting a White Man's War," 73–74. The complicated matter of the Iroquois is discussed in Bernstein, "Walking in Two Worlds," 45–54; see also 79–84 for Indian code talkers.

42. Author's interview with Robert S. Youngdeer, Feb. 21, 1985; author's interview with Joseph George, April 24, 1985; "Casualties and Awards for Valor among Indians in Military Service," RG 75, no. 64A-528, Box 254, NA. Two

other sources indicate that sixteen Eastern Cherokees died in the war. See James Rideway to Edward L. Wright, July 18, 1947, Box 23, CA, and Woods, "War and the Eastern Cherokee." For Charles George's heroism, see *Cherokee One Feather*, Nov. 18, 1987.

43. Author's interview with Robert S. Youngdeer, Feb. 21, 1985; author's interview with Jefferson Thompson, June 14, 1985.

44. Bernstein, "Walking in Two Worlds," 71.

45. Council Records, Jan. 12, 1942; Clyde M. Blair to CIA, Jan. 15, 1942; Jan. 15, April 1, 1944, Box 12, CA; Council Records, July 15, 1943; Holm, "Fighting a White Man's War," 73; " 'Best Damn Soldiers in the Army'—Opinion of Indian Troopers," *Asheville Citizen-Times*, Nov. 29, 1942; Bernstein, "Walking in Two Worlds," chap. 4.

46. " 'Best Damn Soldiers in the Army'—Opinion of Indian Troopers," *Asheville Citizen*, Nov. 29, 1942; Holm, "Fighting a White Man's War," 73.

47. Blair to A. C. Cooley, June 23, 1942 (quotation), Box 17, CA; Mary U. Chiltoskey (quotation), from author's interview with Goingback and Mary U. Chiltoskey, April 18, 1985; author's interview with Tom Underwood, April 24, 1985. Blythe was chief during the years 1931–47, 1955–59, and 1963–67.

48. Clyde M. Blair to CIA, Aug. 17, 1942, Box 12, CA.

49. Bernstein, "Walking in Two Worlds," 272. Agency officials reported only about one hundred Cherokee males enrolled in such programs. James Rideway to Edward L. Wright, July 18, 1947, Box 23, CA. See also Joe Jennings to George P. LaVatta, June 7, 1946, ibid.

50. Most of this information is in Joe Jennings to Donald Q. Palmer, Nov. 7, 1946, Box 46, CA. Additional information came from author's interview with Goingback and Mary U. Chiltoskey, April 18, 1985; also *Cherokee One Feather*, Oct. 5, 1988, 23. Efforts of Indian veterans in Arizona and New Mexico to secure the vote are discussed in Bernstein, "Walking in Two Worlds," 255–61.

51. Joe Jennings to Donald Q. Palmer, Nov. 7, 1946, Box 46, CA; author's interview with Goingback and Mary U. Chiltoskey, April 18, 1985.

52. Ibid.

53. Ibid.

54. Clyde M. Blair to William A. Brophy, June 2, 1945, Box 12; Joe Jennings to George P. LaVatta, June 7, 1946, Box 23, CA.

55. Examples include Council Records, Oct. 9, 11, 15, 1945; Oct. 19, 1946; and Oct. 12, 1948.

56. Council Records, Oct. 4, 1943; Oct. 8, 11, 1945; Feb. 18, 1946; Bauer, *Land of the North Carolina Cherokees*, 52–53.

57. Catherine Bauer to Dan Tompkins, Jan. 26, 1947, Tompkins Papers, WCU; Bauer, *Land of the North Carolina Cherokees*, 53. See also chapter 7.

58. Jennings to CIA, Sept. 5, 1946, Box 13; Jennings to William Zimmerman,

April 29, 1947 (quotation), Box 23, CA. No one disputed Bauer's right to be on the roll.

59. Joe Jennings to E. D. Bennett, Jr., July 16, 1948, Box 23, CA.

60. Blair to CIA, Sept. 16, 1941, Box 12, CA.

61. Parris to Mrs. Elliston P. Morris, July 21, 1951, Governor Scott Papers, Box 86, Cherokee Historical Association folder, NCDAH; Council Records, March 13, 1948; author's interview with Tom Underwood, April 24, 1985; *State of North Carolina: 1949 Session Laws and Resolutions* . . . (Raleigh, 1949), chap. 1064, pp. 1224–25; Larry R. Stucki, "Will the 'Real' Indian Survive? Tourism and Affluence at Cherokee, North Carolina," in *Affluence and Cultural Survival*, ed. Richard F. Salisbury and Elisabeth Tooker (Washington, D.C.: American Ethnological Society, 1984), 58–59.

62. Parris to Mrs. Elliston P. Morris, July 21, 1951, Governor Scott Papers, Box 86, NCDAH; Council Records, March 13, 1948.

63. Kermit Hunter, *Unto These Hills* (Chapel Hill: University of North Carolina Press, 1951), 100; author's interview with Tom Underwood, April 24, 1985; Stucki, "Will the 'Real' Indian Survive?" 62–65. The most savage scholarly attack on the CHA is Larry French, "Tourism and Indian Exploitation: A Social Indictment," *Indian Historian* 10(1977): 17–29.

64. Samuel Selden to H. E. Buchanan, Dec. 7, 1948 (quotation); Joe Jennings to Governor R. Cherry, Jan. 6, 1949, both in Governor Cherry Papers, Box 52, NCDAH.

65. *Knoxville News-Sentinel*, July 5, 1950; *Chattanooga Times*, July 9, 1950; Bauer, *Land of the North Carolina Cherokees*, 54.

66. Ibid.

67. *Asheville Citizen*, July 2, 1950.

68. *Knoxville News-Sentinel*, July 5, 1950.

69. Ibid.; "Fact Sheet on Attendance," Cherokee Historical Association.

70. Author's interview with Tom Underwood, April 24, 1985.

71. Jennings to Dr. Edward J. Johnson, Sept. 5, 1950, Box 23, CA.

72. Ibid. The preceding year the Museum of the Cherokee Indian hosted a conference of the North Carolina Anthropological and Archaeological Society. H. E. Wheeler to "Dear Friends," Nov. 14, 1949, Box 31, CA.

73. Governor Scott to Governor Browning, Dec. 3, 1952; copy of letter of Hunter to Browning, Dec. 12, 1952, both in Governor Scott Papers, Box 112, Cherokee Historical Association folder, NCDAH.

74. Extended accounts of Tsali are in John R. Finger, *The Eastern Band of Cherokees, 1819–1900* (Knoxville: University of Tennessee Press, 1984), 21–28, and John R. Finger, "The Saga of Tsali: Legend versus Reality," *North Carolina Historical Review* 56(Winter 1979): 1–18. See also Bauer, *Land of the North Carolina Cherokees*, 24–25, 54–55.

CHAPTER 7

1. Eastern Band of Cherokee Indians, Council Records, Oct. 18, 1938, microfilm, NCDAH. See also William P. McCoy to Dan Tompkins, Feb. 26, 1947, Tompkins Papers, WCU. Much of this chapter is taken from my forthcoming article "Termination and the Eastern Band of Cherokees," *American Indian Quarterly*.

2. Bauer's views are expressed in detail in his *Land of the North Carolina Cherokees* (Brevard, N.C.: George E. Buchanan, 1970).

3. Council Records, February 1939; 76 Cong., 1 sess., *Senate Report* 1047, Serial 10295 (Washington, D.C.: Government Printing Office, 1939); 76 Cong., 3 sess., House of Representatives, Committee on Indian Affairs, *Hearings . . . on S. 2103* (Washington, D.C.: Government Printing Office, 1940), 5–7, 405–6.

4. 76 Cong., 3 sess., *Hearings . . . on S. 2103*, 35–36, 39–40, 52–53.

5. Ibid., 52–53, 240, 405–6, 424–28; Kenneth R. Philp, *John Collier's Crusade for Indian Reform, 1920–1954* (Tucson: University of Arizona Press, 1977), 203–5.

6. Philp, *John Collier's Crusade for Indian Reform*, 205–8; Alison R. Bernstein, "Walking in Two Worlds: American Indians and World War II" (Ph.D. diss., Columbia University, 1986), chap. 5.

7. Author's interview with Goingback and Mary U. Chiltoskey, April 18, 1985.

8. Larry W. Burt, *Tribalism in Crisis: Federal Indian Policy, 1953–1961* (Albuquerque: University of New Mexico Press, 1982), chap. 1; Donald L. Fixico, *Termination and Relocation: Federal Indian Policy, 1945–1960* (Albuquerque: University of New Mexico Press, 1986), chap. 1.

9. 79 Cong., 2 sess., Senate, *Hearing . . . on S. 1093 and S. 1194* (Washington, D.C.: Government Printing Office, 1946), 4.

10. Fixico, *Termination and Relocation*, 31–32.

11. Catherine Bauer to Dan Tompkins, Jan. 26, 1947, Tompkins Papers. See also her letter of Oct. 8, 1946, to Tompkins.

12. McCoy to Hoey, Jan. 26, 1947, Clyde R. Hoey Papers, Box 150, Duke University.

13. S. Lyman Tyler, *A History of Indian Policy* (Washington, D.C.: Government Printing Office, 1973), 163–64. Donald Fixico says the Zimmerman Plan became "the blueprint to abrogate the federal-Indian trust relationship" (*Termination and Relocation*, 33).

14. *House Report* 2503, 82 Cong., 2 sess., Serial 11582 (Washington, D.C.: Government Printing Office, 1953), 158, 161.

15. *Asheville Citizen*, Feb. 26, 1947 (quotation); Bauer, *Land of the North Carolina Cherokees*, 53.

16. John C. McCoy to Tompkins, Feb. 2, 1947; Walter R. McCoy telegram to representatives of Swain and Jackson counties, Feb. 24, 1947, Tompkins Papers.

17. *Asheville Citizen*, Feb. 26, 1947. Pearson McCoy claimed that all but one of the Cherokees at the hearings were government employees. McCoy to Dan Tompkins, Feb. 26, 1947, Tompkins Papers. The federal government spent

$304,700 on Eastern Cherokee education during fiscal year 1951–52. North Carolina State Board of Public Welfare, "Report of a Social Study of the Eastern Band of Cherokee Indians" (Raleigh, 1952), 4.

18. Bauer to chairman and committee members, March 17, 1947 (quotation), Tompkins Papers; see also Bauer, *Land of the North Carolina Cherokees*, 47, 52–53; Catherine Bauer to Dan Tompkins, Oct. 8, 1946, Tompkins Papers; and Clyde M. Blair to CIA, Sept. 23, Nov. 3, 1942; Blair to Fred H. Daiker, Dec. 7, 1942, Box 12, CA. The case was *U.S. v. Parton and Tahquette*. Webb had long been a problem for agents attempting to uphold federal authority, and his decision in this case owed much to Bauer's own arguments about the nonreservation status of Cherokee lands.

19. Bauer to chairman and committee members, March 17, 1947, Tompkins Papers.

20. Jennings to Zimmerman, April 29, 1947, Box 23, CA.

21. Ibid.

22. Council Records, Oct. 10, 1946.

23. Ibid., Oct. 8, 1947.

24. Ibid., Oct. 16, 1947.

25. Fixico, *Termination and Relocation*, chap. 2 (quotation on p. 27).

26. Ibid., 31; *House Report* 2503, Serial 11582, 273; Docket no. 282, *The Eastern Band of Cherokee Indians, Petitioner, v. The United States of America, Defendant,* Answer, Jan. 1956, William Holland Thomas Collection, WCU; "Cherokees Vote to Accept Land Settlement," *Asheville Citizen*, June 16, 1972; ibid., May 12, 1973. See also chapter 8.

27. Fixico, *Termination and Relocation*, chap. 4; Kenneth R. Philp, "Dillon S. Myer and the Advent of Termination: 1950–1953," *Western Historical Quarterly* 19(Jan. 1988): 37–59 (quotation on p. 37).

28. Philp, "Dillon S. Myer and the Advent of Termination," 48–49; Kenneth R. Philp, "Stride toward Freedom: The Relocation of Indians to Cities, 1952–1960," *Western Historical Quarterly* 16(April 1985): 175–90; Fixico, *Termination and Relocation*, chap. 7.

29. Karen I. Blu, *The Lumbee Problem: The Making of an American Indian People* (New York: Cambridge University Press, 1980), 33–34; W. McKee Evans, "The North Carolina Lumbees: From Assimilation to Revitalization," in *Southeastern Indians since the Removal Era*, ed. Walter L. Williams (Athens: University of Georgia Press, 1979), 63. The Lumbees had only limited federal recognition and therefore did not receive BIA assistance.

30. John Gulick, *Cherokees at the Crossroads* (Chapel Hill: University of North Carolina Press, 1960), 23. Comments of various individuals, including Brown, in *Asheville Citizen*, Feb. 2, 1961; see also *Greensboro Daily News*, Feb. 2, 1961.

31. Examples include author's interviews with Robert S. Youngdeer, Feb. 21, 1985, and Richard Welch, April 17, 1985; biographical information on Frell Owl, *Ashe-*

ville Citizen, Aug. 26, 1962. For comments on emigrants from Paint Town, see Gulick, *Cherokees at the Crossroads*, 84–87.

32. Philp, "Dillon S. Myer and the Advent of Termination," 51–52; Tyler, *History of Indian Policy*, 168–72.

33. *House Report* 2680, 83 Cong., 2 sess., Serial 11747 (Washington, D.C.: Government Printing Office, 1954), 281–82.

34. Ibid.; North Carolina, "Report of a Social Study of the Eastern Band of Cherokee Indians," 4, 9.

35. *House Report* 2680, Serial 11747, 281–82.

36. Ibid., 282–83.

37. Ibid., 26–28; Bauer, *Land of the North Carolina Cherokees*, 56.

38. *House Report* 2680, Serial 11747, 29–30 (quotation on p. 30); Tyler, *History of Indian Policy*, 169–71.

39. Tyler, *History of Indian Policy*, 172–81; Burt, *Tribalism in Crisis*, passim; Fixico, *Termination and Relocation*, chaps. 5–6 and 8, esp. pp. 180–81. The Menominee story is in Nicholas C. Peroff, *Menominee Drums: Tribal Termination and Restoration, 1954–1974* (Norman: University of Oklahoma Press, 1982).

40. Tyler, *History of Indian Policy*, 182–85; Burt, *Tribalism in Crisis*, 24–25; Fixico, *Termination and Relocation*, chap. 6.

41. Harry McMullen and Ralph Moody to Umstead, Nov. 12, 1953, RG 75, no. 71A-2720, Box 85, FRCS. Moody was apparently unaware that all Indians were United States citizens.

42. *Asheville Citizen-Times*, Aug. 29, Sept. 5, 1954.

43. Bauer, *Land of the North Carolina Cherokees*, 56–57; *Asheville Citizen-Times*, July 4, 1954; *Asheville Citizen*, Nov. 12, 1954; "Tarheel of the Week: Chief Osley Saunooke," Raleigh *News and Observer*, Aug. 29, 1954.

44. "Tarheel of the Week: Chief Osley Saunooke," Raleigh *News and Observer*, Aug. 29, 1954; Saunooke obituary, *Asheville Citizen*, April 16, 1965. For concern over the hospital, see Thelma H. Bell to CIA, June 2, 1954, RG 75, no. 59A-643, Box 13, NA.

45. Hildegard Thompson, "Report of conference held with officials in the State Department of Education, Raleigh, North Carolina," Oct. 19, 1954, RG 75, no. 59A-643, Box 13, NA. See also Thompson to Dr. William Gilbert, Sept. 12, 1955, RG 75, no. 61A-182, Box 123B, NA.

46. Hildegard Thompson, "Report of conference," Oct. 19, 1954, RG 75, no. 59A-643, Box 13, NA.

47. Ibid.

48. Wayne T. Pratt to Chief, Branch of Education, Sept. 8, 1955, RG 75, no. 61A-182, Box 123B, NA.

49. Nov. 12, 1954.

50. Comments of E. S. Saunooke, *Asheville Citizen-Times*, Sept. 5, 1954; editorial, *Knoxville Journal*, Nov. 19, 1954; Cherokee letters to editor, *Asheville Citizen*,

Nov. 15, 1954; CIA Emmons to Reed Sarratt, Nov. 24, 1954, RG 75, no. 59A-643, Box 13, NA; ibid., for more material on circumstances surrounding Jennings's transfer and prospects for termination.

51. Buchanan to Hodges, Nov. 18, 1954, Governor Hodges Papers, Box 97, NCDAH.

52. Bill Sharpe to Kerr, Nov. 17, 1954, accompanying letter of Harry E. Buchanan to Governor Luther H. Hodges, Nov. 18, 1954, Governor Hodges Papers, Box 97, NCDAH; see also Harold E. Fey, "The Cherokee Trail of Tears," *Christian Century* 72(June 8, 1955): 680–82.

53. Emmons to Reed Sarratt, Nov. 24, 1954, RG 75, no. 59A-643, Box 13, NA; Governor Luther H. Hodges to Bill Sharpe, Nov. 26, 1954, Governor Hodges Papers, Box 97, NCDAH; Bauer, *Land of the North Carolina Cherokees*, 57–59; Fey, "Cherokee Trail of Tears," 682.

54. *Asheville Citizen*, Dec. 22, 1954. Fred Bauer later remarked, with at least a kernel of truth, that there were ulterior motives for the CHA's support of corporate landownership: "Only by holding the lands as a unit could the grandiose plans of the [CHA] be carried out" (*Land of the North Carolina Cherokees*, 60).

55. Fey, "Cherokee Trail of Tears," 682.

56. Swan to George A. Shuford, Feb. 8, 1955, George A. Shuford Papers, Duke University.

57. Tahquette to George A. Shuford, Nov. 26, 1955, Shuford Papers.

58. 84 Cong., 1 sess., House of Representatives, *Hearing before the Subcommittee on Indian Affairs . . . Pursuant to H. Res. 30* (Washington, D.C.: Government Printing Office, 1955). Haley, the chairman of the Committee on Interior and Insular Affairs' Subcommittee on Indian Affairs, also conducted hearings on possible termination of Florida's Seminoles. See Harry A. Kersey, Jr., "From Near Termination to Self-Determination: The Florida Seminoles, 1953–1957," paper read at November 1988 meeting of the Southern Historical Association, Norfolk, Va.

59. Fixico, *Termination and Relocation*, chaps. 8–9; Tyler, *History of Indian Policy*, 186–88; Burt, *Tribalism in Crisis*, chaps. 8–10.

60. Quoted in *Asheville Citizen*, Sept. 4, 1962; obituary of Osley Saunooke, *Asheville Citizen*, April 16, 1965.

CHAPTER 8

1. Memorandum of Albert Huber, BIA Chief of Credit, June 7, 1956, enclosed with letter of Richard D. Butts to Morrill M. Tozier, June 18, 1956, RG 75, no. 62A-523, Box 8, NA.

2. North Carolina State Board of Public Welfare, "Report of a Social Study of the Eastern Band of Cherokee Indians" (Raleigh, 1952), 15; Harold E. Fey, "The Cherokee Trail of Tears," *Christian Century* 72(June 8, 1955): 680–82 (quotation on 682); 84 Cong., 1 sess., House of Representatives, *Hearing before the Subcommittee on Indian Affairs . . . Pursuant to H. Res. 30* (Washington, D.C.: Government Printing Office, 1955), 61; Mary Sikorsky to whom it may concern, Dec. 16, 1959, Governor Luther Hodges Papers, NCDAH; Larry R. Stucki, "Will

the 'Real' Indian Survive? Tourism and Affluence at Cherokee, North Carolina," in *Affluence and Cultural Survival*, ed. Richard F. Salisbury and Elisabeth Tooker (Washington, D.C.: American Ethnological Society, 1984), 59.

3. *Asheville Citizen*, Feb. 27, 1952; Carol White to Officers and Trustees, Cherokee Historical Association, Sept. 18, 1953, Governor William B. Umstead Papers, Box 3, NCDAH; *North Carolina Session Laws*, 1951, chap. 1164; ibid., 1953, chap. 962.

4. Richard D. Butts to Morrill M. Tozier, June 18, 1956, RG 75, no. 62A-523, Box 8, NA.

5. *Senate Report* 2486, 81 Cong., 2 sess. Serial 11372 (Washington, D.C.: Government Printing Office, 1950–51); *Asheville Citizen*, Sept. 17, 1950 (quotation).

6. 84 Cong., 1 sess., *Hearing . . . Pursuant to H. Res. 30*, 60; act of Aug. 5, 1955, 69 U.S. Stat. 539.

7. Richard D. Butts to Leon V. Langan, June 15, 1956, RG 75, no. 61A-182, Box 10; Butts to CIA, May 23, 1957, RG 75, no. 64A-528, Box 15, NA. Saddlecraft later became Cherokees Industry.

8. Butts to CIA, May 23, 1957, RG 75, no. 64A-528, Box 15, File 7916, NA; *Asheville Citizen*, Dec. 3, 1959; John Parris interview of Thompson in "The Scars Have Healed," *Asheville Citizen*, Dec. 3, 1959. The Harn Corporation later became White Shield.

9. *Asheville Citizen*, Feb. 12, 1961.

10. North Carolina, "Report of a Social Study of the Eastern Band of Cherokee Indians"; Hester A. Davis, "Social Interaction and Kinship in Big Cove Community, Cherokee, N.C." (M.A. thesis, University of North Carolina, Chapel Hill, 1957), 4; Carol White to Officers and Trustees, Cherokee Historical Association, Sept. 8, 1953, Governor Umstead Papers, Box 3, NCDAH.

11. A summary of these findings, along with a list of participants and their scholarly output, is in John Gulick, *Cherokees at the Crossroads* (Chapel Hill: University of North Carolina Press, 1960).

12. John L. Grant, "Behavioral Premises in the Culture of Conservative Eastern Cherokee Indians" (M.A. thesis, University of North Carolina, Chapel Hill, 1957), 1–5; Davis, "Social Interaction and Kinship in Big Cove Community," 27, 45–46.

13. Grant, "Behavioral Premises in the Culture of Conservative Eastern Cherokee Indians," 38–39.

14. Annie Cofield Gardner, "Social Organization and Community Solidarity in Painttown, Cherokee, N.C." (M.A. thesis, University of North Carolina, Chapel Hill, 1958), 49–52.

15. Grant, "Behavioral Premises in the Culture of Conservative Eastern Cherokee Indians," 52–71.

16. Ibid., 48; Davis, "Social Interaction and Kinship in Big Cove Community," 19–20, 47, 50; North Carolina, "Report of a Social Study of the Eastern Band of Cherokee Indians," 9.

17. Gardner, "Social Organization and Community Solidarity in Painttown," 72–74; North Carolina, "Report of a Social Study of the Eastern Band of Cherokee Indians," 9–10.

18. Raymond D. Fogelson, "A Study of the Conjurer in Eastern Cherokee Society" (M.A. thesis, University of Pennsylvania, 1958), part 2, esp. pp. 111–12; quotation in "Last of Old-Time Cherokee Medicine Men Is Gone," *Asheville Citizen*, June 12, 1958.

19. Raymond D. Fogelson, "The Cherokee Ball Game: A Study in Southeastern Ethnology" (Ph.D. diss., University of Pennsylvania, 1962), chap. 8, app. F; Harriet Jane Kupferer, *The "Principal People," 1960: A Study of Cultural and Social Groups of the Eastern Cherokee*, Bureau of American Ethnology Bulletin 196 (Washington, D.C.: Government Printing Office, 1966), 241; Gulick, *Cherokees at the Crossroads*, 113–14; North Carolina, "Report of a Social Study of the Eastern Band of Cherokee Indians," 11–12; *Knoxville Journal*, Sept. 29, 1988.

20. Davis, "Social Interaction and Kinship in Big Cove Community," 15; Gardner, "Social Organization and Community Solidarity in Painttown," 3, 18; Sharlotte Neely Williams, "Ethnicity in a Native American Community" (Ph.D. diss., University of North Carolina, Chapel Hill, 1976), 26–27.

21. Davis, "Social Interaction and Kinship in Big Cove Community," 111–17; Gardner, "Social Organization and Community Solidarity in Painttown," 27, 85, 88–89, 104–7, 110–12, 115–16, 133–34.

22. Gardner, "Social Organization and Community Solidarity in Painttown," 39–41. There were 104 households in Paint Town.

23. Author's interview with James Cooper, April 17, 1985; Chief Osley B. Saunooke to CIA [Glenn] Emmons, Nov. 5, 1954, RG 75, no. 59A-643, Box 14; Richard D. Butts to CIA, April 30, 1956, RG 75, no. 62A-523, Box 8; Rev. Ewell Payne to CIA Emmons, May 1, 1956, RG 75, no. 62A-523, Box 8, NA. In 1961 there were twenty-one churches on the reservation, eleven of them Baptist. See "Cherokees Show a Great Pride, Respect," *Charlotte Observer*, May 21, 1961.

24. Gardner, "Social Organization and Community Solidarity in Painttown," 33, 63; "North Carolina Agricultural Extension Service Annual Narrative Report, Cherokee Indian Reservation 1959," [n.d.], RG 75, no. 67A-721, Box 13, FRCS. Other more or less contemporary reports listed more than six hundred families on the reservation.

25. *House Report* 2503, 82 Cong., 2 sess., Serial 11582 (Washington, D.C.: Government Printing Office, 1953), 1155; North Carolina, "Report of a Social Study of the Eastern Band of Cherokee Indians," 15–16; Gulick, *Cherokees at the Crossroads*, 18–19; Enclosure, "To Break the Cycle," with Don Y. Jensen to George H. Esser, Jr., Jan. 21, 1964, RG 75, no. 68A-2045, Box 266, FRCS; Darrell Fleming's comments in *Greensboro Daily News*, Feb. 12, 1961.

26. Quinn to H. Rex Lee, March 2, 1959, RG 75, no. 66A-641, Box 118, FRCS. For similar social delineations, see Kupferer, *"Principal People,"* 311–12; Harriet J. Kupferer, "The Isolated Eastern Cherokee," *Midcontinent American Studies Jour-*

nal 6(Fall 1975): 128–29; and Gulick's summary of Robert Thomas's continuum in *Cherokees at the Crossroads*, 127 ff.

27. Quinn to H. Rex Lee, March 2, 1959, RG 75, no. 66A-641, Box 118, FRCS.

28. Robert K. Thomas, "Eastern Cherokee Acculturation," May 1958, unpublished paper for the Cross-Cultural Laboratory of the Institute for Research in Social Sciences, University of North Carolina, Chapel Hill, 19–24, summarized in Gulick, *Cherokees at the Crossroads*, 127 ff.; Kupferer, *"Principal People,"* 245–47, 309–17. For related matters see Stucki, "Will the 'Real' Indian Survive?" 60–62, and Laurence French and Jim Hornbuckle, eds., *The Cherokee Perspective* (Boone, N.C.: Appalachian Consortium Press, 1981), 28.

29. North Carolina, "Report of a Social Study of the Eastern Band of Cherokee Indians," 10–11; Kupferer, *"Principal People,"* 240, 320–21.

30. 84 Cong., 1 sess., *Hearing . . . Pursuant to H. Res. 30*, 8–9, 18–21, 38–45, 60–62; Grant, "Behavioral Premises in the Culture of Conservative Eastern Cherokee Indians," 98–103; act of Aug. 21, 1957, 71 Stat. 374; Bauer to SI Frederick A. Seaton, May 7, 1958, RG 75, no. 67A-721, Box 103, FRCS; Kupferer, "Isolated Eastern Cherokee," 130; Thomas, "Eastern Cherokee Acculturation," 24.

31. *Asheville Citizen*, June 17, 1959; Kupferer, *"Principal People,"* 232.

32. SI Stewart L. Udall, Aug. 6, 1963, regarding publication of revised blood quantum requirements, RG 75, no. 69A-3351, Box 117; Myrtle C. Jenkins to whom it may concern, May 14, 1963, RG 75, no. 67A-721, Box 103; "Study Report— Cherokee Agency," May 13–17, 1968, RG 75, no. 75-73-1, Box 50, FRCS.

33. *Asheville Citizen*, Oct. 1, 1964; R. W. Quinn to Tribal Government Section, BIA, Jan. 22, 1965, RG 75, no. 71A-2720, Box 85, FRCS.

34. William B. Benge to Chief, Office of Tribal Operations, May 3, 1965, RG 75, no. 71A-2720, Box 85, FRCS; R. M. Pennington to Don Y. Jensen, July 23, 1965, ibid., with draft of constitution; council resolution of October 1966, ibid.; Krenzke to Jarrett Blythe, Nov. 22, 1966, RG 75, no. 71A-2720, Box 85, FRCS.

35. Williams, "Ethnicity in a Native American Community," chap. 3.

36. *Asheville Citizen*, Sept. 6, 1963; April 16, 1965; Oct. 4, 1967; April 15, 1977; Bob Terrell's column "Only Yesterday," *Asheville Citizen*, April 15, 1975; *Charlotte News and Observer*, Oct. 10, 1965; *Asheville Citizen*, April 15, 1977.

37. Enclosure, "To Break the Cycle," with Jensen to George H. Esser, Jan. 21, 1964, RG 75, no. 68A-2045, Box 266, FRCS.

38. Johnny Long, "The O.E.O. on the Cherokee Indian Reservation," senior seminar paper, Dec. 8, 1983, submitted to Dr. Ronald D. Eller, Mars Hill College; Williams, "Ethnicity in a Native American Community," 78.

39. Quoted in *Charlotte News and Observer*, Oct. 10, 1965.

40. Charles D. Johnson to CIA Robert Bennett, Aug. 11, 1967, RG 75, no. 70A-2935, Box 106; Robert M. Farring, Jr., to Branch of Tribal Operations, April 18, 1968 (quotation), RG 75, no. 75-73-1, Box 50; Charles B. Rovin to Theodore Krenzke, July 8, 1968, RG 75, no. 72A-8022, Box 79, FRCS.

41. Krenzke to Branch of Social Service, July 16, 1968, RG 75, no. 72A-8022, Box 79, FRCS.

42. *Asheville Citizen*, Nov. 27, 1963; Kupferer, "Isolated Eastern Cherokee," 128.

43. *Asheville Citizen*, May 24, 1964; *Charlotte News and Observer*, Oct. 10, 1965 (quotation).

44. "Breakdown on Permanent and Seasonal Indian Employment," Oct. 1, 1965, RG 75, no. 69A-3351, Box 118; Carol White to CIA Robert L. Bennett, Aug. 2, 1967, RG 75, no. 73A-1106, Box 53; "Study Report—Cherokee Agency," May 13–17, 1968, RG 75, no. 75-73-1, Box 50, FRCS.

45. Cherokee Indian Agency Annual Council Report, October 1966, 1, 27, RG 75, no. 73A-1106, Box 53, FRCS; *Asheville Citizen*, April 7, 1969.

46. Krenzke's comments on the 1968 figures are in an interview appearing in the *Asheville Citizen*, Sept. 5, 1970; see also Cherokee Project Proposal submitted to Assistant SI, Public Land Management, Aug. 26, 1970, p. 2, RG 75, no. 75-75-4, Box 40, FRCS. See Jarrett Blythe's comments on spoken Cherokee, *Charlotte News and Observer*, Oct. 10, 1965.

47. An excellent discussion of the Eastern Band's legal status, including concurrent jurisdiction, is in Zelma Barrow to Chief of Tribal Operations, BIA, Jan. 15, 1965, RG 75, no. 71A-2720, Box 85, FRCS. The ten major crimes are murder, manslaughter, rape, incest, assault with a deadly weapon, arson, burglary, robbery, larceny, and Indian-related offenses involving intoxicants.

48. Richard D. Butts to Governor Luther H. Hodges, Jan. 30, 1959, Governor Hodges Papers, NCDAH; CIA Glenn Emmons to Senator B. Everett Jordan, March 27, 1959, RG 75, no. 61A-182, Box 9, NA.

49. CIA Glenn Emmons to Senator B. Everett Jordan, March 27, 1959, RG 75, no. 61A-182, Box 9, NA.

50. Butts to Hodges, Jan. 30, 1959; Robert E. Giles, Administrative Assistant for Hodges, to Butts, Feb. 4, 1959, Governor Hodges Papers, NCDAH.

51. Zelma Barrow to Chief of Tribal Operations, BIA, Jan. 15, 1965, 8–9, RG 75, no. 71A-2720, Box 85, FRCS.

52. *Asheville Citizen*, Sept. 10, 1964; May 9, 1965; Cherokee Indian Agency Annual Council Report, October 1966, 7, RG 75, no. 73A-1106, Box 53, FRCS; act of general assembly, June 2, 1965; various materials on Cherokee fisheries are in RG 75, no. 68A-2045, Box 267, FRCS.

53. *Asheville Citizen*, Sept. 16, 1964 (quotation); *New York Times*, Dec. 29, 1968.

54. Quoted in *New York Times*, Dec. 29, 1968.

55. *Asheville Citizen*, March 26, 1964; materials on possible consolidation in RG 75, no. 68A-2045, Box 267, FRCS; CIA Glenn Emmons to Hon. George A. Shuford, July 2, 1956; Shuford to Emmons, July 3, 1956, both in George A. Shuford Papers, Duke University. See also Sharlotte Neely Williams, "The Role of Formal Education among the Eastern Cherokee Indians, 1880–1971" (M.A. thesis, University of North Carolina, Chapel Hill, 1971), 44.

56. Don Y. Jensen to H. P. Davis, Oct. 5, 1965, RG 75, no. 68A-2045, Box 267, FRCS.

57. Ibid. (quotation); *Asheville Citizen*, July 16, 1965.

58. Taylor to Hickel, Sept. 22, 1970, RG 75, no. 72A-8022, Box 79, FRCS.

59. Cherokee Project Proposal submitted to Assistant SI, Public Land Management, Aug. 26, 1970, RG 75, no. 175-75-4, Box 40, FRCS.

60. Krenzke to CIA, July 17, 1970, RG 75, no. 75-75-4, Box 39, FRCS; Williams, "Role of Formal Education," chap. 8.

61. *Asheville Citizen*, March 15, 1970.

62. Author's interview with Muskrat, Feb. 21, 1985; author's interview with Jonathan L. Taylor, April 8, 1985; author's interview with Richard Welch, April 17, 1985.

63. Author's conversations with several different Cherokees.

64. Stucki, "Will the 'Real' Indian Survive?" 62–65; Laurence French, "Tourism and Indian Exploitation: A Social Indictment," *Indian Historian* 10(Fall 1977): 19–24.

65. William Bruce Wheeler and Michael J. McDonald, *TVA and the Tellico Dam, 1936–1979: A Bureaucratic Crisis in Post-industrial America* (Knoxville: University of Tennessee Press, 1986), 84.

66. Ibid., 134, 148–50.

67. Ibid., 150–56; *Asheville Citizen*, Aug. 30; Sept. 20, 1972; *Knoxville News Sentinel*, Sept. 15, 1972; Peter Matthiessen, *Indian Country* (New York: Viking Press, 1984), 105–26; *Cherokee One Feather*, Jan. 4, 1989.

68. Quoted in Wheeler and McDonald, *TVA and the Tellico Dam*, 152.

69. Ibid., 152–55.

70. Ibid., 177–78.

71. Ibid., 211–15; Ben Oshel Bridgers, "An Historical Analysis of the Legal Status of the North Carolina Cherokees," *North Carolina Law Review* 58(August 1980): 1010–11.

72. 28 *Indian Claims Commission*, 386–98; *Asheville Citizen*, June 16, 1972; May 12, 1973.

73. Francis Paul Prucha, *The Great Father: The United States Government and the American Indians*, 2 vols. (Lincoln: University of Nebraska Press, 1984), vol. 2, chaps. 43–44.

74. Ibid., 2: 1112.

75. Bauer to Taylor, Aug. 27, 1970, RG 75, no. 75-73-1, Box 50, FRCS; Bauer, *Land of the North Carolina Cherokees* (Brevard, N.C.: George E. Buchanan, 1970); *Asheville Citizen*, June 1, 1971.

76. Prucha, *Great Father*, 2: 1160.

CHAPTER 9

1. Figures provided by Wilbur Paul, superintendent of the Cherokee BIA agency. Of the 9,590 enrollees, 2,672 lived off reservation. Reservation acreage in Swain

County is 29,341.87; Jackson County, 19,347; Cherokee County, 5,571; and Graham County, 2,249. In addition, there are 112.16 reservation acres in Swain County belonging to the United States for its agency responsibilities, making a total of 56,621.03 acres.

2. Muskrat to Eastern Area Director, July 27, 1979; see also Robert A. Benzel to Eastern Area Director, March 26, 1979; both in CACF.

3. Evanelle Thompson to Eastern Area Director, Aug. 4, 1982, CACF.

4. *Cherokee One Feather*, Jan. 13, 1988.

5. Ibid., Sept. 21, 1988.

6. Ibid., May 31, 1989.

7. Marketing survey, ibid.; Jeff Muskrat to Eastern Area Director, Sept. 7, 1982, p. 3, CACF; *Waynesville Mountaineer*, May 9, 1983; *Cherokee One Feather*, Nov. 21, 1984; Jan. 9, May 15, Aug. 14, 1985; Jan. 22, 1986; information regarding gross income and the tribe's share is in *Cherokee One Feather*, April 8, 1987. A somewhat condescending and cynical view of Cherokee Bingo is Paul Hemphill, "The Bingo Trail," *Southern Magazine*, July/Aug. 1989, 30–32, 76–79.

8. *Asheville Citizen-Times*, Jan. 31, Sept. 25, 1987; *Cherokee One Feather*, April 23, May 7, 14, 28, July 30, Sept. 3, 1986; Jan. 28, Feb. 4, 11, April 8, 22, Sept. 30, Nov. 4, 1987; Taylor's comments and statistics, *Cherokee One Feather*, March 16, 1988.

9. *Cherokee One Feather*, March 16, May 18, 25, 1988; Sept. 13, 20, Nov. 1, 22, 1989; Jan. 3, 1990.

10. Ibid., Sept. 2, 1987, p. 23; May 11, Sept. 7, 1988.

11. Ibid., Nov. 28, 1984; May 6, 1985; June 18, 25, 1986. Ray Cucumber, the new general manager of the museum, angrily resigned in June 1986 in a dispute over his authority and also called the museum "a well-planned promotional tool by TVA" (ibid., June 4, 1986).

12. "Many-Splendored Chief," *Asheville Citizen*, May 19, 1979; author's interview with Lambert, April 8, 1985; author's interview with Joseph George, April 24, 1985.

13. *Asheville Citizen*, Aug. 15, 1980.

14. *Cherokee One Feather*, Jan. 22, 29, Feb. 19, 1986; July 6, 1988. See also ibid., March 30, 1988.

15. Muskrat to Harry A. Rainbolt, Aug. 4, 1978; Muskrat to Area Director, Oct. 22, 1982, CACF.

16. Report by Community Injury Control Program (n.d.); copy in author's possession.

17. Author's interview with King, May 9, 1988; Patricia Grant report on alcohol abuse, in author's possession.

18. Muskrat to Ed Lentz, May 24, 1979, CACF. Unemployment figures vary; for examples see Muskrat to Area Director, April 5, 1982; April 9, May 4, 1984, CACF;

Cherokee One Feather, March 8, 1989, 1. CETA stands for the Comprehensive Employment and Training Act of 1973.

19. Muskrat to Ed Lentz, May 24, 1979, CACF; see also comments of Darrell Fleming, "Cherokee Show a Great Pride, Respect," *Charlotte Observer*, May 21, 1961.

20. Jesse O. McKee and Steve Murray, "Economic Progress and Development of the Choctaw since 1945," in *After Removal: The Choctaw in Mississippi*, ed. Samuel J. Wells and Roseanna Tubby (Jackson: University of Mississippi Press, 1986), 122–36. For problems with mortgages, see Jim Hummingbird to Area Director, Nov. 8, 1983, CACF.

21. *Cherokee One Feather*, Nov. 12, 1986.

22. Ibid. (quotation); July 6, 1988; Jan. 3, 1990.

23. Dr. Aty Badker to Dr. Larry Isaac, Jr., BIA Eastern Area Records, Cherokee Central School, Oct. 8, 1985, Broyhill Building, Arlington, Va.

24. Author's interview with Richard Welch, April 17, 1985; *Cherokee One Feather*, Nov. 30, 1988 (quotation); June 7, 1989.

25. Concern over this issue appears in the *Cherokee One Feather*, Dec. 5, 1984; April 24, Aug. 21, 28, Sept. 11, Nov. 20, 27, Dec. 4, 1985; Jan. 8, 15, Feb. 26, March 19, Sept. 24, Oct. 15, 1986.

26. Bradley to Acting Director, Office of Indian Education Programs, June 13, 1985, Folder "32, F Cherokee Central School," Department of the Interior, Main Building.

27. *Cherokee One Feather*, Sept. 11, 1985; Feb. 3, 1988; Jeff Muskrat to Denver Service Center, National Park Service, May 4, 1979, CACF.

28. *Cherokee One Feather*, Nov. 11, 1988.

29. Ibid., May 27, 1987. Dr. G. Peter Boyum, an orthopedic surgeon in Stillwater, Minnesota, was apparently the first enrolled Eastern Cherokee to earn the M.D. (in 1970). Ibid., July 15, 1987.

30. *Asheville Citizen*, July 10, 1976.

31. Ibid., Jan. 15, Feb. 6, 1977.

32. Ibid., Feb. 6, 1977.

33. Regarding the bingo controversy, see *Asheville Citizen*, Jan. 31, 1987; *Cherokee One Feather*, April 23, May 7, 14, 28, July 30, 1986; Jan. 28, Feb. 4, 11, Sept. 30, 1987. For McCoy and Taylor, see *Cherokee One Feather*, Sept. 16, 23, 1987.

34. Author's interview with Jim Cooper, April 17, 1985. Chief John A. Crowe initiated consideration of a new constitution in 1979. *Asheville Citizen*, June 15, 1979. Subsequent resolutions regarding the constitution are discussed in Jim Hummingbird, Acting Superintendent, to Area Director, Feb. 10, 1984, CACF.

35. *Cherokee One Feather*, May 23, Sept. 5, 26, Oct. 17, 31, Nov. 7, 1984; June 4, 1986; author's interviews with Youngdeer, Feb. 21, 1985; and Sequoyah, April 24, 1985.

36. Council Resolution 132, May 8, 1986. The tribal charter, with proposed changes

in boldface, appears in *Cherokee One Feather*, Aug. 6, 1986; see also issues of Aug. 20, Sept. 3, 10, Oct. 8, 15, 1986.

37. *Cherokee One Feather*, Sept. 10, Oct. 15, 1986. Sharlotte Neely Williams, "Ethnicity in a Native American Community" (Ph.D. diss., University of North Carolina, Chapel Hill, 1976), chap. 3.

38. "A Chief's Mission: Off-season Jobs," *Knoxville News-Sentinel*, Jan. 31, 1988. Taylor said much the same thing in his interview with author, April 8, 1985.

39. *Cherokee One Feather*, Oct. 28, 1987; June 22, 29, 1988.

40. Author's interview with Muskrat, Feb. 21, 1985. Taylor's comments on IHS funding are in *Cherokee One Feather*, Feb. 15, 1989. Taylor was for many years the tribe's health care officer.

41. *Cherokee One Feather*, March 13, 1985; April 12, July 5, Sept. 13, Nov. 29, 1989.

42. *Cherokee One Feather*, Feb. 27, March 6, July 10, 1985; March 26, 1986; June 3, 1987; March 22, 1989; "Maggie Wachacha: The Cherokees Venerate Their Beloved Women," *Winston-Salem Journal*, Aug. 24, 1986; Carmaleta Littlejohn Monteith, "The Role of the Scribe in Eastern Cherokee Society, 1821–1985" (Ph.D. diss., Emory University, 1985). Mrs. Gloyne died in April 1985.

43. Ben Oshel Bridgers, "An Historical Analysis of the Legal Status of the North Carolina Cherokees," *North Carolina Law Review* 58(August 1980): 1114–22; *Asheville Citizen*, June 15, 1979; July 11, 1980; Dec. 11, 1987; Jeff Muskrat to Area Director, Aug. 9, 10, 1979; April 23, 1982, CACF; *Cherokee One Feather*, Dec. 9, 16, 1987; June 28, Aug. 23, 1989.

44. *Cherokee One Feather*, Oct. 10, 1984; Aug. 1, 1985; Jan. 29, 1986; Jan. 7, 1987; Aug. 24, Sept. 28, 1988; Dec. 13, 1989; North Carolina Commission on Indian Affairs, "A Historical Perspective about the Indians of North Carolina and an Overview of the Commission of Indian Affairs," *North Carolina Historical Review* 56(Spring 1979): 183–87; Ruth Wetmore, "The Role of the Indian in North Carolina History," *North Carolina Historical Review* 56(Spring 1979): 173–76.

45. *Knoxville News-Sentinel*, April 6–8, 1984; *Asheville Citizen*, April 4, 1984; *U.S.A. Today*, April 4, 1984; Jeff Muskrat to Area Director, March 20, 1984, CACF.

46. *Knoxville News-Sentinel*, April 6, 1984.

47. Examples in *Cherokee One Feather*, June 26, July 10, 1985, April 1, Dec. 9, 1987; May 11, 25, June 15, 29, Aug. 24, Sept. 21, Oct. 5, 12, 19, Nov. 2, 16, 1988; Jan. 4, 1989; see also comments of Robert K. Thomas, *Cherokee One Feather*, Nov. 8, 1989.

48. *Cherokee One Feather*, Jan. 30, April 24, June 12, 1985; July 20, 1988.

49. "Cherokee to Decline to Share Name," *Asheville Citizen*, Aug. 8, 1978; see also Jeff Muskrat to Area Director, Feb. 13, 1984, CACF, regarding the "alleged" Indians of Hoke County, North Carolina; and *Cherokee One Feather*, Aug. 17, Oct. 5, 12, 1988; Feb. 22, March 1, 8, 15, 22, 1989; "Viewpoint," *Charlotte Observer*, Oct. 5, 1988. Lumbee recognition as Indians is in 70 U.S. Stat. 254–55.

50. Author's interview with Muskrat, Feb. 21, 1985.

51. Author's interview with King, May 9, 1988.

52. Author's interview with Calonehuskie, Aug. 1, 1988; see also comments of Gilliam Jackson in "Cultural Identity for the Modern Cherokees," *Appalachian Journal* 2(Summer 1975): 280–81.

53. *Cherokee One Feather*, Aug. 28, 1985. Southwestern Tech has since become Southwestern Community College.

54. Ibid., Feb. 24, 1988.

55. Hemphill, "Bingo Trail," 77.

56. "Cherokee Autonomy Could Be Twenty Years Away," *Asheville Citizen-Times*, Jan. 20, 1985; Leon Jones to John Wahnee, Agency Principal, Jan. 28, 1987, BIA Eastern Area Records, Cherokee Central School, Broyhill Building, Arlington, Va.

57. "Cherokee Autonomy Could Be Twenty Years Away," *Asheville Citizen-Times*, Jan. 20, 1985.

58. In 1983 Jeff Muskrat estimated that commercial properties near the high school and agency headquarters were worth $20,000 to $25,000 an acre. Muskrat to Area Director, Jan. 4, 1983, CACF. For comments on tourism's impact and Cherokee identity, see Larry R. Stucki, "Will the 'Real' Indian Survive? Tourism and Affluence at Cherokee, North Carolina," in *Affluence and Cultural Survival*, ed. Richard F. Salisbury and Elisabeth Tooker (Washington, D.C.: American Ethnological Society, 1984), 58–71; Laurence French and Jim Hornbuckle, eds., *The Cherokee Perspective* (Boone, N.C.: Appalachian Consortium Press, 1981), and John Witthoft, "Observations on Social Change among the Eastern Cherokees," in *The Cherokee Indian Nation: A Troubled History*, ed. Duane H. King (Knoxville: University of Tennessee Press, 1979), 215–20.

Bibliographical Essay

THE CHEROKEES are the subject of an enormous scholarly and popular literature, most of which deals with tribal acculturation during the eighteenth and nineteenth centuries and the tragedy of removal. Raymond D. Fogelson's *The Cherokees: A Critical Bibliography* (Bloomington: University of Indiana Press, 1978) is still a good starting point, but of course it does not reflect the considerable output of the past decade. A few of the more important and accessible scholarly books are Grant Foreman, *Indian Removal: The Emigration of the Five Civilized Tribes of Indians* (Norman: University of Oklahoma Press, 1953); Duane H. King, ed., *The Cherokee Indian Nation: A Troubled History* (Knoxville: University of Tennessee Press, 1979); Henry Thompson Malone, *Cherokees of the Old South: A People in Transition* (Athens: University of Georgia Press, 1956); William G. McLoughlin, *Cherokees and Missionaries, 1789–1839* (New Haven: Yale University Press, 1984), and idem, *Cherokee Renascence in the New Republic* (Princeton: Princeton University Press, 1986); Gary E. Moulton, *John Ross: Cherokee Chief* (Athens: University of Georgia Press, 1978); Theda Perdue, *Slavery and the Evolution of Cherokee Society, 1540–1866* (Knoxville: University of Tennessee Press, 1979); John Philip Reid, *A Law of Blood: The Primitive Law of the Cherokee Nation* (New York: New York University Press, 1970); Morris L. Wardell, *A Political History of the Cherokee Nation, 1838–1907* (Norman: University of Oklahoma Press, 1938); Thurman Wilkins, *Cherokee Tragedy: The Story of the Ridge Family and the Decimation of a People* (New York:

Macmillan, 1970); and Grace Steele Woodward, *The Cherokees* (Norman: University of Oklahoma Press, 1963).

Much sparser is the literature on the Eastern Band of Cherokees. After almost a century, James Mooney's classic *Myths of the Cherokee*, Nineteenth Annual Report of the Bureau of American Ethnology (Washington, D.C.: Government Printing Office, 1900), is still a treasure trove of ethnographic detail and insight. A recent comprehensive study of the Band's earlier history is John R. Finger, *The Eastern Band of Cherokees, 1819–1900* (Knoxville: University of Tennessee Press, 1984). There are surprisingly few accounts of recent Eastern Cherokee history and none covers the entire twentieth century. Two that are especially useful in discussing the Band's confusing legal status are George E. Frizzell, "The Politics of Cherokee Citizenship, 1898–1930," *North Carolina Historical Review* 61(April 1984), and Ben Oshel Bridgers, "An Historical Analysis of the Legal Status of the North Carolina Cherokees," *North Carolina Law Review* 58(August 1980). Bridgers is the tribal attorney, and anyone interested in a current assessment of the Band's status should make contact with him at the firm of Haire and Bridgers in Sylva, North Carolina.

Other important sources with a historical focus include Catherine L. Albanese, "Exploring Regional Religion: A Case Study of the Eastern Cherokee," *History of Religion* 23(May 1984); Fred B. Bauer's polemical *Land of the North Carolina Cherokees* (Brevard, N.C.: George E. Buchanan, 1970); Joan Greene, "Federal Policies in the Schools of the Eastern Cherokees, 1892–1932" (M.A. thesis, Western Carolina University, 1986); Gaston Litton, "Enrollment Records of the Eastern Band of Cherokee Indians," *North Carolina Historical Review* 17(July 1940); Carmaleta Littlejohn Monteith, "The Role of the Scribe in Eastern Cherokee Society, 1821–1985" (Ph.D. diss., Emory University, 1985); Sharlotte Neely, "Acculturation and Persistence among North Carolina's Eastern Band of Cherokee Indians," in *Southeastern Indians since the Removal Era*, ed. Walter L. Williams (Athens: University of Georgia Press, 1979); Henry M. Owl, "The Eastern Band of Cherokee Indians before and after the Removal" (M.A. thesis, University of North Carolina, Chapel Hill, 1929); John Parris, *The Cherokee Story* (Asheville, N.C.: Stephens Press, 1950); Russell Thornton, "Tribal History, Tribal Population, and Tribal Membership Requirements: The Cases of the Eastern Band of Cherokee Indians, the Cherokee Nation of Oklahoma, and the United Keetowah Band of Cherokee Indians in Oklahoma," Newberry Library Conference on "Toward a Quantitative Approach to American Indian History," Feb. 19–21, 1987, Occasional Papers Series 8 (Chicago: Newberry Library, 1987); Charles J. Weeks, "The Eastern Cherokee and the New Deal," *North Carolina Historical Review* 43(July 1976); and William W. Wood, Jr., "War and the Eastern Cherokee," *Southern Indian Studies* 2(1950). See also the articles in the Special Cherokee Issue of the *Appalachian Journal* 2(Summer 1975).

Anthropological works focusing on the twentieth-century Eastern Cherokees include James Mooney and Frans M. Olbrechts, *The Swimmer Manuscript: Cherokee Sacred Formulas and Medicinal Prescriptions*, Bureau of American Ethnology Bulletin 99 (Washington, D.C.: Government Printing Office, 1932); William H. Gilbert, Jr., *The Eastern Cherokees* (Washington, D.C.: Government Printing Office, 1943); and a number of theses, dissertations, articles, and unpublished papers by Hester A. Davis, Raymond D. Fogelson, Annie Cofield Gardner, John L. Grant, Charles H. Holzinger, Harriet J. Kupferer, Paul Kutsche, Robert K. Thomas, Sharlotte Neely Williams, and John Witthoft; these are cited throughout the present work, especially in chapters 4, 8, and 9. A descriptive and interpretive overview incorporating some of these works is John Gulick's now outdated *Cherokees at the Crossroads* (Chapel Hill: University of North Carolina Press, 1960, 1973). A recent analysis of tourism and its impact is Larry R. Stucki, "Will the 'Real' Indian Survive? Tourism and Affluence at Cherokee, North Carolina," in *Affluence and Cultural Survival*, ed. Richard F. Salisbury and Elisabeth Tooker (Washington, D.C.: American Ethnological Society, 1984). Related to this is the denunciation of the Cherokee Historical Association and tribal elites by Laurence French, a sociologist, in his "Tourism and Indian Exploitation: A Social Indictment," *Indian Historian* 10(Fall 1977). French and Jim Hornbuckle also provide some good insights on the modern Band in their coedited volume *The Cherokee Perspective* (Boone, N.C.: Appalachian Consortium Press, 1981).

Essential to any scholarly investigation of the Eastern Band is the vast collection of correspondence, data, and other materials accumulated by the Bureau of Indian Affairs. These are readily accessible for the period from the 1890s into the early 1950s in Record Group 75 at the Federal Records Center in East Point, Georgia. Materials for a later period are stored at the Federal Records Center in Suitland, Maryland, but are less conveniently filed and scattered throughout many boxes. For current or very recent records on specific aspects of the Band, it may be necessary to visit appropriate offices within the Department of the Interior's main building in Washington or the BIA's Eastern Area Office in nearby Arlington, Virginia. For daily correspondence from the BIA's Cherokee agency, one should consult the

Chronological File of the agency superintendent. In addition, I used the National Archives in Washington for Eastern Cherokee data from World War II into the termination era. The National Archives has also published two pertinent microfilms: Microcopy 685, "Records Relating to the Enrollment of Eastern Cherokees by Guion Miller, 1908–1910," and Microcopy 1059, "Selected Letters Received by the Office of Indian Affairs Relating to the Cherokees of North Carolina, 1851–1905." Council Records of the Eastern Band are available on microfilm from the North Carolina Division of Archives and History, Raleigh, and in manuscript form at the Museum of the Cherokee Indian, Cherokee, North Carolina.

Other important archival materials are the Governors Papers at the North Carolina Division of Archives and History; the Josiah William Bailey Papers, Clyde Roark Hoey Papers, and George Adams Shuford Papers at Duke University; the George Stephens Papers at the University of North Carolina, Chapel Hill; and the Dan Tompkins Papers and Zebulon Weaver Papers at Western Carolina University. East Tennessee State University has recently acquired the Joe Jennings Papers, which contain material relating to Jennings's term as BIA superintendent at Cherokee; this acquisition was too late for my use, and I instead relied on Jennings's many letters found in other repositories. Also useful is the collection of photographs in the Museum of the Cherokee Indian.

By far the most important printed primary materials are the many documents and reports published by the United States Senate and House of Representatives as part of the Congressional Serial Set. Along with periodic congressional hearings, these offer wide-ranging information and insights on social and economic conditions among the Band as well as detailed assessment of political and legal changes. They are cited throughout the text of this work and are easily accessible through comprehensive indexes found in most research libraries.

Newspapers are another critical source of information on the modern Cherokees, and special clipping files are at Western Carolina University, the Asheville Public Library, and the North Carolina Room at the University of North Carolina, Chapel Hill. Partial runs of the *Jackson County Journal* (Sylva) and the *Bryson City Times* are available, as well as complete microfilm sets of the *Asheville Citizen* and *Citizen-Times*. Anyone hoping to keep up on the latest developments within the Band must consult the *Cherokee One Feather*, published weekly by the tribe. Articles on the Band also appear periodically in newspapers in Knoxville, Chattanooga, Charlotte, Winston-Salem, Raleigh, and other regional cities.

Finally, essential though these written sources are, no scholar can really get a "feel" for the Cherokees' recent past and their current prospects without repeatedly visiting the reservation and making contact with tribal members from all walks of life. Some are reluctant to be interviewed by white historians and anthropologists, but many are quite willing to talk informally about their personal experiences and insights. These interviews and conversations made the research for this book particularly worthwhile and confirmed that history is indeed a living discipline.

Index

Acculturation: in 1900, 11–16; impact of industry on, 17–18; in Progressive Era, 24–30, 32–33; in World War I, 34–41, 43; in postwar period, 43–45, 49; in 1920s, 53, 56–74; in 1930s, 77, 84; and opposition to New Deal, 88–89, 96; and tourism, 102–4; in World War II, 108–10; and voting, 110–12; and termination, 120–22; in 1950s, 141–45; and "Great Society," 147–48; today, 181–85. *See also* Education

Adams, A. M., 76

Agriculture, 102, 110, 152; in 18th century, 6; in 1900, 7–8, 19; orchard, 19–20; in 1920s, 54; revival of, 75–76; New Deal plans for, 81; training in, 110; in 1950s, 141, 143; in 1960s, 150. *See also* Livestock

AIF (American Indian Federation), 89–90, 118

AIM (American Indian Movement), 154, 157

Albanese, Catherine L., 15

Alcohol, 15, 30–32; moonshine, 38, 53; drunkenness, 58; during Prohibition, 66; in 1960s and 1970s, 153; in 1980s, 163–64, 166–67. *See also* Health

Allotment: as issue in Progressive Era, 7, 10, 22, 24–25; tribe agrees to, 44; nonenactment of, 46–52, 118; and IRA, 79

Anthropologists, 56–57, 59, 127, 139–42, 184. *See also names of individuals*

Appalachian Railroad, 20, 61, 79, 84, 100–101

Arneach, Molly, 115

Arrowmont School, 82

Asheville, first mentioned, 1; *passim*

Aspinall, Wayne N., 135

Automobile: and related industries, 54; and early tourism, 54–56, 63, 74, 98; impact of, after World War II, 114; ownership of, 56, 140–41; accidents in, 166–67. *See also* Tourism

Axe, John, 12

Bailey, Josiah, 90

Baker, Fred A., 48

In the Indians of the Southeast series

William Bartram on the Southeastern Indians
Edited and annotated by Gregory A. Waselkov and Kathryn E. Holland
Braund

Deerskins and Duffels
The Creek Indian Trade with Anglo-America, 1685–1815
By Kathryn E. Holland Braund

Searching for the Bright Path
The Mississippi Choctaws from Prehistory to Removal
By James Taylor Carson

Cherokee Americans
The Eastern Band of Cherokees in the Twentieth Century
By John R. Finger

Choctaw Genesis, 1500–1700
By Patricia Galloway

The Southeastern Ceremonial Complex
Artifacts and Analysis
The Cottonlandia Conference
Edited by Patricia Galloway
Exhibition Catalog by David H. Dye and Camille Wharey

The Invention of the Creek Nation, 1670–1763
By Steven C. Hahn

An Assumption of Sovereignty
Social and Political Transformation among the Florida Seminoles, 1953–1979
By Harry A. Kersey Jr.

The Caddo Chiefdoms
Caddo Economics and Politics, 700–1835
By David La Vere